Colloquial
Finnish

The Colloquial Series

The following languages are available in the Colloquial series:

Albanian	Japanese
Amharic	Korean
Arabic (Levantine)	Latvian
Arabic of Egypt	Lithuanian
Arabic of the Gulf and Saudi Arabia	Malay
	Norwegian
Basque	Panjabi
Bulgarian	Persian
* Cambodian	Polish
* Cantonese	Portuguese
* Chinese	Romanian
Czech	* Russian
Danish	Serbo-Croat
Dutch	Slovak
English	Slovene
Estonian	Somali
French	* Spanish
German	Spanish of Latin America
* Greek	Swedish
Gujarati	* Thai
Hindi	Turkish
Hungarian	Ukrainian
Indonesian	* Vietnamese
Italian	Welsh

Accompanying cassette(s) are available for the above titles.

* Accompanying CDs are also available.

Colloquial
Finnish

The Complete Course
for Beginners

Daniel Abondolo

with dialogues by Hanna Björklund and Elina Multanen

London and New York

First published 1998
by Routledge
11 New Fetter Lane, London EC4P 4EE

Simultaneously published in the USA and Canada
by Routledge
29 West 35th Street, New York, NY 10001

© 1998 Daniel Abondolo

Typeset in Times Ten by Florencetype Ltd, Stoodleigh, Devon
Printed and bound in Great Britain by Clays Ltd, St Ives PLC

British Library Cataloguing in Publication Data
A catalogue record for this book is available from the British Library

Library of Congress Cataloging in Publication Data
 Abondolo, Daniel Mario
  Colloquial Finnish : the complete language course / Daniel
 Abondolo.
  p. cm. – (The colloquial series)
  ISBN 0–415–11391–1 (pack). – ISBN 0–415–11389–X (pbk).
– ISBN 0–415–11390–3 (audio cassettes)
  1. Finnish language–Spoken Finnish. 2. Finnish language–Textbooks
for foreign speakers–English. I. Title. II. Series.
PH135.A26 1997
494'. 54183421–dc20   96–32137
                                                          CIP

ISBN 0–415–11389–X (book)
ISBN 0–415–11390–3 (cassette)
ISBN 0–415–11391–1 (book and cassette course)

Contents

Acknowledgements   vii
List of abbreviations and symbols   ix
About this book   1
The sounds of Finnish   4

1 **Tutustutaan**   9
  Making contact
2 **Ei, kiitos!**   27
  No thanks
3 **Ole hyvä!**   42
  Help yourself!
4 **Paikasta toiseen**   55
  Getting around and about
5 **Mitä me ostetaan?**   72
  What'll we buy?
6 **Mennääks kiskalle!**   91
  Let's go to the kiosk!
7 **Eiks ookki ihana päästä kotiin
  joulunviettoon!**   111
  Isn't it great to get home for Christmas!
8 **Huonosta vielä huonommaksi**   127
  From bad to worse
9 **Aika ja tila**   144
  Time and space
10 **Mitä tehtäs tänään?**   161
  What'll we do today?

11 Yhä nopeammin   178
More and more quickly

12 Maton alla tuntuu olevan jotain   194
There seems to be something under the carpet

13 Mikä laulaen tulee . . .   208
Easy come . . .

14 Karhut voi kai olla vaarallisiakin   222
Bears can be dangerous, I suppose

15 Vakavia asioita   237
Serious matters

16 Älköön sanottako!   252
Let it not be said!

Key to exercises   267
Appendix: Finnish names   277
Finnish–English glossary   279
English–Finnish glossary   292
Glossary of grammatical terms   300
Index   305

Acknowledgements

I wish to thank the following people for much help I have received during the preparation of this book. Among the many native speakers who have helped me, Hanna Björklund and Elina Multanen deserve special mention: it is they who provided most of the dialogue materials, on which the grammar sections are largely based, and with whom I have had many profitable discussions over points of suitability and style. Other native speakers who have helped me over the years are Matti Koskiala, Heikki and Eeva Sarmanto, and, most recently, Tuomo Lahdelma. I also thank the numerous teachers of Finnish who have helped me, first and foremost Aili Flint, who is a language-teaching paragon, but also Eila Hämäläinen and Fred Karlsson, Hannele Branch, Carol Rounds, and Sirkka Betts. This is also the place to express my gratitude to those colleagues, conversant with both language-teaching and with Finnish, who made valuable suggestions, namely Stefan Pugh, Ian Press, and Peter Sherwood; to the superb copy-editing of Jenny Potts; and to Simon Bell, Kate Hopgood, and the rest of the editorial team at Routledge for getting the book started and through various hurdles.

Abbreviations and symbols

Abbreviations

The names of the cases are always abbreviated with uppercase letters, as follows:

ABL	Ablative	ILL	Illative
ADE	Adessive	INE	Inessive
ALL	Allative	N	Nominative
ELA	Elative	P	Partitive
ESS	Essive	TRA	Translative
G	Genitive		

Singular and plural are indicated by a preposed lowercase s or p, e.g. sG = genitive singular, pILL = plural illative.

The codes s1 s2 s3 p1 p2 p3 refer to first, second, and third persons singular and plural.

Other abbreviations:

adj	adjective	pass	passive
adv	adverb	PR	participial construction
cd	conditional	ps	present
dir	directive	pt	past
ind	indefinite	ptcpl	participle

Examples:

s1 pt   first person singular past, e.g. **mä men|i|n** '*I went*'.
s2 pIne   second person singular form of plural inessive, e.g. **tasku|i|ssa|si** '*in your pockets*'.

Symbols

|	(upright line) is used to separate the morphemes, i.e. the minimal meaningful units of words, e.g. English *tree|s, friend| li|ness*, Finnish **puu|t, ystävä|llis|yys**.
Q	is found at the ends of morphemes, and stands for a variety of phonetic and grammatical effects: see Unit 2.
X	see Q.
>	stands for 'changes to' or 'is read as', e.g. pp > p is 'pp changes to p'.

About this book

This book aims to provide you with the basics you need to communicate in Finnish. That means grammatical nuts-and-bolts, some useful vocabulary, and an idea of how to guess at the meanings of words you haven't heard before. It is not a phrase-book or a tourist's guide to Finland; plenty of those are already available, and besides, all the phrase-books in the world won't get you communicating if you aren't equipped with the rules.

Finnish is the first language of some five and a half million people. Most speakers live in Finland, but there are also significant enclaves in Sweden, Estonia, and Norway, and in the area around Lakes Michigan and Superior in the United States and Canada.

In the European context, Finland presents a rich paradox: geographically northern, it is culturally like neither Sweden nor Norway; geographically eastern, it is like neither Poland nor Ukraine. The main reason for this uniqueness is Finnish culture, borne and permeated by the Finnish language.

Neither Germanic (like Swedish, German, or English) nor Slavonic (like Polish and Ukrainian), Finnish is a Uralic language, and is thus related to Estonian, Saam (Lappish), and (much more distantly) to Hungarian. Most of Finnish vocabulary will therefore probably be new to you; the learning curve flattens out fairly soon, however, because once you enter the intermediate stages you will find Finnish vocabulary richly systematic and therefore relatively easy to learn.

Some of the grammar, too, is quite different from that of most European languages. But there is nothing intrinsically difficult about it; it is simply unfamiliar. We'll hit a few of the high spots here to give you some idea of what's in store.

Finnish pronunciation presents few novel challenges, and the spelling is for the most part perfectly consistent. For English

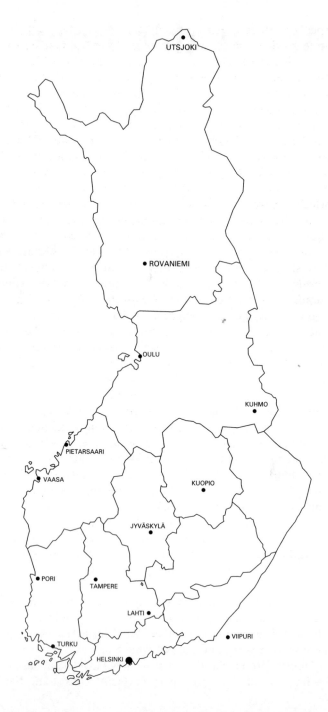

UTSJOKI

ROVANIEMI

OULU

KUHMO

PIETARSAARI

VAASA

KUOPIO

JYVÄSKYLÄ

PORI

TAMPERE

LAHTI

VIIPURI

TURKU

HELSINKI

speakers, there are few unfamiliar sounds. Many will be relieved to learn that Finnish word-stress is always on first syllable.

Finnish words take on many forms, and some Finns like to try to frighten foreigners with tales of sesquipedalian (i.e. polysyllabic) adjectives and case systems with fifteen-plus members. And in fact, Finnish nouns can and do take some fifteen different endings depending on their role in the sentence. The word for 'Finland', for example, **Suomi**, can also be **Suomesta**, **Suomeen**, and **Suomessa**, corresponding to English '*from* Finland', '*to* Finland', and '*in* Finland'. But nothing as complicated as Latin or even Russian or German need be feared, for the endings, or suffixes, which appear at the end of this word (and which we shall segment in this book as **Suome|sta, Suome|en, Suome|ssa**) are essentially the same for *all* nouns, in both singular and plural. There is no grammatical gender, even in the third person singular pronoun: Finnish does not distinguish 'she' from 'he', or 'her' from 'him'. The Finnish verb is also quite straightforward, particularly when compared with that of English, French, or Spanish. There is only one irregular verb (or one-and-a-half).

The Finnish lexicon is exceptionally rich, in part because of the built-in machinery which the language has for making and modifying words, in part because of its openness to foreign borrowings and the creativeness of its slang. If you are interested in folk poetry, you probably already know that Finnish is the key to the world's largest archive of orally transmitted verbal art.

It is perhaps useful to stress that like any language, Finnish is more than a means of communication. It is also an object which can be studied for its own sake. You don't need to devote the rest of your life to studying it, but the more thought and work you invest into Finnish itself, the more communication will become not only easier but more pleasurable.

The sounds of Finnish

The basic rule for good pronunciation of Finnish is: don't rush; give all the sounds their due time and attention.

Vowels 🔊

The letters **i e a o u y ä ö** stand for sounds which are always pronounced fairly *short, but never mumbled or clipped*, regardless of position. *Always long* are the sounds written **ii ee aa oo uu yy ää öö**, i.e. the same eight letters doubled.

The vowels may be classified roughly according to their manner of articulation as *high* (**i y u**), *mid* (**e ö o**), and *low* (**ä a**); *front* (**i y e ö ä**) vs. *back* (**u o a**); and *rounded* (**y ö u o**) vs. *unrounded* (**i e ä a**).

Listen to the recording and do your best to imitate these samples, concentrating on the vowel marked with italics. Remember to stress the first syllable, regardless of what else is going on later on the word.

Finnish		Meaning	Pronounced as in German	Pronounced a bit as in English
i	k*i*va	smashing	bitte	'bit' (especially Australian)
ii	k*ii*tos	thanks	biete	'bead'
u	k*u*va	picture	gucke	'cook' (especially Australian)
uu	k*uu*ma	hot	Schuhe	(billed and) 'cooed'
y	k*y*lä	village	Hütte	–
yy	t*yy*li	style	müde	–
ee	vet*ee*n	into the water	gäbe	'square', but with no trace of an 'r'

oo	tal**oo**n	into the house	*ohne*	'north', but with no trace of an '*r*'
öö	keitti**öö**n	into the kitchen	*Höhle*	–

aa	pat**aa**n	into the pot	*Ahnung*	'palm'
ää	pes**ää**n	into the nest	–	'ban', but longer

e	k**e**li	road conditions	*Bett*	'bet'
o	K**o**li	(placename)	*solle*	–
ö	k**ö**li	keel	*Hölle*	–

a	k**a**la	fish	*knapp*	'palm,' but shorter
ä	k**ä**si	hand	–	'bat'

The letter-sequences **ie**, **uo**, **yö** represent diphthongs. You may first attempt them by simply pronouncing a good Finnish **i**, **u**, or **y** followed by a good Finnish **e**, **o**, or **ö**. Avoid allowing the diphthong to 'centre', i.e. do not pronounce (as in Leeds or New York 'near', 'cure') the second vowel as a *schwa* (like the second vowel in 'sofa'). Avoid, also, the temptation to lengthen the second vowel at the expense of the first (as in Italian *miele*, *buono*).

ie	k**ie**li	language	–	cf. Jamaican 'face'
uo	S**uo**mi	Finland	–	cf. Jamaican 'goat'
yö	s**yö**dä	to eat	–	–

Here are some more examples to practise. Make sure you can clearly hear the difference in length (of the vowels, again, in italics):

English	*Short*	*Long*	*English*	*Contrast*
pig	s**i**ka	s**ii**ka	herring	i : ii
of a row	riv**i**n	riv**ii**n	into a row	i : ii
of a name	nim**e**n	nim**ee**n	into a name	e : ee
of a fish	kal**a**n	kal**aa**n	into a fish	a : aa
of a poem	run**o**n	run**oo**n	into a poem	o : oo
of sorrow	sur**u**n	sur**uu**n	into sorrow	u : uu
expenses	k**u**lut	k**uu**lut	you belong	u : uu
summer cabin	m**ö**kki	r**öö**ki	fag, cigarette	ö : öö
wrinkle	r**y**ppy	r**yy**ppy	(alcoholic) drink	y : yy

Consonants

Most of the consonants also come in *short* and *long* varieties. Between vowels, the long consonants are written double. For example:

who?	**kuka**	**kukka**	flower
worm	**mato**	**matto**	rug
help	**apu**	**vappu**	May Day
heap	**kasa**	**kassa**	cash register
beer	**olut**	**ollut**	been

When two different consonants occur next to one another, either the first or the second is long. Length is indicated in spelling as follows.

1 If the first consonant is pronounced short and the second consonant is pronounced long, the second consonant is written double. Examples:

linssi	lens	**teltta**	tent
kantta	lid (sP)	**helppo**	easy
kartta	map	**marssi**	march
ankka	domesticated duck	**korppu**	floppy disk
lamppu	lamp	**herkkä**	sensitive, touchy
valssi	waltz	**palkka**	salary

2 In the reverse scenario, that is, if the first consonant is pronounced long and the second is pronounced short, *both consonants are written single*. Practise these examples:

länsi	west	**tunti**	hour
hanki	snowcrust	**norsu**	elephant
lampi	pond	**korpi**	backwoods
tylsä	stupid	**itse**	self
halko	log	**yskä**	cough
pelto	field	**halpa**	cheap

Special attention should be paid to the following letters:

h represents a sound much like English 'h' in 'hut', except when written to the left of another consonant letter, when it represents a *voiceless velar fricative* (as in German *Bach*) or a *voiceless palatal fricative* (as in German *ich*), depending, as in German, on the surrounding vowels. Listen to these words and try to copy the differences:

sohva	sofa	**pihvi**	steak
lahti	bay	**tyhjä**	empty
kirahvi	giraffe		

b, **d**, **g**   represent sounds much like those of English 'bait', 'date', and 'gate', except that the sequence **ng** stands for a long *velar nasal* [ŋː], not a sequence of velar nasal plus [g]. If you distinguish the medial sounds of 'finger' and 'singer', it's the latter sound you want, but with a longer pronunciation. Examples:

Helsingissä   in Helsinki   **ongelma**   problem

n in **nk** stands for velar [ŋ] as in English 'ba*n*k'.

You will also come across the letter š, used to represent the initial sound of English 'ship'; it is used only in foreign words such as **šekki** 'cheque', **šakki** 'chess'.

Glottal stop and its consequences

The Finnish alphabet has no symbol for the *glottal stop* which is pronounced by most Finns at the ends of forms such as **istu!** 'sit!' or **palaute** 'feedback'. (Glottal stop is commonly heard in London, e.g. instead of 't' in 'ci*t*y' and 'no*t* a lo*t*'). In Finnish, the glottal stop often attaches to following consonants, making them longer; it has other, grammatical, effects, as well. To help you to acquire a good pronunciation and to render Finnish grammar more transparent, this book writes the glottal stop in grammatical sections and in the vocabularies as **Q**.

Nuts and bolts, and a few symbols

Many Finnish words will look long to you at first, but in most instances they break up readily into smaller, recurring, parts with which you will quickly become familiar. To help you to see these smaller parts clearly, a vertical stroke (|) is liberally applied throughout this book, e.g. marking off the Finnish suffix **sto** in both **kirja|sto** 'library' and **laiva|sto** 'fleet' – words that are easy to remember once you've learned that **kirja** is 'book' and **laiva** 'ship'. In grammatical sections, a right-pointing arrowhead (>) will indicate change, as you might expect (an English example would be 'y' > 'ie' in 'library' > 'librarie|s'). In the vocabulary sections the arrow (→) leads you from a *colloquial* form to a *more formal* Finnish form.

Finnish suffixes usually have more than one form. In order to capture this variety, in the grammatical sections of this book they are written with capital letters representing the sounds which vary. So for example the suffix **sto** (as in **kirja|sto** above) is **stö** in **ympäri|stö** 'environment' (from **ympäri** 'around'); in this suffix therefore the varying vowel (**o**, **ö**) is written with capital **O**, and the non-varying consonants **st** are written in lower case: **=stO**. In the suffix **=iME**, the reverse scenario applies: in this suffix the vowel **i** does not vary, and is therefore written in lowercase, but capital **M** and **E** are intended as reminders that we do not have simple **m** and **e** here (the **e** alternates with zero, and the **m** with **n**: see page 89).

A note on slang

The 'colloquial Finnish' presented in this book is a range of varieties of Finnish as spoken by younger people in Finland today, particularly in urban areas, when they are speaking casually and naturally. Very little slang is presented, as this would simply double one of your first tasks, namely the acquisition of the working parts of a basic vocabulary; and once you have learned the basic (colloquial *and* formal) word for 'hand', **käsi**, you will not find it especially difficult to slot in slang terms for the same thing, e.g. **tassu**, **handu**, **känny**.

Dictionaries

The glossaries at the back of this book provide the essential forms you'll need to complete the course. Soon enough, however, you'll want to find out more, and you're in luck: Finns are excellent dictionary-makers, and a wide range of sizes and types are available. If you go to Finland you can nose around in search of bargains in the second-hand bookshops (**divari|t**) you'll find in every city.

1 Tutustutaan

Making contact

In this unit you will learn:

- how to say what country you're from, what you do, and how to ask the same about others
- how to say 'yes'
- one way to express possession
- how vowels in a Finnish word cooperate with one another (vowel harmony), and how consonants fight (consonant compression)

Dialogue ▣▣

Esittäytyminen

Introducing yourself

Juuso and Paul introduce themselves to each other

JUUSO: Hyvää päivää. Juuso Virtanen.
PAUL: Hyvää päivää. Paul Smith. Hauska tutustua.
JUUSO: Hauska tutustua.

JUUSO: *Good day. (I'm) Juuso Virtanen.*
PAUL: *Good day. (I'm) Paul Smith. Pleased to meet you.*
JUUSO: *Pleased to meet you.*

To introduce yourself in Finnish, you say your name. It's polite to preface your name with a greeting such as the following, and to offer to shake hands:

Hyvää huomenta!	(lit. 'Good morning'), said in the morning
Hyvää päivää!	(lit. 'Good day'), said throughout the day, until it's time for
Hyvää iltaa!	(lit. 'Good evening'), said in the evening

Usually, the phrase **Hauska tutustua** (Pleased to meet you) gets thrown in as well. Here's another example, with the 'I'm' (**Mä olen**) explicitly stated:

IRMA: Hyvää päivää. Mä olen Irma Ojala.
SOPHIE: Hyvää päivää. Sophie Grant. Hauska tutustua.

IRMA: *Good day. I'm Irma Ojala.*
SOPHIE: *Good day. I'm Sophie Smith. Pleased to meet you.*

In less formal contexts, the greetings **hei** or **moi** are used, and surnames dispensed with:

MASA: Moi. Mä olen Masa.
HANNU: Moi. Hannu.

MASA: *Hi. I'm Masa.*
HANNU: *Hi. (I'm) Hannu.*

Follow-up will usually consist of saying where you're from and what you do for a living. Let's go back to Paul and Juuso:

JUUSO: Oletteko te englantilainen?
PAUL: Olen.

JUUSO: *Are you English?*
PAUL: *Yes* (lit. I am).

Here's the follow-up to the conversation between Irma and Sophie:

IRMA: Oletteko te opettaja?
SOPHIE: Olen.

IRMA: *Are you a teacher?*
SOPHIE: *Yes* (lit. I am).

Formal Finnish doesn't really have a word that works like English 'yes'. Instead, the key word in the question is repeated. See also below, 'Answering "yes" to yes/no (**-kO**) questions'.

Exercise 1 Build short dialogues in which the Finns and foreigners listed below introduce themselves to each other. Use the greetings given above, and the phrases **Oletteko te X** 'Are you X?' and **Olen** 'Yes (I am)'; don't forget **Hauska tutustua**. Here are some nationalities to start with:

suomalainen	Finnish, a Finn
kiinalainen	Chinese, a Chinese
italialainen	Italian, an Italian
irlantilainen	Irish, an Irish (wo)man
belgialainen	Belgian, a Belgian
ruotsalainen	Swedish, a Swede
puolalainen	Polish, a Pole
venäläinen	Russian, a Russian
unkarilainen	Hungarian, a Hungarian
eestiläinen	Estonian, an Estonian
sveitsiläinen	Swiss, a Swiss
englantilainen	English, an Englishman
egyptiläinen	Egyptian, an Egyptian
amerikkalainen	American, an American
somalialainen	Somali, a Somali
kanadalainen	Canadian, a Canadian
saamelainen	Sami, a Sami ('Lapp')
australialainen	Australian, an Australian
romaani	Romany (Gipsy), a Rom
ranskalainen	French, a Frenchman
walesilainen	Welsh, a Welsh (person)
saksalainen	German, a German
skotlantilainen	Scottish, a Scot

Some Finnish names

Women:

Marja Mäkinen
Satu Salokangas
Eila Elstelä
Raija Nieminen

Men:

Hannu Huttunen
Pekka Virtavuori
Raimo Santala
Heikki Karapää

Some foreigners' names
Nigel Baker
Albert O'Rourke
Wilfred Owen
Angus Salmon
Françoise Peugeot
Renate Porsche
Sergio Lamborghini
Yuri Yavlinsky
Jorge González
Seiji Nakamura
Jawaahir Maxamed
Annike Rätsep
Wang Wei

Language points

To make statements like 'I am English' or 'I am an engineer', you have to know (1) how to use personal pronouns; (2) how to use the verb 'is'; (3) vocabulary for nationalities, countries, and occupations. These are the three areas which we shall explore in the next three sections.

Personal pronoun basics

English pronouns distinguish three subject persons, 'I' – 'you' – '(s)he/it' and singular from plural ('I' vs. 'we', 'he' vs. 'they'). So do Finnish pronouns, but the gender distinction 'he/she' is absent. On the other hand, other distinctions are important. We'll summarize these distinctions under four points:

1 *Full vs. cropped*: 'I' is either **minä** or **mä**; 'you', if addressed to a friend, is either **sinä** or **sä**. In other words, alongside the full-length forms **minä** and **sinä** are shorter, or 'cropped' forms; the cropped forms are more colloquial.

2 'He', 'she', 'it' are all **se** in colloquial Finnish, and 'they' is **ne**. In more formal style, **se** and **ne** are used only when referring to animals or things; for humans, **hän** is used in the singular and **he** in the plural.

3 The third person pronouns (**hän**, **he**, **se**, **ne**) are not usually omitted; the others may be omitted if they are not stressed, but to include them (in their cropped forms, of course) is more colloquial.

4 When speaking to one person, you may express distance, politeness, or formality by using the second person plural. (In colloquial contexts, you use the second person plural only when addressing more than one person.)

The singular subject pronouns are a bit complex, so we'll overview them diagrammatically:

Subject person	s1	mä	minä	
	s2	sä	sinä	(te + p2)
	s3	se	hän	humans
			se	other
	colloquial ↔ formal contexts			

How to say 'am', 'are', and 'is': the verb ole- 'is'

The most frequently used verb in Finnish is the verb **ole-** 'is'. Here are its present-tense forms in more formal Finnish:

Singular		*Plural*	
1 **(minä) ole|n**	I am	**(me) ole|mme**	we are
2 **(sinä) ole|t**	you are	**(te) ole|tte**	you are
3 **hän/se on**	(s)he/it is	**he ovat**	they are

Finnish has no future tense, so English equivalents of **minä olen** also include 'I will/shall be'.

As mentioned in the preceding section, the p2 form **(te) ole\|tte** is used not only when addressing more than one person, but also to express politeness when addressing a single person.

As mentioned in the previous section, colloquial Finnish uses **se** to refer to people, as well, and the cropped pronoun forms **mä** and **sä** are frequent. There are also two other differences: for 'they are', colloquial Finnish has **ne on** instead of **he ovat**; and for 'we are' colloquial Finnish has **me ollaan**. More on these forms in later units.

Vocabulary building

Countries and nationalities

You have already met several names of nationalities above, and you will probably have noticed that they all end in either **lainen** or **läinen**.

This is because **lainen/läinen** is a suffix by means of which Finnish derives nationality names from simpler, shorter words, usually names of countries. The form with **a** is used if the word to which the suffix is added contains an **a**, **o**, or **u** (thus **tanskallainen, puolallainen**) and the form with **ä** is used elsewhere (thus **venälläinen, sveitsilläinen**). This sort of matching-up of vowels is called *vowel harmony*; you'll learn more about it later on in this unit.

For now, you can use the table below to revise nationality names while you learn the country names on which they are based; if in doubt, refer back to the exercise at the beginning of this unit. Notice the irregularities – unexpected **-a-**, **-jä** – in the words for 'Finnish', 'Swedish', and 'Russia'.

Nationality	Country	Nationality	Country
suom*a*llainen	Suomi	saksallainen	Saksa
ruots*a*llainen	Ruotsi	belgiallainen	Belgia
venälläinen	Venä*jä*	puolallainen	Puola
eestilläinen	Eesti	unkarillainen	Unkari
englantillainen	Englanti	sveitsilläinen	Sveitsi
amerikkallainen	Amerikka	egyptilläinen	Egypti
kanadallainen	Kanada	somaliallainen	Somali
australiallainen	Australia	saamellainen	NB
ranskallainen	Ranska	romaani	NB
		walesillainen	Wales
		skotlantillainen	Skotlanti

As the example **Wales/walesilainen** (pronounced [valesilainen] or [veilsiläinen]) shows, an **-i-** is added to foreign words which end in a consonant in order to ease the attachment of the suffix; another example is **Gabon/gabonilainen**.

Occupations

Like names of nationalities, names for occupations are usually derived words. Such words are derived from simpler words by means of *derivational suffixes*, which we shall distinguish by prefixing them with an equals sign (=). Common derivational suffixes which form occupation names are **=isti** and **=ikko**, both of which are usually added to stems which you will either recognize or be able to guess:

pianisti pianist (**piano** 'piano')
klarinetisti clarinetist (**klarinetti** 'clarinet')
kontrabasisti double-bassist (**kontrabasso** 'double bass')

muusikko	musician	**matemaatikko**	mathematician
mekaanikko	mechanic		
poliitikko	politician	**akateemikko**	academic

Tip: The vowel in the syllable immediately preceding the occupation-forming suffix **=ikko** is usually long: **m***uu***sikko**, **matem***aa***tikko**, **pol***ii***tikko**.

Also easy to recognize and remember are:

diplomaatti	diplomat
insinööri	engineer
poliisi(konstaapeli)	police (constable)

but probably not:

tulkki	interpreter

The ending **ri** is frequent:

tuomari	judge	**leipuri**	baker
maalari	painter	**lääkäri**	doctor

The suffix **=jA** (for capital 'A' see pages 17–18), which is added to verbs, is the closest Finnish equivalent to the English '**=er**' of 'writer' or the '**=or**' of 'director'. In later units, you will meet some of the verbs from which these occupation names are derived:

opetta|ja	teacher	**valokuvaa|ja**	photographer
kirjaili|ja	writer	**maanviljeli|jä**	farmer
runoili|ja	poet	**sairaanhoita|ja**	nurse
asianaja|ja	solicitor, lawyer	**toimisto-**	office worker
ohjaa|ja	(film) director	**työnteki|jä**	
tarjoili|ja	waiter	**opiskeli|ja**	student

The compound-element **mies** (man; husband) is also common, whether the person is a man or a woman:

laki|mies	jurist (**laki** 'law')
meri|mies	sailor (**meri** 'sea')
posti|mies	mail carrier (**posti** 'post, mail')
palo|mies	firefighter (**palo** 'fire which destroys a building')
lehti|mies	journalist (**lehti** 'leaf; newspaper')

Finally, some older terms are made with **seppä** 'smith':

puu|seppä	joiner (**puu** 'tree; wood')
lukko|seppä	locksmith (**lukko** 'lock')
kello|seppä	watchmaker (**kello** 'clock, watch')

Putting it all together

You have now met the three basics you need to know in order to say 'I am English', 'Harriet is an engineer', even 'The Frenchman is a musician.' The neutral, normal way is to string the three items together, subject–verb–predicate, in precisely that order. Thus we have subject (**minä**, **Harriet**, **ranskalainen**), then verb (**olen**, **on**, **on**), and finally predicate (**englantilainen**, **insinööri**, **muusikko**):

> Minä olen englantilainen.
> Harriet on insinööri.
> Ranskalainen on muusikko.

Notice that both subject and predicate are in the *nominative*.

Exercise 2 Now combine and revise what you have learned in the preceding sections by translating the following Finnish sentences into English:

1 Minä olen englantilainen.
2 Minä olen insinööri.
3 Mä olen skotlantilainen muusikko.
4 Sä olet ulkomaalainen.
5 Te olette italialainen diplomaatti.

Exercise 3 Put into Finnish:

1 Are you a doctor?
2 She is a Hungarian director.
3 I am an English businessman.
4 He is a French mathematician.
5 I'm a Canadian student.

Exercise 4 Use analogy, guesswork, and – if desperate – the answers in the back of this book to fill in the missing items in each line of the table below.

	Nationality	*English*	*Country*	*English*
1	——	Danish	**Tanska**	Denmark
2	**kreikkalainen**	Greek	——	Greece
3	——	Norwegian	**Norja**	Norway
4	——	Dutch	**Hollanti**	Holland
5	**albanialainen**	Albanian	——	Albania
6	——	Ukrainian	**Ukraina**	Ukraine

| 7 —— | Turkish | **Turkki** | Turkey |
| 8 —— | Portuguese | **Portugali** | Portugal |

Asking yes/no questions: -ko (and vowel harmony)

As you have seen, the Finnish for 'Are you?' is **oletteko**; in other words, the verb form **olette** 'you are' plus a suffix **-ko** (more colloquial: **-ks**). This is the standard way to form yes-or-no questions in Finnish: you attach this suffix to the word you're asking about. Thus **Onko se tämä?** (more colloquial: **Onks se tää?**) simply asks 'is it this?', in other words whether or not it is this (**tämä/tää**), but **Tämäkö se on?** (more colloquial: **Tääks se on?**) singles out 'this', something like 'Is it this!? and not that'.

Now, this suffix is not always -ko. Like =**lainen**/=**läinen** and indeed most Finnish suffixes, it has two shapes. The difference between the two shapes lies in the vowel: for this suffix the shapes are **-ko** and **-kö**. Which shape you use depends on the vowels of the word to which the suffix is attached. The rule may be stated quite simply in two parts: (1) if the word has any of the vowels **u**, **o**, **a**, you use **-ko**, e.g.:

Onko se italialainen?	Is (s)he Italian?	(**On** contains **o**, so -**ko**)
Pariisiko?	Paris?	(**Pariisi** contains **a**, so -**ko**)
Lontooko?	London?	(**Lontoo** contains **o**, so -**ko**)
Turkuko?	Turku?	(**Turku**, the name of Finland's former capital, contains **u**, so -**ko**)

(2) otherwise, you use **-kö**:

| **Sveitsikö?** | Switzerland? | (no **u**, **o**, **a** in Sveitsi, so -**kö**) |

In compound words, it is the vowels of the last word which are decisive. For example, the word **lukko|seppä** 'locksmith' takes **-kö** because the last member of this word, **seppä** 'smith' has no **u**, **o**, **a**: **Lukkoseppäkö te olette?** 'Are you a *locksmith*?'

To save time and space, we shall refer to the question suffix as

-**kO**, with the upper-case **O** to serve as a reminder that the vowel is **o** or **ö** depending on vowel harmony. Similarly, whenever a suffix has **a** or **ä** depending on vowel harmony, we shall write **A**, and upper-case **U** will refer to the vowel pair **u** and **y**.

For a minor refinement of the vowel-harmony rule given above, see Unit 10.

Exercise 5 Ask politely (i.e., use **te** and the second person plural form of the verb) whether someone is

1 Finnish
2 a locksmith
3 Russian
4 a policeman
5 French

Exercise 6 Ask these questions in Finnish, laying emphasis on the italicized words by attaching the appropriate form of -**kO**:

1 Is he *Japanese*?
2 Are you an *engineer*?
3 Is he a *firefighter*?
4 Are you *German*?
5 Is she a *politician*?

Answering 'yes' to yes/no (-kO) questions

You answer in the affirmative by repeating the verb form, if this is what was being questioned:

Oletteko te suomalainen?	Are you Finnish?
Olen.	Yes.

If the yes/no-question suffix -**kO** was added to any word other than the verb, you say **niin**; it is more polite to repeat the questioned word, as well:

Ruotsalainenko sä olet?	Are you *Swedish*?
Niin, ruotsalainen.	Yes, I am.

Finally, there is simple **joo**. This corresponds more to English 'yeah' than to 'yes', i.e. it is used only in informal, colloquial contexts:

Oletsä suomalainen?	Are you Finnish?
Joo.	Yeah.

How to say 'Irma's friend', 'the capital of France', etc.: the genitive case and an introduction to nominal stem-types

Have a look at these sentences:

Mikä *sen opettajan* **nimi on?** What's *that teacher's* name?

Kuka tuo on? Who's that?
Se on *Irman* **ystävä.** That's *Irma's* friend.

The words **se|n**, **opettaja|n**, and **Irma|n** are all in the *genitive* case. The genitive corresponds to the 's' of English 'Irma's friend' and the 'of' of 'the capital of France'.

To form the genitive of any Finnish *nominal* (= noun or adjective) you add -**n**. So 'Irma's friend' is **Irma|n ystävä** (where **ystävä** is 'friend') and 'the capital of France' is **Ranska|n pääkaupunki** ('France's capital', where **pääkaupunki** is 'capital'). The rest of this section shows you how to do this.

Non-alternating stems

For thousands of nominals like **Irma** and **Ranska**, you just add the -**n** to the 'citation form'. (This is the form of the nominal which is listed in dictionaries. It is also called the nominative singular, so we shall use the abbreviation sN.)

These nominals all have *citation forms* ending in vowels, and their shapes do not vary, or at least they vary in predictable ways (for the most widespread predictable way see *consonant compression*, below). We shall call them *non-alternating* stems because their stem endings remain unchanged to the left of the genitive singular (= sG) suffix -**n**. All nominals that end in **a**, **ä**, **o**, **ö**, **u**, and **y** (or their long equivalents **aa**, **ää**, **oo**, **öö**, **uu**, **yy**) are non-alternating. Examples:

citation form (sN)	sG	English
kala	kala|n	fish
kesä	kesä|n	summer
talo	talo|n	house
hölmö	hölmö|n	fool
savu	savu|n	smoke
levy	levy|n	record, disc

Any adjective modifying a noun must agree with that noun in case. So both 'green' and 'house' are in the genitive in

vihreä|n talo|n ovi   the door of the green house
                                 (**vihreä** 'green')

and both 'green' and 'door' are in the nominative in

talo|n vihreä ovi   the green door of the house

Exercise 7 Have a go at translating these possessive phrases into English. You'll need the words listed just above, plus these: **pyrstö** 'tail', **ovi** 'door', **maku** 'taste', **loppu** 'end', **pöllö** 'owl', **siipi** 'wing', **koko** 'size'.

1 kala|n pyrstö
2 talo|n ovi
3 kala|n maku
4 kesä|n loppu
5 pöllö|n siipi
6 levy|n koko

Alternating stems

These are nominals whose stem endings change when to the left of the genitive singular suffix. Most are easy to spot, once you know what to look for. In this lesson you have already met one very common type: nominals ending in =**lAinen** such as **ranskalainen** 'French', **egyptiläinen** 'Egyptian'. These and *all* Finnish nominals (except **kymmenen** 'ten') that have citation forms ending in **nen** have a stem that ends in **se**, and it is to this stem that case suffixes are added. Have a look at these forms:

sN   **ranskalainen**   **egyptiläinen**
sG   **ranskalaise|n**   **egyptiläise|n**

It's best to learn the groupings of alternating stems gradually; we'll discuss them as they come up. For another important group of alternating stems see the section on **e**-*stems* later in this unit.

Boxes with tight lids: consonant compression

In the preceding section, you saw how adding the genitive singular -**n** can trigger changes in alternating stems. This section introduces you to another kind of alternation which this and other suffixes can trigger.

If you examine the nominative and genitive singular of the following three stems, you will notice that something is happening to the **t**.

citation form (sN)	sG	English	consonant alternation
katu	**kadu|n**	street	t ~ d
hattu	**hatu|n**	hat	tt ~ t
hinta	**hinna|n**	price	nt ~ nn

The -**t**- of **katu** 'street' is said to 'weaken' to -**d**- in the genitive **kadu|n** 'of a street'; in parallel fashion, the -**tt**- of **hattu** 'hat' weakens to -**t**- in the genitive **hatu|n** 'of a hat', and the consonant cluster -**nt**- of **hinta** is -**nn**- in the genitive **hinna|n**.

One way to think of this 'weakening' is that it is a kind of *compression*. It is as if Finnish words were boxes full of various consonants and that suffixes like -**n** were tight-fitting lids: putting such a 'lid' onto the end of a 'box' that is already full crams the 'consonant contents' of that word into a tighter, more compressed shape.

What kind of word is a 'full box'? One that has very little 'space' at the end, i.e., any word ending in a short vowel.

What kind of suffix is a 'tight lid'? Any suffix which consists of a single consonant (like our -**n**) or begins with two consonants. With certain exceptions which we will detail as we go along, adding any such suffix causes compression of any **p**, **t**, or **k** inside the 'box'. For example, long **pp** compresses to **p**:

kauppa	shop
kaupa|n	sG

and short **p** preceded by a vowel compresses to **v**:

apu	help
avu|n	sG

The **p** of **vapaa** 'free' is not compressed when we add the tight lid -**n**, because the long vowel (**aa**) at the end provides plenty of vowel space:

vapaa	free
vapaa|n	sG

These and other, parallel alternations (which we shall call *consonant compression*) are quite regular. Consonant compression is not difficult to acquire, because (1) it is regular (the rules will be introduced as we go), and pervades most of the grammar and lexicon of the Finnish language; (2) it operates in parallel (for example, all longs compress to shorts); (3) it is restricted: every alternation pair involves a **p**, **t**, or **k**; no other consonants undergo compression.

For ease of reference, all consonant changes due to compression are set out below. Read it through now, not with an aim to memorizing it, but merely in order to become more acquainted with the sorts of changes which are involved.

The changes are illustrated here by the form of the genitive, so what we have is a list of possessive noun phrases. Each consists of a noun in the genitive singular followed by another in the nominative singular. The consonant compression which is illustrated in each case is listed in the column on the right.

1 Long **pp**, **kk**, **tt** compress to short **p**, **k**, **t**:

		Compression
kauppa 'shop'	**kaupa|n ovi** 'the door of the shop'	**pp > p**
lukko 'lock'	**luko|n hinta** 'the price of the lock'	**kk > k**
tyttö 'girl'	**tytö|n nimi** 'the girl's name'	**tt > t**

Since this type (**pp > p**, **kk > k**, **tt > t**) involves the *length*, i.e. the quantity, of the consonants, we shall call it *quantitative* compression. Quantitative is the only kind of compression which affects personal names (**Pekka** 'Peter', **Peka\|n** 'Peter's') and most foreign words.

All other types of compression are *qualitative* i.e. involve a change in the nature of the consonant. They are:

2 To the right of a nasal (**m**, **n**, [ŋ], see page 7), compressed **p**, **t**, **k** assimilate, i.e., they copy the nasal:

rumpu 'drum'	**rummu|n pärinä** 'the beating of the drum'	**mp> mm**
Helsinki 'Helsinki'	**Helsingi|n historia** 'the history of Helsinki'	**nk > ng** [ŋŋ]
hinta 'price'	**hinna|n romahdus** 'the collapse in (lit. of) the price'	**nt > nn**

3 Otherwise, **p** (unless preceded by **s**) compresses to **v**:

apu 'help'	**avu|n tarvitsija** 'one in need (lit. "a needer") of help'	**p > v**
halpa 'cheap'	**halva|n hotelli|n osoite** 'the address of a cheap hotel'	**p > v**

4 (a) A **k** between two **u**'s or **y**'s also compresses to **v**:

puku 'dress, suit' **puvu|n hinta** 'the price of   **k** > **v**
                                   the dress'
kyky 'ability'   **kilpailukyvy|n ylläpitäminen**   **k** > **v**
                                   'the sustaining of the ability
                                   to compete'

4 (b) but between other vowel combinations, compressed **k** melts
into the surrounding vowels:

laki 'law'   **lai|n periaate** 'the principle of **k** > (melts)
                                   the law'

(Pronunciation note: the -**i**- of **lai|n** is quite long, as if in memory
of the **k** which has been compressed.)

4 (c) If preceded by **l** or **r**, single **k** either compresses to nothing:

härkä 'ox'   **härä|n häntä** 'the tail of the ox' **k** > **0**

4 (d) or (if followed by **e**) to **j**:

solki 'buckle'   **solje|n hinta** 'the price of the   **k** > **j**
                                   buckle'

5 (a) A **t** preceded by a vowel compresses to **d**:

koti 'home'   **kodi|n kalusto** 'the furniture   **t** > **d**
                                   of the home'

5 (b) Preceded by an **l** or **r**, compressed **t** assimilates to those
consonants:

kulta 'gold'   **kulla|n hinta** 'the price of gold' **lt** > **ll**
parta 'beard'   **parra|n ajelu** 'the shaving of   **rt** > **rr**
                                   a beard'

More alternating stems: e-stems

E-stems are a very important class of alternating stem. They are
all bisyllabic nominals whose citation form ends in **i**, but which
have **e** in the genitive singular. This kind of alternating stem is
more difficult to spot than the **ranskalainen** type because there are
plenty of imposters, i.e. bisyllabic nominals with citation forms
ending in **i** which have **i** in the genitive singular. Compare these
three pairs of nominals:

Non-alternating		*Alternating (e-stems)*
sN	**rivi** 'row'	**kivi** 'stone'
sG	**rivi|n**	**kive|n**
sN	**pommi** 'bomb'	**tammi** 'oak'
sG	**pommi|n**	**tamme|n**
sN	**tuoli** 'chair'	**nuoli** 'arrow'
sG	**tuoli|n**	**nuole|n**

From a citation form in final **i** you cannot be sure whether a nominal is an **e**-stem or not, so brute memorization is in order. When you learn a new nominal, you should make at least a mental note of its genitive singular. To assist you in this, all alternating stems are clearly marked in the vocabularies in this book. **E**-stems are marked with an extra **e**; thus 'arrow' is listed as **nuoli** *e*.

Tip: A good rule of thumb will help, however: the older the concept expressed by the word, and the more central it is to traditional Finnish culture, the greater the chances that it will be an **e**-stem; have another look at the six examples given above. (Counterexamples exist, of course, but they are few. Among the more egregious: the word for 'oxygen', **happi**, is an **e**-stem, but 'mother', **äiti**, isn't!)

There is one more vital complication which concerns **e**-stems. Most of them (see the short list at the end of this section) which have a citation form ending in **si** have stems ending in **te**. For example, the stem of **käsi** 'hand' is **käte-**; its genitive singular is therefore **käde\|n**, with regular **t > d** compression; contrast non-alternating **lasi** 'glass' (stem: **lasi**), with sG **lasi\|n**. In the vocabularies, nouns like **käsi** will be indicated thus: **käsi** *te*.

Here's a short list of some of the most common **e**-stems:

vesi *te*	water	**ääni** *e*	voice, sound
käsi *te*	hand	**pieni** *e*	small
uusi *te*	new	**nimi** *e*	name
vuosi *te*	year	**väki** *e*	people
tosi *te*	true, truth	**henki** *e*	spirit, life,
kansi *te*	lid, cover		person
viisi *te*	five	**tuli** *e*	fire
kuusi *te*	six	**hetki** *e*	moment
		pilvi *e*	cloud
mieli *e*	mind	**järvi** *e*	lake
kieli *e*	language, tongue	**sieni** *e*	mushroom; sponge

siipi *e*	wing	**kivi** *e*	stone
suuri *e*	great, large	**kuusi** *e*	spruce
nuori *e*	young	**suomi** *e*	Finnish language
puoli *e*	half; side	**Suomi** *e*	Finland
lehti *e*	leaf; newspaper	**veri** *e*	blood

Exercise 8 Practise forming the genitive singular and revise vocabulary by translating these phrases into Finnish:

1 the taste of French wine
2 the colour (**väri**) of money
3 the door of the small house
4 the house's small door
5 the capital of Sweden
6 the doctor's Italian friend
7 the history of London
8 the new price of the dress
9 the price of a new dress
10 the musician's beard

How to say where people are from: the elative case (-stA)

Mi|*stä* **maa**|*sta* **sä olet kotoisin?** What country are you *from*?
Mä olen kotoisin Espanja|*sta.* I'm *from* Spain.

To say what country you are originally from, you use the adverb **kotoisin** 'by domicile', but you must also put the name of the country into the *elative case*.

The suffix of the elative case is -**stA**. The uppercase **A** means that its vowel is susceptible to vowel-harmony changes. The two consonants **st** at the beginning of this suffix mean that it is a 'tight lid' and will therefore cause consonant compression.

Let's look at a few more examples:

Me olemme kotoisin Sveitsi|*stä.* We are from Switzerland.
Se on kotoisin Hollanni|*sta.* (S)he is from Holland.
   (**nt** > **nn** compression)
Ne on kotoisin Amerika|*sta.* They are from America.
   (**kk** > **k** compression)

Exercise 9 Make up short exchanges in which people ask each other what country they're from. Use the vocabulary given in the section above about nationalities. Don't forget to harmonize your vowels and to compress your consonants, as appropriate!

Reading

Try to understand as much of these short snippets of Finnish as you can without peeking at the vocabulary at the back of the book. The only new words are **ja** 'and' and **mutta** 'but'.

1 Pekka on suomalainen. Se on insinööri. Pekan ystävä, Jeanne, on pianisti. Jeanne on kotoisin Belgiasta.
2 Hyvää päivää! Mä olen Jorge Rodriguez.
   Hyvää päivää! Satu Pennanen. Hauska tutustua.
   Hauska tutustua.
   Oletteko te Espanjasta kotoisin?
   Nimi on espanjalainen, mutta mä olen kotoisin Amerikasta.

2 Ei, kiitos!
No thanks!

In this unit you will learn:

- about expressing likes and preferences
- more about nominal stems
- how to say 'before' and 'after'
- how to talk about 'doing things' to things and people: expressing the direct object
- how to say 'no', and to express dislike
- basic numeracy
- another way to express possession

Language points

Expressing likes and preferences: the present tense of verbs

Minä pidän kahvista.	'I like coffee.'
Minä pidän teestä.	'I like tea.'

To say that someone likes something, you use the verb **pitä-** and put the person or thing liked into the elative case (-stA), which you have already met in the preceding unit. As you would expect from having studied the verb **ole-** 'to be', the present-tense forms of the verb **pitä-** vary according to person, number, and formality.

These three dimensions are summarized in the following chart. The forms within the heavy lines are relatively formal, and those outside the heavy lines are relatively informal and colloquial. The dotted line separates forms with singular subject (to its left) from those with a plural subject (to its right).

colloquial/informal			formal
person			
1	**pidän**	**pidetään***	**pidämme**
2	**pidät**	**pidätte**	
3	**pitää**		**pitävät**

singular	plural

* You will learn how to build and use forms like **pidetään** in Unit 5.

Thus 'I like coffee' is **M(in)ä pidä|n kahvi|sta**, and '(S)he likes gold' is **Hän/Se pitä|ä kulla|sta** (remember that the personal pronouns have full and cropped forms, and that **hän** is more formal than **se** when referring to people).

You should notice two things about these verb forms. One is nothing new: the **-t-** of **pitä-** is compressed to **-d-** whenever a 'tight-lid' suffix is added. The other is the form for the third person. This form is made by lengthening the vowel at the end of the verb stem; contrast the form **on** of the verb **ole-** 'is', which you learned in the previous unit.

This lengthening is the regular ending of the third person present tense for all verbs other than **ole-** that end in a single vowel. Here are some more examples, given in colloquial style:

se etsi|i	(s)he is searching	**ne etsi|i**	they are searching
se näke|e	(s)he sees	**ne näke|e**	they see
se kestä|ä	it lasts	**ne kestä|ä**	they last
se puhu|u	(s)he speaks	**ne puhu|u**	they speak
se sano|o	(s)he says	**ne sano|o**	they say

Since this notion of 'lengthening of the preceding vowel' is often useful in talking about Finnish, we shall use a symbol for it: **#**, and we shall refer to all the various forms of the third person suffix (**-i**, **-e**, **-ä**, **-u**, **-o**, etc.) as **-#**.

More formal Finnish has a distinct suffix for the third person plural: **-vАt**. Thus in more formal contexts you will hear and see:

hän pitä|ä   (s)he likes, holds   **he pitä|vät**   they like, hold

hän puhu|u (s)he speaks, talks **he puhu|vat** they speak, talk
hän näke|e (s)he sees **he näke|vät** they see

Exercise 1 Here are the Finnish names of some things to like:

kahvi	coffee	**talvi** *e*	winter
tee	tea	**kesä**	summer
viini	wine	**syksy**	autumn
viina	spirits	**kevät**	spring (stem: **kevää**!)

Now put into Finnish:

1 I like coffee.
2 Do you like tea?
3 She likes spring(time).
4 I like spirits, he likes wine.
5 We like Finland.

Exercise 2 To practise some of the verb forms introduced above, put the following into Finnish. Don't forget to compress consonants as necessary!

1 I say
2 We see
3 Do you (polite) like Paris?
4 They are talking (formal).
5 She is talking about (use **-stA**) Finland.
6 Do you see?

Preferences

To state preferences such as 'I prefer coffee', you use the adverb **mieluummin** 'more gladly' with whatever verb is appropriate. So 'I prefer coffee' is **Mä juo|n mieluummin kahvia**, more literally 'I drink coffee more gladly'. Study these examples:

Mä pidän televisio|sta, mutta mä kuuntelen mieluummin radio|ta.
'I like television, but I prefer to listen to the radio.'

Ne pitää vede|stä, mutta ne juo mieluummin viini|ä.
'They like water, but they prefer to drink wine.'

Exercise 3 State your own preferences among the activities listed.

Example: **Mä pidän ranskasta, mutta mä puhun mieluummin ruotsia.**

'I like French, but I prefer speaking Swedish.'

For now, don't worry about the endings on the things drunk, eaten, and watched; these are explained later in this unit (direct objects).

1 drinking (**juo-**) water or milk (**maito**)
2 eating (**syö-**) fish or cheese (**juusto**)
3 watching (**katsele-**) television or listening to the radio
4 speaking English or Finnish
5 listening to the clarinet (**klarinetti**) or the piano

More on alternating stems: X-stems and Q-stems

The capital of Finland is **Helsinki**, and the Finnish word for 'tyre' is **rengas**. Now have a look at these two words in their genitive forms:

Helsingi|n historia	the history of Helsinki
renkaa|n hinta	the price of a tyre

X-stems

In the previous unit you saw how the consonants of many Finnish words become compressed when certain suffixes are added, for example the **nk** of **Helsinki** becomes **ng** when the 'tight-lid' suffix **-n** is added: **Helsingi|n** 'of Helsinki; Helsinki's'.

For a noun like **rengas** 'tyre', whose stem ends in a consonant, the reverse scenario applies. The **-ng-** in this stem is *already compressed*, because the **s** at the end of the stem acts like a 'tight lid'. When you add a tight-lid suffix to such a stem, the **s** changes to the vowel **A**, and since this provides more vowel space at the end of the stem, there is room for the **ng** to 'decompress' into its plain state **nk**. The genitive singular is therefore **renkaa|n**, and the elative ('out of the/a tyre') is **renkaa|sta**.

This alternation of **s** with **A** is characteristic of a large number of stems. We shall use the letter X to refer to the alternation **s/A** and shall refer to stems of this kind as *X-stems*. To save space and time in the vocabularies of each unit, we shall write **renkaX** instead of spelling out the citation form **rengas** and the genitive singular **renkaa|n**.

Here are a few more examples, with the citation and genitive singular forms listed together for you to compare. In each instance, the compressed consonants are in *italics*:

	'comb'	'tooth'	'sun'	'king'	'war'	'slow'
sN	kampa	ha*mm*as	aurinko	kuni*ng*a*l*s	sota	hi*d*as
sG	ka*mm*a*l*n	hampaa*l*n	auri*ng*o*l*n	kuninkaa*l*n	so*d*a*l*n	hitaa*l*n
stem	kampa	hampaX	aurinko	kuninkaX	sota	hitaX

Note on verbs. Many verbs, too, end in X; this X behaves slightly differently from the X found in nouns. At this point you need only know that to the left of all of the suffixes you have met so far, it is read as **A**. Thus from the stem haluX- 'wants' you may form 'I want': **mä halua**l**n**. (In verbs ending in XE, X is read as **n**: from kylmeXE- we have **kylmenee** 'it's getting cold'. More on verb stems in the next unit.)

Q-stems

There is a large set of words which – like X-stems – have a stem which ends in a tight lid, but which – unlike X-stems, which end in **s** in the citation form – are written as if they ended in the vowel **e**. If you listen carefully, you will hear most Finns pronounce a consonant (glottal stop, in fact; see the section on pronunciation, page 7) after this **e**. We shall call these stems Q-stems, and write their final tight lid as Q when giving their stems in the vocabularies.

When a tight-lid suffix is added, the sequence eQ is read as **ee**. Consonant compression and decompression occur exactly as in the X-stems. Compare the forms (once again, compressed consonants are in italics):

	'shore'	'wrist'	'custom'	'need'	'war'	'rain'
sN	ranta	ri*nn*e	tapa	tar*v*e	sota	sa*d*e
sG	ra*nn*a*l*n	rintee*l*n	ta*v*a*l*n	tarpee*l*n	so*d*a*l*n	satee*l*n
stem	ranta	rinteQ	tapa	tarpeQ	sota	sateQ

Exercise 4 To say 'after the lesson' you put the noun that means 'lesson', **tunti**, into the genitive and add the word **jälkeen**, thus **tunni**l**n jälkeen**. Develop your facility for Finnish stem-types while you learn how to say:

1 after the sauna   **sauna**
2 after the war   **sota**
3 after breakfast   **aamiainen**
4 after the exam   **koe** (stem: **kokeQ**)
5 after the break   **tauko**

Direct objects

Mä juon *kahvi*|**a.**   I'll drink *some coffee.*
Mä maksan *lasku*|**n.**   I'll pay *the bill.*

To say things like 'I'll drink some coffee' or 'I'll pay the bill' in Finnish, you have to know how to form the direct object. In the second example, you put the word for 'bill', **lasku**, into the genitive: **lasku|n.**

But the genitive will not do for the first example. This is because 'some coffee' refers to a vague amount of coffee, not a known, specific, finite, definite portion; and this is the sort of direct object which the genitive marks. Thus **Mä juon kahvi|n** would mean 'I'll drink the coffee', where a specific portion – say, a particular cup of coffee, perhaps even already poured – is meant.

To express 'some coffee' you need to use the *partitive case.* To form this, see the next section.

How to form the (singular) partitive

This case form is vital, but building it can be a bit complicated, so it's a good idea to start practising early. This section begins with a survey of the ways in which the partitive is formed. You should read these through with an aim to getting the general picture; don't bother trying to memorize them. The section to follow (Using the partitive) is a brief introduction to some of the uses of the partitive. Once you've read through to the end, do the exercises by referring back to this section.

We may think of the suffix of the partitive singular as -**TA**, with **A** standing, as always, for **a** and **ä** according to vowel harmony and with uppercase **T** standing for a **t** which is idiosyncratic in that it alternates with zero. The suffix thus has two subtypes, -**tA** and -**A**.

You can tell which subtype of this suffix to add, -**tA** or -**A**, by knowing the stem of the nominal to which you want to attach it.

The suffix is -**tA** if the stem ends in a long vowel or diphthong:

sN	sP	
maa	**maa**|**ta**	earth, land
kuu	**kuu**|**ta**	moon
tie	**tie**|**tä**	road, way
vapaa	**vapaa**|**ta**	free
tienoo	**tienoo**|**ta**	region
paluu	**paluu**|**ta**	return

filee	fileeǀtä	fillet
revyy	revyyǀtä	(stage) revue
korkea	korkeaǀta	high

Stems that end in any single vowel other than **e** take **-A**:

kala	kalaǀa	fish
kesä	kesäǀä	summer
talo	taloǀa	house
sähkö	sähköǀä	electricity
katu	katuǀa	street
levy	levyǀä	record, disk
kasetti	kasettiǀa	casette

If a nominal stem ends in **e** (really **e**, and not Q! – see Q-stems, discussed above), you must examine the consonant to the left of this **e** in order to determine how to proceed:

1 If that consonant is a single dental consonant (**s, t, T, n, l** or **r**, as mentioned on page 6) preceded by a vowel or by any of the consonants **n, l,** or **r**, delete the final **e** and add **-tA**. We'll refer to such stems as *dental stems*.

2 Otherwise just add **-A**, leaving the stem-final **e** intact.

You can revise the nominative and genitive as you compare them with the partitive singular forms of the following nominals (compressed consonants in italics):

stem	vete	kiele	suure	suomalaise	ääne	kante	purte
sN	vesi	kieli	suuri	suomalainen	ääni	kansi	pursi
sG	ve*d*eǀn	kieleǀn	suureǀn	suomalaiseǀn	ääneǀn	ka*nn*eǀn	pu*rr*eǀn
sP	vetǀtä	kielǀtä	suurǀta	suomalaisǀta	äänǀtä	kantǀta	purtǀta

'water' 'language' 'great'   'Finnish' (adj.) 'voice' 'lid, cover' 'sail'

stem	oluTe	lahte	Suome	onne	järve
sN	olut	lahti	Suomi	onni	järvi
sG	olueǀn	lah*d*eǀn	Suomeǀn	onneǀn	järveǀn
sP	olutǀta	lahteǀa	Suomeǀa	onneǀa	järveǀä

'beer'   'bay'   'Finland'   'joy'   'lake'

If the stem ends in a consonant, the suffix is **-tA**; Q is read as **t** and X is read as **s**:

stem	kirjeQ	hampaX
sN	kirje	ha*mm*as

sG	kirjee|n	hampaa|n
sP	kirjet|tä	ha*mm*as|ta
	'letter'	'tooth'

This treatment of the formation of the partitive leaves rather a few loose ends, but these will be handled individually. For example, **lohi** *e* 'salmon' acts like a dental stem (**lohi\|ta**), and **lumi** *e* 'snow' not only acts like a dental stem but its **m** changes to **n** (**lun\|ta**). All such deviations will be noted in the vocabulary lists.

Exercise 5 To say 'before the lesson' you use the word **ennen** followed by the noun that means 'lesson', **tunti**, in the partitive, thus **ennen tunti\|a**. Practise your partitives while you learn how to say:

1 before the sauna
2 before the war
3 before breakfast
4 before the exam
5 before the break

If you have forgotten any of the vocabulary, look back at exercise 4.

Using the partitive

The partitive has an enormous range of uses, but they may all be placed under the headings incompleteness, vagueness, and negativity. What follows here is a checklist of the more important instances of these headings; further discussion will follow in appropriate sections, as indicated. For now, just read through this section to get a general idea of what the partitive is for.

The partitive singular marks:

1 The greater bulk of something of which only a part is specified, e.g. **lasi olut\|ta** 'a glass of beer', **kuudes helmikuu\|ta** 'the sixth of February', **missä päin Helsinki\|ä** 'whereabouts in Helsinki?', **vähäksi aika\|a** 'for a little while'. Here we may also place **kolme poika\|a** 'three boys', literally something more like 'a threesome of boy'. Note the word order of this type of construction, with the word which is in the partitive second. For details, see Unit 7 (numerals) and Unit 9 (time expressions).

2 The domain of which most prepositions (and some postpositions) are the specific: **ilman apu\|a** 'without assistance', **ennen sota\|a** 'before the war', **tie\|tä pitkin** 'along the road'. For more on prepositions and postpositions see Unit 9.

3 The outdone member of a comparison: **puulta kovempi** 'harder than wood', **minula vanhempi** 'older than me'. In this construction the word in the partitive comes first; you'll learn more in Unit 8.

4 An indefinite quantity or entity, e.g. **leipälä** '(some) bread', contrast sN **leipä** 'the bread; bread (in general); a(n entire) loaf of bread'.

5 Any direct object which is not fully acted upon, even if it is itself a definite quantity and entity. Thus **Mä syön leipälä** can mean not only 'I'm eating some bread' but also 'I'm eating the loaf (but haven't finished).' Here belong activities which have no specific goal or clear outcome, as in **Se rakastaa Irmala** '(S)he loves Irma', **Se raapii päältälän** 'He scratches his head', **Mä ajan autola** 'I'll drive the car.' Contrast **Mä ajan auton korjaamoon** 'I'll drive the car into the repair-shop', an activity with a clear goal and an outcome whose success can be assessed.

6 Any direct object whatsoever, if the verb is negated: **Mä en syö¹ leipälä** 'I won't eat any bread, I won't eat the bread', **Se ei maksa¹ laskula** '(S)he won't pay the bill.' For superscript letters see the Pronunciation Note on page 37.

7 Indeterminacy in the subject, provided that the verb is negated: **Ei täällä asuᵏ ketään Pekkala**. 'There's no (one named) Pekka living here.'

Exercise 6 You can't speak an entire language, you can only speak parts of it. So it is not surprising that the direct object of 'I speak Finnish' is put into the partitive: **Mä puhun suomela**.

You already have met the names of many languages in section Unit 1: they are usually identical (but note that they are not capitalized) with the names of the countries in which they are spoken by the majority. Complete these sentences by supplying the partitive form of the appropriate language name.

1 András on unkarilainen; se puhuu___.
2 Irma on kotoisin Italiasta; se puhuu___.
3 Poliitikko on ruotsalainen; se puhuu___.
4 Poliisi on ranskalainen; se puhuu___.
5 Victor on kotoisin Hollannista; se puhuu___.

Exercise 7 Since the partitive marks direct objects which are not completely affected, one way to express the idea that someone is still in the middle of doing something is to put the direct object in the partitive. Thus:

Heikki maksaa lasku|a.
Heikki is paying the bill (right now; he hasn't finished yet).

Use the following vocabulary to build similar sentences:

Subjects: **Jari**, **Anna**, **Jussi**, **Satu**

Verbs

katso-	looks at, watches	**luke-**	reads
etsi-	looks for	**kirjoitta-**	writes
pese-	washes	**kuuntele-**	listens to
maalaX-	paints	**syö-**	eats

Direct objects:

omena	apple	**kasetti**	casette
kynä	pen	**postikortti**	postcard
lattia	floor	**levy**	record; disc
lehti e	newspaper	**talo**	house
kirja	book	**televisio**	television

How to say 'no': the negative verb and its associates

At the beginning of this unit you learned that 'I like coffee' is **Mä pidän kahvista**. But what if you don't? You will want to be able to say 'I don't like coffee', and for this you need to know how to negate verbs in Finnish.

There are two parts. The first is the negative verb, **e-**; it is to this little stem that you attach the personal endings. Here is the paradigm for colloquial Finnish:

	Singular	*Plural*
1	e|n	e|mme
2	e|t	e|tte
3		e|i

Once again, one form serves for both singular and plural in the third person (more formal Finnish has plural **ei|vät**). Just the word **ei** on its own is used to mean 'no', as in **Ei, kiitos** 'No, thanks.'

The second part is called the *connegative*. To form this, you add the suffix **-Q** to the stem of whatever verb you want to negate. So, the connegative of **pitä-** is **pidä** (with compression **t** > **d** because of the tight-lid suffix **-Q**; compare the **d** of **sade** 'rain' in the section on Q-stems, above).

Put the two parts together and you have a negated verb, for example:

Mä en pidä kahvista.
I don't like coffee.

Such a statement is a bit blunt, so it is best to preface it with something like **Anteeksi, mutta ...** (Sorry, but ...), or **Valitettavasti** (Unfortunately).

Pronunciation note: in the speech of most Finns, the **Q** at the end of the connegative copies any consonant to its right. It is as if we were to write **Mä en pidä[k] kahvista.**

Now have a look at these short dialogues:

Juotko sä viiniä?
Ei, kiitos. Valitettavasti mä en pidä viinistä.

Will you have (lit. drink) some wine?
No, thanks. Unfortunately I don't like wine.

Otatko kahvia?
Ei, kiitos. Mä juon mieluummin teetä.

Will you have (lit. take) some coffee?
No, thanks. I'd rather have some tea.

Exercise 8 Write some short dialogues of your own, in which liked and disliked beverages and foods are offered and declined. Be as polite as you can by using **valitettavasti**, **anteeksi**, and **kiitos**.

The cardinal numerals and how to use them

The basic cardinal numerals are:

1	**yksi** (stem: **y***h***te**)	6	**kuusi** *te*
2	**kaksi** (stem: **ka***h***te**)	7	**seitsemän** (stem: **seitsemä**)
3	**kolme** (stem: **kolme**)	8	**kahdeksan** (stem: **kahdeksa**)
4	**neljä**	9	**yhdeksän** (stem: **yhdeksä**)
5	**viisi** *te*	10	**kymmenen** (stem: **kymme***n***e**)

100	**sata**
1000	**tuhat** (stem: **tuhante**; sG **tuhanne|n**, sP **tuhat|ta**)

Notice the rather unexpected forms of the stems of the words for 'one', 'two', and 'seven' to 'ten'.

The teens are made by adding **+toista** to the names of the basic numerals: thus 'eleven' is **yksitoista** and 'eighteen' is **kahdeksantoista**.

To use the numerals with nouns, you put the noun which refers to the thing counted into the partitive singular. For example:

kaksi talo|a	two houses
kolme tyttö|ä	three girls
neljä nime|ä	four names
viisi suomalais|ta	five Finns

'Twenty' is **kaksi\|kymmentä**, i.e. 'two tens': 'two' plus the partitive of **kymmenen** 'ten'; note that the phrase is written together. Similarly:

kolme\|kymmentä\|viisi 'thirty-five'
neljä\|kymmentä\|seitsemän 'forty-seven'
viisi\|sataa\|kuusi '506'
kahdeksan\|sataa\|neljä\|toista '814'
tuhat\|yhdeksän\|sataa\|kolme\|kymmentä\|seitsemän '1937'

You'll learn more about numerals in Units 7 and 11.

More on possession: how to say 'I have a cat'

You have already learned that to say something like 'Irma's cat' in Finnish you must put the owner, Irma, into the genitive case: **Irma\|n kissa**. In this section we shall be looking at how Finns express things like 'Irma has a cat.'

From an English perspective it's not at all straightforward, for Finnish doesn't have a verb 'to have'. What Finnish speakers do instead is this: they simply say that the possession 'is', and put the possessor into the adessive case (suffix **-llA**, attached just like the elative **-stA**). So 'Irma has a cat' is **Irma\|lla on kissa**.

Here are some more examples:

Lapse|lla on koira.	The child has a dog. (**lapsi** *e* 'child'; **koira** 'dog')
Kaisa|lla ei ole koira|la.	Kaisa doesn't have a dog.
Mei|llä on aika|la.	We have time.
Onko su|lla aika|la?	Do you have time?
Häne|llä ei ole lasi|la.	(S)he doesn't have a glass.
Peka|lla ei ole raha|la.	Pekka hasn't any money.

Minulla on kaksi siskoa.   I have two sisters.

Notice the adessive forms of the personal pronouns: **meillä** for first person plural (and similarly, **teillä** and **heillä** for second and third persons plural); and **minulla** for first person singular (cropped form: **mulla**) and **sinulla** (**sulla**) for second person singular. The (formal) third person singular pronoun **hän** is a dental stem: **hänellä**. Informal **se** and **ne** have the adessives **sillä** and **niillä**.

If both possessor and possession are thought of as concrete and inanimate, the possessor goes into the *inessive case*. This is formed with the suffix **-ssA**, which you attach just like the elative **-stA**.

Tässä ruuassa ei ole makua.
This food has no flavour.

Tässä pöydässä on vain kolme jalkaa.
This table has only three legs.

Contrast:

Mikä ero on sanoilla 'järvi' ja 'lampi'?
What difference do the words 'järvi' and 'lampi' have? (i.e.,
    What's the difference between 'järvi' and 'lampi'?)

Miksi sillä tehtaalla on se nimi?
Why does the factory have that name?

When the personal pronouns are the possession, they take the suffix **-t**, for example:

Sulla on aina minut.   You'll always have me.

You will learn more about this **-t** in Unit 5.

Exercise 9 This exercise is designed to help you to acquire facility in discussing possession. The task is to convert, say, 'Irma's cat is white' to 'Irma has a white cat' (or the reverse).

Model: **Irman kissa on valkoinen.**
        Irmalla on valkoinen kissa.

1 Presidentin auto on iso.
2 Onks sulla tummaa olutta?
3 Talossa on vihreä ovi.
4 Baarimikon vaimo on ruotsalainen.
5 Onko teillä pieni asunto? (Use Teidän for 'your'.)

These further examples are chiefly for later reference, but don't be afraid to have a look at them now:

Minulla on parempi ajatus.	I have a better idea.
Minulla on lippuja.	I have some tickets.
Minulla on liput.	I have the tickets.
Liput on minulla.	*I* have the tickets.
Mulla on sulle joltain kiinostavaa.	I have something interesting for you.
Heillä ei ole miltään sanomista.	They have nothing to say.
Kuinka monta lasta teillä on?	How many children do you have?
Rouva Salmisella on sukua Ruotsissa.	Mrs Salminen has family in Sweden.
Hänellä on koko yö edessään.	(S)he has the whole night ahead of him/her.
Onko teillä aivan oma sauna?	Do you have your very own sauna?
Jokaisella on oma makunsa.	Everyone has his/her own taste.
Kaikella on rajansa.	Everything has its limits.
Onks sulla mun osoitteeni?	Do you have my address?
Eikö hänellä ole velikin?	Doesn't (s)he have a brother, as well?
Onko teillä kaikki muut huonekalut?	Do you have all the rest of the furniture?
Haluan että se on jollakulla.	I want someone to have it.
Hänellä on veitsi kädessään.	(S)he has a knife in his/her hand.
Sen miehellä on suu kuin kalalla.	Her husband has a mouth like a fish (has).

Exercise 10 Say in Finnish:

1 (S)he has a lot of money (**raha**).
2 Pekka has many friends.
3 We have family (use **sukua** 'some kin') in Lappi.
4 Do you have a dog?

Exercise 11 Make up three sentences naming things you do and don't have. Use the **-llA ole-** construction, e.g. **Minulla ei ole omaa asuntoa, mutta mulla on rahaa pankissa.**

Exercise 12 Study this model:

Minulla on radio, mutta siinä ei ole kelloa.
I have a radio, but it doesn't have a clock/there's no clock in it.

The form **siinä** is the inessive of **se**. Use this to make up similar sentences on the model above.Take pairs from among the following words:

auto	car	**kuppi**	cup
raha	money	**lompakko**	billfold, wallet
kahvi	coffee	**musteQ**	ink
postimerkki	stamp	**bensiini**	petrol
kynä	pen	**kuori** e	envelope

Basic word order

The two basic word orders. In Unit 1, you met one basic word order for declarative sentences, namely subject – verb – predicate, as in **Minä olen englantilainen** 'I am English'. Direct objects fit in the 'predicate' slot, e.g. **Minä syön voileivän** 'I'll eat a sandwich.'

In this unit, you have met the other basic word order, namely X – verb – subject, as in **M(in)ulla on kaksi kissaa** 'I have two cats.' The 'X' here can be any word or expression which refers to a person, place, or time. This word order is neutral and normal not only with sentences which express ownership, but also in any context in which the existence of the subject, i.e. the presence of the subject at that place and time, is more important than what the subject is doing.

3 Ole hyvä!

Help yourself!

In this unit you will learn:

- how to make, accept, and decline offers, and other common conversational formulae
- how to make requests and how to give commands (imperative)
- how to ask who, what, where, when, why
- how to use the first infinitive

Language points

Two short exchanges

Saisko olla kahvia?
Kiitos.

Would you like some coffee?
Thanks.

Ota kahvia.
Kiitos.

Have some coffee.
Thanks.

Making and accepting offers

In the first exchange above, someone is offering his or her guest some coffee. Since it's *some* coffee, we have the partitive **kahvia**. The actual offering is being done by the little formulaic word

saisiko (more colloquial variants include **saisko, saiskos**). This construction is always polite and thus never out of place.

The second exchange illustrates another common way of offering something, especially food or drink. Once again, we have **kahvi|a** in the partitive; but this construction is different in that **ota** is a command: it is the imperative of the verb **otta-** 'takes'. Later on in this unit you will find an outline of the various forms of the imperative and an overview of verbal stem types, but for now you should practise making various offers.

Exercise 1 Write your own exchanges, in which you offer a friend some of the following, using **saisiko** and **ota**. (You can urge your friend to take more by inserting **vielä: Ota vielä piirakkaa!** 'Have some more pie/pastry!') Write the friend's replies, either accepting (**Kiitos kyllä, Kyllä kiitos**) or declining (**Kiitos ei, Ei kiitos**). Declining can be brusque, so mitigation is often given, for example: **Kiitos ei, syön hyvin vähän makea|a** 'Thank you no, I eat very little (that is) sweet' or **Juon hyvin vähän viini|ä** 'I drink very little wine'.

mehu	juice	**tee**	tea
viini	wine	**sokeri**	sugar
juusto	cheese	**kerma**	cream
kakku	cake	**maito**	milk

A few more short exchanges

Saisinko voileivän?
Totta kai!

Could I have a sandwich?
(Indeed you may.) (i.e. 'Yes.')

Saanko sokeria?
Olkaa hyvä.

May I have some sugar?
Here you are. (or: Help yourself.)

To request something, you use **saa|n|ko**, or, more polite, **sa|isi|n|ko**. These are both first-person forms of the verb **saa-** 'gets' and would translate literally into something like 'May I (get)?' and 'Might I (get)?'. (You'll find out about the **isi** of **sa|isi|n|ko** in Unit 10.) The thing requested is the direct object of the sentence, and is therefore put into the accusative (which, so far, is the same as the genitive; but see below) or the partitive.

It is put into the accusative (i.e., the genitive) if it is a whole, individual, countable, self-contained thing such as a sandwich (**voileiväln**, lit. 'butter bread', above); it is put into the partitive if it is stuff which comes in various indefinite quantities, like sugar (**sokerila** above). The difference is basically one of whole versus part, and English usually handles this with 'a(n)' or 'the' versus 'some':

Saisinko lasiln? May I have *a* glass or May I have *the* glass?
Saisinko vetltä? May I have *some* water?

Compare

Saisinko lasila? (at the glazier's) May I have *some* glass?

Exercise 2 Write your own short exchanges, in which you request the following, using the genitive or partitive direct object form as appropriate. Have your collucutor accede, either with **Totta kai!** (Yes indeed) or **Olkaa hyvä**, a formula you use whenever you hand anything to anyone.

sämpylä	roll	**leipä**	bread
kahvi	coffee	**lusikka**	spoon
voi	butter	**lautanen** *se*	plate
hillo	jam	**suola**	salt

Issuing commands: the imperative

At the beginning of this unit, you learned that **ota** 'take!' is grammatically an imperative. This section shows you how to make imperative verb forms.

There are two forms commonly used, singular and plural. As in other tenses and moods of the verb, you use the plural form when talking to more than one friend, or to be polite when speaking to one or more relative strangers; you use the singular form only when talking to one friend.

The suffixes of these two types of imperative are -**Q** for the singular and -**kAA** for the plural. Study the imperatives of these four verbs:

Stem	*Imperative*		*English*
otta-	**ota!**	singular	Take!
	otta|kaa!	plural/formal	
tilaX-	**tilaa!**	singular	Order!
	tilat|kaa!	plural/formal	
mene-	**mene!**	singular	Go!
	men|kää!	plural/formal	
vie-	**vie!**	singular	Take (away)!
	vie|kää!	plural/formal	

As these forms show, adding -**Q** to a verb stem can have two kinds of effect. It compresses consonants (e.g. the **tt** > **t** in o*t*a!) and it changes **X** to **A** (e.g. the second **a** of **tila***a***!**).

On the other hand, the suffix of the plural imperative -**kAA** causes no compression (since by virtue of its shape it is not a tight lid) and it changes **X** to **t** (e.g. **tila***t***kaa!**). It also deletes any **e** at the end of a verb stem, provided that this **e** is preceded by **l**, **n**, **r**, or **s**, as in **men\|kää**, above.

Before you begin to practise using verbs in the imperative, a word about direct objects is in order. So far, you have seen that a direct object that is conceived of as complete is put in the accusative (= genitive), e.g. **Mä syön voileiväin** 'I'll eat the sandwich', but is put into the partitive if only part is affected or the activity is vague in some way, e.g. **Mä syön leipä\|ä** 'I'll eat some bread.'

In imperative sentences, things are slightly different. The partitive is used in the same way, e.g. **Syö leipä\|ä!** 'Eat some bread!'; but the accusative which marks the complete direct object of an imperative verb does not resemble the genitive. Instead, it is identical with the citation form, e.g. **Syö voileipä!** 'Eat the sandwich!'

The personal pronouns are yet another matter. These are put in the partitive if the activity is incomplete or vague, e.g. **Auta minu\|a!** 'Help me!' (**autta-** 'helps'); but they take their own special suffix, -**t**, when they are complete objects or the activity is easily assessed or measured, e.g. **Vie minu\|t ulos!** 'Take me outside!'

Don't worry too much about all these details just now; they will coalesce in your mind as you work through other points, and all will be revised in Unit 5. For now, have a look at a few more examples of direct objects with the imperative:

Complete direct objects

Täyttä⎮kää tämä lomake!	Fill in this form! (**täyttä**- 'fills', **lomakkeQ** 'form to be filled in')
Avaa suu!	Open (your) mouth! (**avaX**- 'opens', **suu** 'mouth')
Sammuta lamppu!	Turn out the lamp! (**sammutta**- 'extinguishes', **lamppu** 'lamp')

Incomplete direct objects

Avaa suu⎮ta vähän enemmän!	Open your mouth a little more!
Tuo kuuma⎮a vet⎮tä!	Bring some hot water! (**tuo**- 'brings', **kuuma** 'hot')
Seuraa hän⎮tä!	Follow him! (**seuraX**- 'follows')

Exercise 3 To practise what you have learned, try telling first a friend, then a relative stranger to do the following things. Remember to soften the command by telling them to 'be good': **Ole hyvä** (singular and informal) or **Olkaa hyvä** (plural and/or formal).

Tell him/her to

1 follow you
2 bring some juice
3 open the door (**ovi** *e*)
4 close (**sulke**-) the window (**ikkuna**)
5 put (**pane**-) the cat out
6 fetch (**hake**-) a doctor
7 take the television away (**pois**)
8 eat some cake
9 help the police
10 forget (**unohta**-) it

Prohibition

To tell someone not to do something, you need the negative imperative, or prohibitive. Like the negative forms you have met so far, this is made of two parts.

For the singular prohibitive, you use **älä** followed by the connegative, a form you already know. Since the verb is negative, *any* direct object will be in the partitive, whether incomplete or not:

Älä mene!	Don't go!
Älä syö leipä⎮ä!	Don't eat any bread! or Don't eat the bread!

Älä suutu!   Don't be (lit. 'get') angry!
(**suuttu-** 'becomes angry')

To build the plural prohibitive, you use **älkää** instead of **älä**, and add **-kO** to the main verb, instead of the usual connegative **-Q**. The plural prohibitives corresponding to the examples above are therefore:

Älkää menkö!
Älkää syökö leipää!
Älkää suuttuko!

Tip: Notice that the suffixes of the connegative and of the singular imperative are identical in shape: they are both **-Q**, a tight-lid suffix. Another pair of lookalikes is the **-kO** used to form the plural prohibitive and the **-kO** which makes yes/no questions; since **-kO** is not a tight-lid shape, these suffixes do not cause compression. Compare:

Ota viiniä!	'Have some wine!' (pronounce: 'ota*v* viiniä')
Älä ota viiniä!	'Don't have any wine!' (pronounce: 'ota*v* viiniä')
Ota|tte|ko viiniä?	'Will you have some wine?' (plural)
Älkää otta|ko viiniä!	'Don't have any wine!' (plural)

Exercise 4 Practise both singular and plural prohibitions by redoing the previous exercise, but this time prohibiting rather than issuing commands: say 'Don't follow me!', etc.

Exercise 5 Get Finns talking about something by asking them to tell (**kerto-**) about (use the elative **-stA**) it. For example: **Kerro Suomen talvesta!** 'Tell (me) about the Finnish winter!' (lit. '. . . Finland's winter'). For such purposes you can turn any verb into a noun by adding **=minen** (**=mise-**) to the stem. Example: **Kerro jotain saunomisesta** 'Tell (me) something about going in the sauna' (**sauno-** 'uses the sauna')

Here are some topics to get you started:

Helsingin historia
hiihto ('skiing') Suomessa
urheilu ('sport') Suomessa

Asking who, what, when, where, and why

You form this type of question by first saying the question word, then the rest of the sentence. Notice that Finnish doesn't invert the way English does:

Kuka se on?	Who is it? (lit. Who it is?)
Milloin se saapuu?	When does it/(s)he arrive? (lit.: When it arrives?)
Mitä sä sanot?	What are you saying?
Mitä ne ottaa?	What'll they have (lit. 'take')?
Miksi te lähdette?	Why are you (plural or formal) leaving?
Missä ne asuu?	Where do they live?
Minne ne menee?	Where are they going?
Mistä se tulee?	Where does it come from?

Study these further examples in order to become more familiar with the pattern and to pick up some more useful vocabulary:

Kuka puuttuu?	Who's missing?
Mistä ne puhuu?	What are they talking about?
Mitä sä teet joka aamu, ennen kun lähdet kotoa?	
What do you do every morning before you leave the house?	
Milloin se tulee takaisin?	When is it/(s)he coming back?
Miksi ne menee pois?	Why are they going away?
Se tietää, kuka sä olet.	(S)he knows who you are.

The most frequently used question words are the various forms of **kuka**, which is used of people, and **mikä**, which is used of things. Both of these words have slightly irregular paradigms; they keep their second syllable (ku*ka*, mi*kä*) only if they would otherwise become monosyllabic, and **kuka** switches to *ke(ne)-* for all cases except the citation form. Here are the case forms you have met so far, listed alongside a few personal pronouns and a noun, for comparison and revision:

	what	who	I, me	(s)he	it; (s)he	house
sN	mi|kä	kuka	m(in)ä	hän	se	talo
sG	mi|n|kä	kene|n	m(in)u|n	häne|n	se|n	talo|n
sP	mi|tä	ke|tä	m(in)u|a	hän|tä	si|tä	talo|a
sELA	mi|stä	kene|stä	m(in)u|sta	häne|stä	sii|tä (!)	talo|sta
sADE	mi|llä	kene|llä	m(in)u|lla	häne|llä	si|llä	talo|lla
sACC	*	kene|t	m(in)u|t	häne|t	*	*

* Remember that the accusative forms of **mi**|**kä** and **se**, like those of all nouns in the singular (like **talo** 'house'), are identical to either their genitive or their nominative singular.

Where are you now? Where are you (coming) from?

As the sentences in the previous section illustrate, the Finnish equivalents of English 'where' are actually case forms of the word for 'what?', **mikä**:

'from where' is simply the elative, **mi**|**stä**, as in **Mistä sä olet kotoisin?** 'Where are you from?' Compare **Mistä maasta sä olet kotoisin?** 'What country are you from?', more literally: 'From-what from-country you are by-domicile?'

'(located) where' is in a case called the *inessive*, with tight-lid suffix -**ssA**. Examples: **Mi**|**ssä sä asut?** 'Where do you live?', **Mi**|**ssä kaupungi**|**ssa sä asut?** 'In what city do you live?', **Mä asu**|**n Lontoo**|**ssa** 'I live in London.'

'(going to) where' is in a case called the *illative*. You will learn how to form and use the illative in the next unit.

Exercise 6 Put these sentences into Finnish. All the vocabulary you need is in the back of the book (and some is already in your head):

1 He is arriving from Turku.
2 They live in Helsinki.
3 They're waiting outside.
4 What does she say?
5 Where do you (plural or formal) live?
6 Where do they sleep?
7 Why are you waiting?

8 When do we leave?
9 Who is coming?
10 They know where we live.

Exercise 7 What if you don't know the answer? If you are asked something you don't know about, you'll want to say either **Mä en tiedä sitä** 'I don't know it' (if it's a matter of facts) or **Mä en tunne sitä** 'I don't know him/her' if it's the more complex matter of people. Since the verb is negated, you specify what or who it is you don't know by putting it into the partitive, for example:

Mikä sen nimi on?	What is her/his name?
Valitettavasti mä en tiedä	Unfortunately, I don't know
sen nimeä.	her/his name.

Now reply to these questions by saying you don't know the answer. To soften the blow, insert **valitettavasti** 'unfortunately' or **Mä olen pahoillani** 'I'm sorry'.

1 Mikä sen osoite on? (**osoitteQ** 'address')
2 Mikä sen puhelinnumero on? (**puhelin|numero** 'telephone number')
3 Minkälainen ihminen sen isä on? (**minkälainen** 'what kind of?' **ihminen** i.e. 'human being, person')
4 Minkä näköinen sen poika on? (**Minkä näköinen X on?** 'What does X look like?')
5 Minkälainen ihminen sen vaimo on? (**vaimo** 'wife')

Exercise 8 More practice with the imperative. Ask a new acquaintance (with whom you are still on formal terms) to:

1 Say something in Finnish (**suome|ksi**).
2 Say something about Helsinki.
3 Read it to you.
4 Sit down.
5 Write you a postcard.
6 Wait outside (**ulkona**).

Exercise 9 Ask the same things as in the previous exercise, this time of a friend (i.e., using the singular forms).

Exercise 10 'Do you mind if I listen to the radio?' – 'Not at all, carry on!' To encourage someone to go ahead and do something, you use the imperative plus **vaan**.

Model

Häiritseekö, jos poltan?
Do you mind (lit. 'Does it disturb') if I smoke?

Ei häiritse. Polttakaa vaan!
Not at all (lit. 'It does not disturb'). Carry on and smoke.

Here are some more things people might want to do. Supply the missing Finnish imperatives:

1 kuuntelen radiota
2 sammutan lampun
3 avaan ikkunan
4 imuroin (**imuroi**- 'hoovers')
5 otan tän ('this') tuolin

Exercise 11 Encourage a stranger to carry on doing the same things as in the previous exercise.

The first infinitive

Yes, Finnish has more than one infinitive, but they are all easy to form if you know the shape of the verb stem. The first infinitive is the most common one in Finnish, and it has more than one English equivalent. A few examples will illustrate the more common uses: 'I want *to go* outside', 'I'm in the habit *of reading* the newspaper in the morning', 'You mustn't *smoke* in a hospital.' More on the uses of the infinitive later on in this unit, and in Unit 10.

You form the first infinitive by adding the suffix -**TAQ** directly to the verb stem. Like the partitive suffix -**TA**, the **t** at the beginning of the first infinitive suffix is idiosyncratic in that it alternates with zero.

You use the **t**-less variant, -**AQ**, if the verb stem ends in any single vowel other than **e**:

sano|**a**	to say	**kysy**|**ä**	to ask
tietä|**ä**	to know	**etsi**|**ä**	to search for
saapu|**a**	to arrive		

The **t**-less variant is also used with verbs which end in **e** preceded by any consonant save **n**, **l**, **r**, **s**, or **X**. Actually, there aren't many verbs of this description; the most common ones are:

lukela	reads	lähtelä	leaves, departs
hakela	fetches, seeks;	kokela	experiences
	applies for	kylpelä	bathes
pätelä	is valid		

From here on, we'll label verbs which belong to these two sets as *class I.*

Otherwise you use -**TAQ**. When this suffix is attached to a verb stem which ends in a long vowel or diphthong (hereafter: *class IV*), the **t** of -**TAQ** compresses to **d** because of the tight-lid **Q** to its right:

saalda   to get
syöldä   to eat
imuroilda   to hoover

When attached to a verb stem ending in **e** preceded by **n**, **l**, **r**, **s** (hereafter: *class III*), the **e** is deleted. Of the resulting clusters, **nt**, **lt**, **rt** (but not **st**, which is immune) are compressed by the **Q** at the end. Here's a step-by-step presentation of the formation of these infinitive forms:

Stem + suffix	After e-deletion	Actual form	Compression	English
mene-tAQ	> mentäQ	> menlnä	nt > nn	goes
opiskele-tAQ	> opiskeltaQ	> opiskellla	lt > ll	studies
pure-tAQ	> purtaQ	> purlra	rt > rr	bites
pääse-tAQ	> päästäQ	> pääsltä	(none)	manages to get (somewhere)

All other verbs (*class II*) follow their own set of rules. These are verbs whose stems end in **X**, **TSE**, or **XE**. To the left of the first infinitive suffix -**TAQ**, these final elements all change to **t**:

X	> t
TSE	> t
XE	> t

The resulting double **tt** is then compressed to **t**. Examples:

haluX-tAQ	> haluttaQ	> haluta	wants
mainiTSE-tAQ	> mainittaQ	> mainita	mentions
tarviTSE-tAQ	> tarvittaQ	> tarvita	needs
kylmeXE-tAQ	> kylmettäQ	> kylmetä	grows cold

Finally, the verbs 'sees' and 'does' are irregular: their infinitives are
näh|dä, teh|dä.

Exercise 12 One good way to firm up your knowledge of the rules
given above is to run them backwards. (That's exactly what you'll
have to do in order to use Finnish dictionaries, since these list verbs
in the first infinitive.) Notice that knowing the rules won't work
with class II verbs: you can't tell, from an infinitive like **mainita**,
whether its stem ends in =**X**, =**TSE**, or =**XE**.

Give the stems for these first infinitives:

1 kieltää
2 niellä
3 tuoda
4 reagoida
5 sanoa

Using the first infinitive: introducing modals

You can simply say that you're going to buy a map (**mä ostan
karta|n**), or you can fine-tune your statement by saying things such
as 'I may buy a map', or 'I want to buy a map', or 'I'm thinking
of buying a map'. We call such constructions modal expressions,
and the verbs used to form them, modal verbs.

There are two basic types of modal construction in Finnish. In
the first type, the subject goes in the nominative just as in a simple
sentence, and the modal verb agrees with it; the verb that expresses
what it is you may do, or want to do, or intend to do is in the
infinitive. Common modal verbs are **voi-** 'is able', **haluX-** 'wants',
and **taita-** 'is capable; probably is/does':

Ne voi ol|la oikea|ssa.
They can be right (lit. 'in right') (= It's possible they're right.)

Mä haluan osta|a uude|n auto|n.
I want to buy a new car.

Pekka taitaa tul|la kotiin aika myöhään.
Pete may come home fairly late.

Sä et taida tunte|a sitä.
You must not know him/her (or: You probably don't know
    him/her; or: I guess you don't know him/her.)

Other examples of modals which form this construction are **ajat-tele-** 'think (of doing)', **aiko-** 'intend', **osaX-** 'know how (to do)', and three very common verbs which are often used in the negative, **ehti-** 'have time (to do)', **jaksa-** 'have strength or stamina (to do)', **viitsi-** 'feel like (doing)', as in **Se ei ehdi nählldä kaikkea** '(S)he doesn't/won't have time to see everything', **Mä en jaksa enää kuunnellla tätä ohjelmaa** 'I can't stand listening to this programme any more', **Etkös viitsi jääldä vielä?** 'Don't you feel like staying (= couldn't you stay) a little longer?'

You will learn the second type of modal construction in Unit 10.

Exercise 13 To say that one is not allowed to do something, you use the structure **ei saa** plus the first infinitive, e.g. **Sairaalassa ei saa polttala** 'One is not allowed to smoke in a hospital.' To express 'one shouldn't' you use **ei pitäis**, as in **Ravintolassa ei pitäis nukkula** 'One shouldn't sleep in a restaurant.' To express impossibility, you use **voi-**: **Ilman vettä ei voi elälä** 'One cannot live without water.' Match up activities (verbs) and circumstances which are mutually inappropriate, then specify why by using **ei voi**, **ei saa**, or **ei pitäis** with the first infinitive. Here is some vocabulary to start you off:

veneessä	in a boat	**ravintolassa**	in a restaurant
ennen uimista	before swimming	**ilman ajokorttia**	without a driver's licence
hyppi-	hops, jumps about	**syö-**	eats
huuta-	shouts	**aja-**	drives

Exercise 14 One of the many uses of English 'must' is to convey the idea that we feel certain, on the basis of evidence or gut feeling, that something is the case: 'You must be tired' expresses commiseration, not a command. This kind of 'must' is conveyed by Finnish **taita-**, e.g. **Sä taidat olla väsynyt** 'You must be tired.'

Practise this construction by putting these into Finnish:

1 She must be Swedish.
2 They must have a big house.
3 You (plural/formal) must need (**tarviTSE-**) some coffee.

4 Paikasta toiseen

Getting around and about

In this unit you will learn:

- how to get about: giving and understanding directions
- how to say where people and things are, where they're from, and where they're going
- about communicating at the post office, in bars, at train stations, and at passport control

---

Dialogue 1 ▒

Kadulla

On the street

*In the street, Nigel asks a stranger, in this case a native of Helsinki (**helsinkiläinen**) for directions.*

NIGEL: Anteeksi, voisitteko sanoa, missä rautatieasema on?

HELSINKILÄINEN: Hetkinen ... se on tuolla, tuon suuren talon takana. Menkää tästä yli ja sitten kääntykää oikealle sanomalehtikojun edestä.

NIGEL: Onko se kaukana?

HELSINKILÄINEN: Ei ole, sinne on vain noin 300 (kolme sataa) metriä.

NIGEL: Kiitoksia paljon.

HELSINKILÄINEN: Ei kestä.

NIGEL: *Excuse me, could you tell me where the railway station is?*

HELSINKILÄINEN: *Hmm ... It's over there, behind that big building.*
Cross over here and then turn to the right in front
of the newsstand.
NIGEL: *Is it far?*
HELSINKILÄINEN: *No, it's only about 300 metres.*
NIGEL: *Thanks very much.*
HELSINKILÄINEN: *Don't mention it.*

Vocabulary

anteeksi	excuse me	**oikea|lle**	to the right
edestä	(X|n **edestä**) in	**rautatie|asema**	railway station
	front of X	**sano-**	says
Ei kestä	You're welcome/	**sanomalehti** e	newspaper
	Don't mention it.	**sinne**	(to) there
hetkinen *se*	moment	**sitten**	then
kaukana	far away	**takana**	(X|n **takana**)
Kiitoksia paljon!	Many thanks!		behind X
koju	booth, small	**tuo**	that
	stand	**tuo|lla**	there
käänty-	turns	**tä|stä**	this way, via
metri	metre		here
mi|ssä	where?	**vain**	only
noin	about,	**voisitteko**	Could you ...?
	approximately	**yli**	across, over

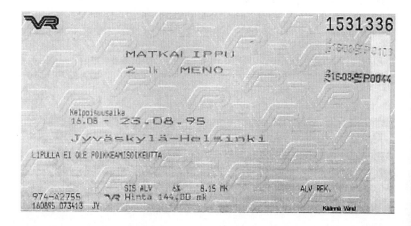

Here are the types of trains you will probably encounter:

kiito|juna	more commonly called an **intercity**; long-distance train
henkilö|juna	passenger train (as opposed to goods train, **tavara|juna**)
pika|juna	long-distance, stopping at main stations
paikallis|juna	local service; stops at all stations

Other useful train vocabulary includes:

info	information office
matkustaja	passenger
tulo	arrival
lähtö	departure
matka|tavara|säilytys	baggage room
ravintola|vaunu	restaurant car
odotus|huone	waiting room
konduktööri	conductor; officially: **junailija**
hätä|jarru	emergency brake
meno-paluu|lippu	return (round-trip) ticket
meno|lippu	single (one-way) ticket
makuu|vaunu	sleeping car
laituri	platform
raide (stem: **raiteQ**)	track

Some signs you are likely to see at railway stations:

LÖYTÖ|TAVARAT	Lost and found
PAIKALLISLIPPUJA	Local tickets
KAUKOLIIKENNE	Long-distance traffic
VAIN PARRANAJOKONETTA VARTEN	For shavers only!
SAAPUVAT	Arriving (trains)
LÄHTEVÄT	Departing (trains)
MIESTEN|HUONE	Men's WC
NAISTEN|HUONE	Women's WC

And here are some phrases that will come in handy:

Matkustan junalla.	I'll travel by train.
Miltä asemalta juna lähtee?	From what station does the train leave?
Miltä raiteelta juna lähtee?	From what track does the train leave?
Mille raiteelle saapuu juna Jyväskylästä?	At what track is the train from Jyväskylä arriving?

Miten pääsen asemalle?	How can I get to the station?
Viekää minut rautatieasemalle.	Take me to the railway station.
Milloin seuraava juna lähtee Turkuun?	When does the next train leave for Turku?
Onko aikaisempaa/myöhempää junaa?	Is there an earlier/later train, at all?
Mistä saa aikataulun?	(From) where can I (lit. 'does one') get a timetable?
Onko tämä paikka vapaa/varattu?	Is this seat (lit. 'place') free/reserved?
Saanko avata ikkunan?	May I open the window?
Sulkekaa ovi!	Close the door!

Once on board and underway, you will probably meet the **konduktööri**, who will call out:

Liput, olkaa hyvät!	Tickets, please!

More useful phrases on board:

Pysähtyykö tämä juna X-ssA?	Does this train stop at X?
Montako minuuttia vielä on junan lähtöön?	How many minutes (are there) still until the train's departure?
Montako minuuttia juna seisoo?	How long will the train be stopping?
Montako tuntia matka kestää?	How many hours does the journey take?
Monesko asema X on?	How many stations does this make? (lit. 'This is the what-th station?')
Koska saavumme Turkuun?	When do we arrive in Turku?
Milloin tullaan perille?	When do we (lit. 'does one') arrive?
Onko juna ajassaan?	Is the train on time?
Pitääkö vaihtaa junaa?	Is it necessary to change train(s)?
Juna saapuu aikataulun mukaan.	The train is arriving according to timetable.
Me ollaan perillä.	We are there (= 'We've arrived.', lit. 'One is . . .')

JYVÄSKYLÄ–TAMPERE–TURKU

VOIMASSA 28.5.–31.12.1995

Juna nro	P102	P104	IC90 [R]	P106	P108	P110	P112	IC92 [R]	P114	P94 [R]	P96	P116	P98/P120
Kulussa	M	M-S	M-L	M-S	M-S	M-S	M-S	M-S	M-S	S	P	M-S	M-S Jy-Tpe / M-P, S Tpe-Tku
Jyväskylä		4.15	6.10	8.10	11.08	13.14	14.18	15.30	16.44	17.57	18.19		20.22
Jämsä		4.50	6.39	8.44	11.44	13.50	14.49	16.01	17.16	18.30	18.56		20.58
Orivesi		5.27	7.13	9.21	12.21	14.27	15.26	|	17.53	|	19.34		21.34
Tampere O		5.55	7.38	9.47	12.47	14.53	15.52	16.54	18.19	19.29	20.00		21.59
Tampere	5.50	6.55		10.00	12.57	15.03	16.31		18.29			20.57	22.03
Toijala	6.15	7.22		10.24	13.22	15.29	16.58		18.56			21.23	22.29
Humppila	|	7.57		10.57	13.53	15.57	17.29		19.26			21.54	23.00
Loimaa	6.54	8.13		11.13	14.07	16.15	17.46		19.43			22.08	23.15
Turku	7.42	8.57		11.54	14.48	16.56	18.28		20.32			22.50	23.56
Turku satama O		1)9.17					1)18.42		1)20.41				

TURKU–TAMPERE–JYVÄSKYLÄ

Juna nro	P89	P101	IC91 [R]	P103	P105	P07	P93	P109/IC95 [R]	P111	P97	P113/P99	P115	P117 (vain 16.6-13.8)
Kulussa	M (14.8.alk)	M-S	M-L	M-S	M-S	M-S	P	M-S	M-P, S	P	P	M-S	M-S
Turku satama				8.45	9.58	12.56					1)19.26	1,2)20.41	1)21.40
Turku		7.00		8.58	10.39	13.40		15.33	17.00		19.37	20.53	21.51
Loimaa		7.42		9.40	10.56	13.40		16.17	17.45		20.21	21.40	22.43
Humppila		7.56		9.54	11.25	13.53		16.31	18.00		20.35	21.55	23.00
Toijala		8.24		10.23	11.51	14.21		17.00	18.29		21.04	22.32	23.28
Tampere O		8.50		10.49		14.47		17.27	18.55		21.31	22.58	23.55
Tampere	6.18	9.00	10.05	11.03	12.03	15.00	16.10	17.32	19.08	20.40	22.20	23.20	
Orivesi	6.44	9.26	|	11.29	12.29	15.26	16.36	17.58	19.34	21.06	22.46	23.47	
Jämsä	7.25	10.02	11.01	12.09	13.05	16.02	17.17	18.31	20.10	21.46	23.19	0.24	
Jyväskylä O	7.57	10.33	11.28	12.39	13.35	16.35	17.48	18.58	20.44	22.16	23.46	0.58	

[R] = LISÄMAKSULLINEN JUNA
IC = INTERCITY
P = PIKAJUNA
– = JUNAN VAIHTO
O = TULOAIKA
M = MAANANTAI
P = PERJANTAI
L = LAUANTAI
S = SUNNUNTAI
Jy = JYVÄSKYLÄ
Tpe = TAMPERE
Tku = TURKU

1) Vain laivamatkustajille laivojen kulkupäivinä
2) Vaihto Turun asemalla

JUHLAPYHIEN MUUTOKSET LÄHEMMIN ASEMLTA.

OIKES AIKATAULUN MUUTOKSIIN PIDÄTETÄÄN

pk-paino oy Tampere

Language points

Saying where things and people are: *local cases* -ssA, -llA

*Lasi*lssa **on mehua.**	There's some juice *in the glass.*
Lasi on *hylly*l*llä.*	The glass is *on the shelf.*

Just as in English we can distinguish between 'in' and 'at' and 'on', so in Finnish, too, we can fine-tune our statements and questions about the locations of things and people. One of the ways to do this in Finnish is to use *local* suffixes. This and the next two sections present one pair of local suffixes each; they are revised in overview towards the end of this unit.

You have already met the adessive (**-llA**) and inessive (**-ssA**) in connection with expressing possession (Unit 2); their use in expressing location is even more frequent.

Normally, 'in' is expressed by means of the inessive suffix **-ssA**, for example:

Suomel**ssa**	in Finland	**hotelli**l**ssa**	in the/a hotel
Englannil**ssa**	in England	**iso**l**ssa lauku**l**ssa**	in a/the big bag
Helsingil**ssä**	in Helsinki		

and 'at' or 'on' is expressed by the adessive suffix **-llA**, for example:

oikeal**lla**	on the right	**asema**l**lla**	at the station
vasemmal**lla**	on the left	**kadu**l**lla**	on the street
merel**llä**	at sea	**toise**l**lla puole**l**lla**	on the other side

Generally speaking, forms with **-ssA** refer to closer, more intimate contact than forms with **-llA**: thus **kaivossa** is 'in the/a well', but **kaivolla** is 'at the/a well'. Larger, relatively open, public places tend to be used with **-llA** (**asema**l**lla** 'at the station', **lentokentä**l**llä** 'at the airport').

Often the shades of meaning are quite subtle, for example:

Ruoka on pöydäl**ssä.**	Dinner is served. (lit. 'The food is "in" the table'.)
Pöydäl**llä on ruokaa.**	There is some food on the table (as it happens).

Note also **maa**l**lla** 'in the country' (as opposed to 'in town'), but **maa**l**ssa** 'on the ground'.

As the example **vuode**l**ssa** 'in a year' shows, the local cases are used in time expressions as well. For example, the amount of time it takes for a certain amount of activity to take place is expressed with **-ssA**, as in:

Se juo kuusi kuppia kahvia päivä|ssä.
(S)he drinks six cups of coffee a day.

Less specific time expressions are often built with the **-llA** suffix:

päivä|llä	during the day(-time)
talve|lla	in winter

Notice also:

ensi/viime/tällä viikolla	next/last/this week
ensi/viime/tässä kuussa	next/last/this month

More on time expressions in Unit 9. Here are some more examples of the local cases in their spatial meanings:

Mi|ssä sinä olet työ|ssä?	Where do you work?' (lit. 'Where are you in work?')
Toinen pullo on vielä hylly|llä.	The other bottle is still on the shelf.
Mä asun Oulu|ssa.	I live in Oulu.
Asutko sinä Tampereella?	Is it in Tampere that you live?

You will notice that some Finnish placenames (like **TampereQ**) take **-llA**, others (like **Oulu**) take **-ssA**. There is no hard and fast rule, and even Finns often disagree! Follow the locals. (All cities outside Finland take **-ssA**: **Lontoo|ssa, Pariisi|ssa**.)

Exercise 1 Give Finnish equivalents for the words in italics:

1 I live *in Helsinki*.
2 The wine is still *in the bottle*.
3 Her gloves are *on the table*.
4 They're still *at the station*.
5 She read fifty letters *in one day*.
6 *in Finland*
7 *in England*
8 *in the summer*
9 *next month*
10 *on the right*

Saying where people and things are from: *source cases* -stA, -ltA

Study the following pairs of sentences:

Witold asuu Puolalssa.   Witold lives in Poland.
Witold on kotoisin Puolalsta. Witold is (originally) from
                                 Poland.

Pullo on hyllyllä.   The bottle is on the shelf.
Ota pullo hyllyltä!   Take the bottle (down) from off
                       the shelf!

Parallel in meaning and form to the suffixes -**ssA** and -**llA**, which indicate location, are -**stA** and -**ltA**, which indicate origin or source, i.e. the place from which someone or something has moved. Here are some more examples:

Ota kahvipannu kaapilsta!
Take the coffee-pot out of the cupboard!

Mä odotan postikorttia Moskovalsta/Heikilltä.
I'm expecting a postcard from Moscow/Heikki.

Oletteko te kaupungilsta vai maalta?
Are you from the city or from the country?

Se puhuu ranskaa, mutta se ei ole kotoisin Ranskalsta.
(S)he speaks French, but (s)he isn't from France.

Se pyytää meilltä rahaa.
(S)he's asking us for money (lit. 'requesting from us money').

You will notice that the forms with -**ltA**, like those with -**llA**, generally refer to less intimate, less concrete contact, e.g. a postcard is normally **Heikiltä** 'from Heikki'; **Heikistä** would be either 'from inside Heikki' (i.e. surgically removed, after he had swallowed it), or more likely, 'about Heikki, on the subject of Heikki'. More examples:

Mä kirjoitan kirjettä Heikilstä.
I'm writing a letter about Heikki.

Mitä te pidätte tästä kaupungilsta?
What do you think of this city?

Milstä sinä saat tätä olutta?
Where do you get this beer from?

Keneltä sinä saat tätä olutta?
'Who do you get this beer from?' (lit. 'From whom . . .')

The **-ItA** suffix is also used in time expressions referring to hours and minutes of the clock, for example:

Suomen tunti alkaa kello kahdelta.
Finnish class begins at two o'clock.

Exercise 2 Give Finnish equivalents for the words in italics:

1 coming *from the station*
2 waiting *at the station*
3 It's now *at the platform.*
4 They're already *on the train.*
5 *at six o'clock*
6 This letter is *about Juuso.*
7 This letter is *from Juuso.*
8 Take the letter *off the table.*
9 Take the spoon *out of the cup.*
10 *on the right*

Saying where people and things are going: *goal cases* -lle, -#n

Parallel to the locational and source suffixes are the goal suffixes **-lle** and **-#n**. Thus just as you use the ablative **-ItA** to say 'from whom', as in

Keneltä tämä kirje on?   Who is this letter from?

you use the allative **-lle** to say 'to whom', as in

Kenelle tämä kirje on?   Who is this letter to?

The vowel of the allative suffix is always **e**, i.e. it does not vary according to vowel harmony:

kadulle   onto the street
levylle   onto the disc

Now notice the similar parallelism of these suffixes:

Witold asuu Puolassa.   Witold lives in Poland. (with the inessive **-ssA**)
Witold menee Puolaan.   Witold is going to Poland. (with the illative **-#n**)

Just as in the third person singular suffix of the verb, the # at the beginning of the illative suffix means that you lengthen any single vowel at the end of a nominal stem:

kaivolon	into the well	**Ruotsilin**	to Sweden
laukkulun	into the bag	**Suomelen**	to Finland
junan lähtölön	until the train's departure		

There are just two hiccups. (1) If the stem is a monosyllable, the illative suffix is -**h#n** followed by a copy of the last vowel:

teelhen	into tea	**voilhin**	into butter
työlhön	to work	**puulhun**	into a tree

(2) With all other nominals, the illative is -**seen**. Thus we have this form of the illative with bisyllabic nominals which end in long vowels or diphthongs, and with Q-stems and X-stems, for example:

vieraalseen huoneelseen   into a strange room (**vieraX**, **huoneQ**)

As with the other suffix pairs you have learned in this unit, the difference between -**lle** and -**#n** is one of degree of intimacy, or closeness of contact, and whether or not the place is relatively open and public. So, for example, you send a letter 'to Heikki', **Heikillle**, and you go 'to (lit. onto) the station', **asemallle**, but you go 'into a room', **huoneelseen**, and pour water 'into a bottle', **pullolon**.

Exercise 3 Give Finnish equivalents for the words in italics, using the correct forms made with -**lle** or -**#n**, as appropriate:

1 Take me *to the station*.
2 Put it back *on(to) the table*.
3 I'll give this *to Eila*.
4 He put it *onto the shelf*.
5 Put your spoon *into the cup*.
6 I'm going *to Denmark*.
7 They're on their way *into town*.

Overview: the local case suffixes

You have now met the main six cases which Finnish uses to express location and motion. Three of the cases (-**llA**, -**ltA**, -**lle**; hereafter: *l-cases*) have at least one **l** in their suffix, and refer to general neighbourhood or surface. The other three (-**ssA**, -**stA**, -**#n**; hereafter:

s-cases) refer to closer proximity, even to contact or interiorness. In the following table, these six cases are represented by forms of the nouns **kirjeQ** 'letter' and **katu** 'street':

	Inside	Surface, neighbourhood
motion towards	**kirjee|seen**	**kadu|lle**
location	**kirjee|ssä**	**kadu|lla**
motion from	**kirjee|stä**	**kadu|lta**

As you study the table, notice the parallels and patterns in the forms. Which differences are due to vowel harmony? Which differences are due to stem types?

Now have a look at the following sentences, which illustrate some of the more important meanings of these forms:

Huomenna ne on *kadu\|lla* taas.
Tomorrow they'll be back *on the street*. (**kadu\|lla** *adessive*: stasis at, or on surface)

Se tulee sisään *kadu\|lta.*
(S)he comes in *from the street*. (**kadu\|lta** *ablative*: motion from neighbourhood or surface)

Se menee ulos *kadu\|lle.*
(S)he goes out *onto the street*. (**kadu\|lle** *allative*: motion towards neighbourhood or surface)

***Kirjee\|ssä* hän sanoo, että Heikki ei tule.**
In the letter (s)he says that Heikki isn't coming. (**kirjee\|ssä** *inessive*: stasis inside)

Valitettavasti mä en ehdi vastata *kirjee\|seen.*
Unfortunately I don't have time to answer the letter. (lit. 'into the letter', i.e. *motion towards inside*!)

Kiitos *kirjee\|stä*!
Thanks for the letter! (lit. 'from inside' the letter, i.e. *motion from inside*!)

As the last two examples show, the notion of motion *to* and *from* is a useful model for thinking about Finnish, but you should not apply it mechanically to English constructions in the hope of creating idiomatic Finnish sentences. For example, in Finnish you find things *from out of* (**-stA**) or *from off* (**-ltA**) places, and you leave them *into* (**-#n**) or *onto* (**-lle**) places:

Se löytää aina rahaa kadulta.
(S)he's always finding money on the street.

Mä jätän mun takin eteiselen.
I'll leave (**jättä-**) my jacket (**takki**) in the entrance hall
(**eteinen** *se*).

Exercise 4 Give Finnish equivalents of the following sentences.
Try to remember the Finnish word before peeking back at the
vocabularies above or resorting to the glossary at the back of this
book:

1 Leave the bag in the entrance hall.
2 I'll put the glass back in(to) the cupboard.
3 Aila is still on the train.
4 I'll write a letter to Juuso.
5 Send a postcard to Heikki in (lit. 'into') London.
6 The timetable is behind the shelf.
7 The car is in front of the station.
8 Take me to Paris.
9 When do we arrive?
10 Is there any juice in the glass?

Dialogue 2 ▣▣

Mikä sen kylän nimi on?

What's the name of that village?

*Celia starts to ask her friend Matti about his family, and ends up
getting a quick lesson in Finnish geography*

CELIA: Asuuko sinun perheesi[1] Helsingissä?
MATTI: Ei asu. Mun perhe asuu maalla, pienessä kylässä.
CELIA: Mikä sen kylän nimi on?
MATTI: Padasjoki. Mun perhe asuu Padasjoella.
CELIA: Onko Padasjoki kaukana Helsingistä?
MATTI: Ei ole. Padasjoelta ei ole pitkä matka Lahteen, joka on
noin sata kilometriä Helsingistä pohjoiseen.
CELIA: Anteeksi, mä en ymmärrä. Mikä se Lahti on?
MATTI: Lahti on pieni kaupunki Hämeen läänissä.
CELIA: Vai niin.

CELIA: *Do your family live in Helsinki?*
MATTI: *No, they don't. They live in the country, in a little village.*
CELIA: *What is the village called? (lit. What is that village's name?)*
MATTI: *Padasjoki. They live in Padasjoki.*
CELIA: *Is Padasjoki far from Helsinki?*
MATTI: *No, not at all. It's not far from Padasjoki to Lahti, which is about 100 kilometres to the north of Helsinki.*
CELIA: *I'm sorry, I don't understand. What is this 'Lahti'?*
MATTI: *Lahti is a small city in the **lääni** of Häme.*
CELIA: *I see.*

[1] **perhee|si** is 'your family'; you'll learn about forms like this in Unit 10.

Vocabulary

asu-	resides, dwells	**lääni**	administrative region
HämeQ	*lääni* in southwest Finland	**matka**	journey, trip; distance
		nimi *e*	name
joka	every, each	**ollenkaan**	at all
kaukana	far away	**perheQ**	family
kaupunki	city, town	**pitkä**	long; tall
kilometri	kilometre	**pohjoinen** se	northern
kylä	village	**ymmärtä-**	understands

Additional vocabulary

Have a look at these basic kinship terms, so you can ask people about their families and tell about your own.

äiti	mother	**eno**	maternal uncle
isä	father	**setä**	paternal uncle
vaimo	wife	**täti**	aunt
mies	husband (! stem: **miehe-**)	**isoäiti**	grandmother
poika	son, boy (sG **poja|n**)	**isoisä**	grandfather
tytär	daughter (! stem: **tyttäre-**)	**naimisissa**	married
sisko	sister	**leski** *e*	widow
veli	brother (! stem: **velje-**)	**leski|mies**	widower
serkku	cousin	**orpo**	orphan

Exercise 5 Make up your own short dialogues, in which people ask one another about their families and where they live. Make sure to ask and say what people do for a living, whether or not they're married, and how many children they have.

Dialogue 3 ▣

Baarissa

In a bar

Kalle would like to order some cider, but they are completely out of it, so he reverts to the default setting and has a beer instead

KALLE:	Onks teillä siiderii?
BAARIMIKKO:	Sori, sitä tulee huomenna.
KALLE:	Yks pitkä sit.
BAARIMIKKO:	Meillä on Koffia[1], Lapin Kultaa, ja Karlsbergia[1].
KALLE:	Lapin Kultaa. Paljoks se maksaa.
BAARIMIKKO:	Yheksäntoista viiskyt[2]. (19,50)

KALLE:	*Do you have any cider?*
BARMAN:	*Sorry. There'll be some coming tomorrow.*
KALLE:	*A large one (= beer), then.*
BARMAN:	*We have Koff, Lapland Gold, and Karlsberg.*
KALLE:	*(Make it) Lapland Gold. How much is that?*
BARMAN:	*Nineteen (marks and) fifty (pennies).*

1 Notice how Finnish handles foreign nouns that have not yet adjusted to Finnish ways, such as *Koff* with its final *f*, and *Karlsberg* with its final *g*: before adding Finnish suffixes such as (here) the partitive, an extra **-i-** is inserted: so **Koff**, partitive singular **Koffila**.

2 **yheksäntoista viiskyt**: the bartender uses allegro forms of the numerals. These are quite common, so practise using them yourself: 1–2–3 are **yks kaks kol**; 5–6 are **viis kuus**; and 10 is **kyt**. Thus 635, **kuusisataakolmekymmentäviisi**, becomes **kuussataakolkytviis**.

Vocabulary

From here on more formal forms, which you will be able to find in Finnish dictionaries (and at the back of this book), are given in the vocabularies to the right of the symbol '→'. For example **sit** → **sitten** means that **sit** is a colloquial form of **sitten**. Rules to help

you to form and recognize such colloquial forms will be introduced
as we go.

siideri	cider
sit → sitten	then
sori	sorry (more 'proper' Finnish has **olen pahoillani**)
pitkä	a 'long', i.e. a large beer
paljoks → paljonko	how much?
maksa-	costs, pays

Exercise 6 Make up your own brief dialogues, in which people
order various drinks in bars. Don't forget to use your numeracy:
ask and give prices.

Dialogue 4 🔲

Postissa

At the post office

*Anneli has gone to the post office to buy some stamps. A **virkailija**
is an 'official'*

ANNELI:	Päivää, mitä maksaa postimerkki Englantiin?
POSTIVIRKALIJA:	Ensimmäisen luokan tavallinen kirje on kolme kakskymmentä.
ANNELI:	Kaks merkkiä Englantiin ja sitte vielä kolme kotimaan sisäiseen postiin.
POSTIVIRKAILIJA:	Ja se tekee[1] kolmetoista markkaa.
ANNELI:	Kiitos. Missä mahtaa olla postilaatikko?
POSTIVIRKAILIJA:	Ovesta[2] ulos ja vasemmalle.
ANNELI:	Kiitos ja näkemiin.

ANNELI:	*Good day. What does a stamp to England cost?*
POSTIVIRKAILIJA:	*A regular first-class letter is three (marks and) twenty (pennies).*
ANNELI:	*(I'll have) two stamps to England, and then three for post within Finland.*
POSTIVIRKAILIJA:	*And that makes thirteen marks.*
ANNELI:	*Thank you. Where might there be a letterbox?*
POSTIVIRKAILIJA:	*(Go) out the door and (turn) to the left.*
ANNELI:	*Thank you and goodbye.*

1 With prices, **teke-** can also mean 'amounts to, adds up to'.
2 The elative is also used to mean 'by way of'.

Vocabulary

ensimmäinen *se*	first	**näkemiin**	goodbye
kaks	→ **kaksi**	**posti**	post, mail
kirjeQ	letter	**sisäinen** *se*	internal
kotimaa	homeland	**sitte**	→ **sitten**
	= Finland	**tavallinen** *se*	ordinary, normal
luokka	class	**ulos**	(moving towards)
mahta-	might		out(side)
markka	mark	**vasemmalle**	to the left
merkki,	stamp	**vielä**	still, yet
postimerkki			

Exercise 7 Can you put these into Finnish without peeking at the dialogue above?

1 out the door and to the left
2 Where might there be a bank (**pankki**)?
3 That makes twenty marks.
4 How much is a stamp to England?

Dialogue 5 ▄▄

Passitarkastus

Passport control

At an entry-point to Finland, Joe answers the questions put to him by an official

VIRKAILIJA: Passinne,[2] kiitos[1].
            (*Joe ojentaa passin*)
VIRKAILIJA: Mistä maasta tulette?
JOE: Amerikasta.
VIRKAILIJA: Kuinka kauan aiotte viipyä Suomessa?
JOE: Kolme viikkoa.
VIRKAILIJA: Mikä on matkan tarkoitus?
JOE: Olen turistimatkalla.
VIRKAILIJA: Missä aiotte asua matkanne[1] aikana?
JOE: Tätini[3] luona Helsingissä, Kulosaaressa.
VIRKAILIJA: (*antaa passin takaisin*) Tervetuloa Suomeen!

OFFICIAL: *Your passport, please.*
            (Joe hands over his passport.)
OFFICIAL: *What country are you coming from?*
JOE: *America.*
OFFICIAL: *How long do you intend to stay in Finland?*
JOE: *Three weeks.*
OFFICIAL: *What is the purpose of (your) journey?*
JOE: *I'm a tourist. (lit. I'm on a tourist trip.)*
OFFICIAL: *Where do you intend to stay during your journey?*
JOE: *At my Auntie's house in Helsinki, on Kulosaari.*
OFFICIAL: (hands back the passport) *Welcome to Finland!*

1 **kiitos**: the official thanks Joe in advance: the implication is that Joe will comply.

2 **passi|nne, matka|nne**: the -nne is a suffix meaning 'your', used especially in more formal contexts; for more, see Unit 10.

3 **täti|ni**: -ni, too, is a possessive suffix; it means 'my'.

Vocabulary

anta-	gives	**takaisin**	back (to origin)
aikana: X|n aikana	at the time of X	**tarkoitus**	purpose, meaning, intent
aiko-	intends	**täti**	paternal aunt
kuinka kauan	for how long?	**Tervetulo|a**	Welcome!
luona: X|n luona	at Xs place	**turisti**	tourist
ojenta-	offers, hands over	**viikko**	week
passi	passport	**viipy-**	stops, stays

5 Mitä me ostetaan?

What'll we buy?

In this unit you will learn:

- about different kinds of shopping
- about talking over the telephone
- how to be less than definite (indefinite forms of the verb)
- more about the form of direct objects
- more alternating noun stems
- how to make plurals

Dialogue 1 💿

Alkossa

At the off-licence

SUSANNA: Mitä me ostetaan sun synttäreitä varten?

MARI: Ku nyt kerta on kakskytviis-vuotis synttärit niin pitää kai ostaa pari pulloa kuohuviiniä.

SUSANNA: Elyseetä vai?

MARI: Joo ja otetaan sit samalla neljä pulloa valkkaria boolia varten.

SUSANNA: Mitä kirkasta sä haluut, kossuu vai jotain muuta votkaa?

MARI: Otetaan vaikka[1] kossuu ja sit saakin[2] melkein riittää.[2] Tässä onkin[3] jo kantamista[3]. Jätetään kaljat ja lonkerot poikien huoleksi.

SUSANNA: *What'll we buy for your birthday party?*

MARI: *Well, since it's my 25th, we really ought to buy a couple of bottles of champagne.*

SUSANNA: *Elysee?*
MARI: *Yeah, and let's buy four bottles of white white, as well, for punch.*
SUSANNA: *What spirits do you want, Koskenkorva or some other vodka?*
MARI: *Let's have some Koskenkorva and that'll probably be pretty much enough. There's enough here to carry as it is. Let's leave the long drinks and beers for the boys to worry about.*

1 **vaikka** Mari uses this little word to introduce a suggestion, while leaving open the possibility that Susanna will have a different idea: 'We could get some Koskenkorva, (or perhaps you'd prefer something else).'

2 **saalkin riittälä** '(it'll) probably be enough'.

3 **Tässä onkin jo kantamista** 'there's enough here to carry already (I'm sure you'll agree)'. In both these expressions, Mari uses the clitic **—kin** to suggest that Susanna won't disagree.

Vocabulary

ALKO	Finnish state	**ku → kun**	
	alcoholic	**ku(n) X, ...**	since X, ... so Y
	beverage	**niin Y**	
	monopoly sales	**kuohulviini**	sparkling wine
	outlet	**lonkero**	long drink
booli	punch	**melkein**	pretty, fairly
Elysee	(brand name)	**muu**	other, else
haluut → haluat		**niin**	so
Xln huoleksi	in Xs care	**nyt**	now
jäteltään	let's leave	**ostala**	to buy
jo	already	**osteltaan**	let's buy
joo	yeah	**oteltaan**	let's take
joltalin	something	**pari**	pair, a couple of
kai	maybe	**pitälä**	it's necessary
kantalmislta	carrying (sP)	**poika**	boy, pG **poiklien**
kerta	(for) once	**pullo**	bottle
kirkkaX	clear, bright;	**riittä-**	is enough, suffices
	alcoholic spirits	**saa**	it is possible; one
koskenkorva	a type of spirits		may
kossu →		**samallla**	at the same time,
koskenkorva			as well
kossulu → kossula		**sit → sitten**	

su|n → **sinun**	your	**valkkari**	white wine
synttäri →	birthday	→ **valkoviini**	
syntymäpäivä		**varten: X-TA**	for X
synttäre|i|tä, pP,		**varten**	
pN **synttäri|t**		**votka**	vodka
tä|ssä	here	**X|vuotis|Y**	Y which is X
vai	or (used in questions)		years old

Language points

Being less than definite: indefinite forms of the verb

Alongside the six personal verb forms you have already learned in Unit 2, Finnish has a seventh, indefinite, form which has two common uses:

1 The most common use of the indefinite, in both formal and colloquial Finnish, is to place the subject of the verb in the background. You may not know who the subject is, or you may simply not like to say. In either case, it's the indefinite you want. Contrast these sentence pairs:

Ne puhu|u suomea.	They speak Finnish. (colloquial; p3)
He puhu|vat suomea.	They speak Finnish. (formal; p3)

Suomessa puhu\|taan suomea.
In Finland, people speak Finnish/Finnish is spoken. (neutral; indef.)

In the first two examples, it is assumed that we know specifically who 'they' (**ne** or **he**) are. In the third example, there is no such definiteness. All that is assumed is that there is more than one person who speaks Finnish.

2 In colloquial Finnish, the indefinite is the regular form for indicating a first person plural subject. Contrast:

Me puhu|mme suomea.	We speak Finnish. (formal)
Me puhu|taan suomea.	We speak Finnish. (colloquial)

Without the subject pronoun **me**, the same form is used to make suggestions, for example **Puhutaan suomea!** 'Let's speak Finnish.'

For all verbs except those of class I, forming the affirmative indefinite is easy: just add **#N** to the first infinitive. So, for example:

	class II	*class III*	*class IV*
1st inf.	**haluta**	**mennä**	**saada**
indefinite	**halutaan**	**mennään**	**saadaan**

Class I verbs are different, so this little trick won't work with them. Compare these infinitive and indefinite forms:

1st inf.	**sano**|a	**luke**|a	**anta**|a
indefinite| **sano**|**taan**	**lue**|**taan**	**anne**|**taan**

You'll see that the indefinite forms for these verbs are different in three ways: (1) their suffix begins with **t**; (2) despite its appearance, this **t** is a tight lid, so it causes compression to its left (**k > 0** in **lue**|**taan**, **nt > nn** in **anne**|**taan**); and (3) this suffix also causes any **A** at the end of the verb stem to change to **e** (**e** in **anne**|**taan**).

Here are some more examples. They are provided with a variety of possible English equivalents in order to give you a taste of the range of meanings.

Class 1 verbs
sano|**taan**	(stem: **sano-**)	it is said; people say
anne|**taan**	(stem: **anta-**)	it is given; people give
kielle|**tään**	(stem: **kieltä-**)	it is forbidden

Class 2 verbs
halu|**taan**	(stem: **haluX-**)	is wanted; people want
maini|**taan**	(stem: **mainitse-**)	is mentioned
vaie|**taan**	(stem: **vaikeXE-**)	one is silent

Class 3 verbs
men|**nään**	(stem: **mene-**)	people go
ol|**laan**	(stem: **ole-**)	people are

Class 4 verbs
saa|**daan**	(stem: **saa-**)	one gets
vie|**dään**	(stem: **vie-**)	get taken (away), is exported
relegoi|**daan**	(stem: **relegoi-**)	gets relegated

Now have a look at these further examples, given with other verb forms for comparison and revision:

Me pide|**tään teestä.**	We like tea. (colloquial)
Me pidä|**mme teestä.**	We like tea. (formal)

Illallisen jälkeen ote|**taan kahvia.**	One has coffee after dinner.
Illallisen jälkeen ne otta|a **kahvia.**	They have coffee after dinner.

Milloin sä mene|t kotiin?   When are you going home?
Milloin men|nään kotiin?   When do/will people go home?
Milloin me men|nään kotiin? When will we go home?
                                  (colloquial)

The negative indefinite consists of two parts: (1) the third person singular of the negative verb, **ei**, plus (2) the connegative indefinite. This latter form is not at all as daunting to form as it sounds: it is the same as the affirmative form, but with a final **-Q** instead of a final **-AN**. Note the parallels:

anne|taan	is given	**halu|taan**	is wanted
ei anne|ta	is not given	**ei halu|ta**	is not wanted
pes|tään	is washed	**tuo|daan**	is brought/imported
ei pes|tä	is not washed	**ei tuo|da**	is not brought/imported

You can hear the effects of the final **-Q** in doubling such as that of **Ei tuoda^P puuta** 'Wood isn't imported.'

Exercise 1 Switch from formal to colloquial, and vice versa.

1 Me asumme Helsingissä.
2 Me mennään maalle.
3 Me haluamme valkoviiniä.
4 Me emme pidä oopperasta.
5 Me ei lueta lehteä.
6 Me puhutaan ranskaa.
7 Me emme tarvitse apua.

Plurals

In this section you will learn how to form and use most of the plural forms of nouns and adjectives. We'll divide it into three subsections to make it easier to absorb.

Plural cases I

The plural nominative (pN) is easy to form: its suffix is **-t**, a tight-lid suffix which attaches to the stem exactly like the **-n** of the genitive singular:

stem	kaupunki	maa	hampaX	rakennukse
sG	kaupungi|n	maa|n	hampaa|n	rakennukse|n
pN	kaupungi|t	maa|t	hampaa|t	rakennukse|t
	'city, town'	'country'	'tooth'	'building'

stem	puhelime-	huoneQ	katu	talve
sG	puhelime|n	huonee|n	kadu|n	talve|n
pN	puhelime|t	huonee|t	kadu|t	talve|t
	'telephone'	'room'	'street'	'winter'

The nominative plural refers to definite things or people, often members of a set. Here are some examples of the pN in action:

Euroopa|n maa|t	the countries of Europe
Rooma|n yö|t	Roman nights (lit. 'the nights of Rome')
Helsingi|n kadu|t	the streets of Helsinki
Suome|n talve|t	Finland's winters
pöydä|n jala|t	the legs of the table (**jalka** leg; foot)
Sirka|n silmä|t	Sirkka's eyes
Venäjä|n uude|t yliopisto|t	Russia's new universities

mone|t edellise|n hallitukse|n uudistukse|t
many of the previous government's innovations/reforms

The plural nominative is also used to mark the plural accusative. So we have, for example, **Mä syön kaikki nämä voileivä|t** 'I'm going to eat up all these sandwiches.' To say 'I'll eat some sandwiches' you need the plural partitive; see 'plural cases III', below.

Exercise 2 Change singular to plural, and vice versa:

1 jalka
2 huoneet
3 kaupunki
4 katu
5 hampaat

Plural cases II:

For the most part, the other suffixes in the plural are the same as those you have already learned for the singular. There is one important difference: they are all preceded by a generic plural marker -i-. This -i- causes certain vowel changes in the stem to its left; for comparison, here are the singular inessive (sINE) and plural inessive (pINE) forms of a few nouns:

Stem	sINE	pINE	Vowel change	Citation form	English
talve-	talve|ssa	talv|i|ssa	e > 0	talvi	winter
käte-	kä*de*|ssä	kä*s*|i|ssä	e > 0	käsi	hand
kaupunki	kaupungi|ssa	kaupunge|i|ssa	i > e	kaupunki	city
kesä	kes*ä*|ssä	kes|i|ssä	ä > 0	kesä	summer
juna	jun*a*|ssa	jun|i|ssa	a > 0	juna	train
sana	sana|ssa	san*o*|i|ssa	a > o	sana	word
asema	asema|ssa	asem|i|ssa	a > 0	asema	station
ystävä	ystävä|ssä	ystäv|i|ssä	ä > 0	ystävä	friend
omena	omena|ssa	omeno|i|ssa	a > o	omena	apple
kännykkä	kännyk*ä*|ssä	kännyk*ö*|i|ssä	ä > ö	kännykkä	cellular phone
maa	ma*a*|ssa	ma|i|ssa	aa > a	maa	country, land
yö	y*ö*|ssä	ö|i|ssä	yö > ö	yö	night

As the table shows, to the left of the plural -i- *all* stem-final **e**'s are deleted (> 0, e.g. **talvi**). TE-stems like **käsi** change their **t** to **s**, as in the singular nominative.

All stem-final **i**'s, as in **kaupunki**, change to **e**.

In bisyllabic words, *all* stem-final **ä**'s are deleted (**kesä**); **a** is deleted only if **u** or **o** is the first or only vowel of the first syllable (**juna**). Otherwise, **a** > **o**, as in **sana**.

In polysyllabic words, **a** and **ä** are sometimes deleted (as in **asema** and **ystävä**), and sometimes change (**a** > **o**, **ä** > **ö**, as in **omena** and **kännykkä**).

The diphthongs **ie**, **yö**, **uo** are shortened to **e**, **ö**, **o**. All long (double) vowels are shortened, e.g. **aa** > **a**, **uu** > **u**. Notice that such long vowels may themselves be from sequences with **Q** or **X** (**huoneQ|i|ssa** > **huone|i|ssa**; **hampaX|i|ssa** > **hampa|i|ssa**). Consonants to the left of such shortened vowels do not get compressed (**mp** of **hampa|i|ssa**); contrast the compressed **ng** of **kaupunge|i|ssa**.

Here are some more examples (compare with the examples given above):

Euroopa|n ma|i|ssa	Sirka|n silm|i|ssä
Helsingi|n kadu|i|lla	Venäjä|n uus|i|lla yliopisto|i|lla
Rooma|n öl|i|ssä	mon|i|ssa edellise|n hallitukse|n
Suome|n talv|i|ssa	uudistuks|i|ssa

As in the singular, the illative presents a few hiccups. Its ending is -**#n** as usual if the generic plural -**i**- to its left is the only vowel; but if there *is* a single stem-final vowel, you use -**h#n** followed by a copy of that vowel. Compare these plural inessive and illative forms:

	-i- alone	*stem-vowel plus -i-*
pINE	silm|i|ssä	sano|i|ssa, ma|i|ssa
pILL	silm|i|in	sano|i|hin, ma|i|hin
pINE	järv|i|ssä	kaupunge|i|ssa
pILL	järv|i|in	kaupunke|i|hin

Finally, if the noun takes -**seen** in the singular illative, its pILL is -**siin**:

sILL	vapaa|seen	huonee|seen	vieraa|seen
pINE	vapa|i|ssa	huone|i|ssa	viera|i|ssa
pILL	vapa|i|siin	huone|i|siin	viera|i|siin

Exercise 3 Convert the following from singular to plural, or vice versa.

1 kirjassa
2 taloissa
3 saarilta
4 lasista
5 pankille
6 hampaisiin
7 taloon
8 työhön
9 veteen
10 jalkoihin

Plural cases, III

The partitive plural refers to indefinite quantities of things or people. Building it is not so very difficult if you bear in mind that it consists of two parts: the generic plural suffix -**i**-, which is added to the nominal stem, followed by the partitive suffix -**TA**. As in the singular, this -**TA** suffix has two basic shapes, with and without the **t**: -**tA** and -**A**.

Which shape you use for any given noun is fairly predictable according to the following rules. You use -**tA**

1 if the nominal ends in a long vowel or diphthong. Vowel changes to the left of -i- apply as usual:

vapaa	vapali|ta	aa > a	free
tienoo	tienol|ta	oo > o	region
ainoa	ainol|ta	oa > o	only
tie	teli|tä	ie > e	road
yö	öli|tä	yö > ö	night
voi	voli|ta	oi > o	butter
maa	mali|ta	aa > a	country

2 if the nominal ends in X or Q:

rikas	rikkal|ta	(stem: rikkaX)	rich
huone	huonel|ta	(stem: huoneQ)	room

3 and *often* if the word is polysyllabic. This is true especially of words ending in **ri**, so from **paperi**, **tuomari**, **traktori** and **professori** we have **paperel|ta** 'papers', **tuomarel|ta** 'judges', **traktorel|ta** 'tractors', and **professorel|ta** 'professors'; but it is also likely if the last syllable is **nA**, **kkA**, or **rA**, or if the word ends in **ijA**. These stems have **a > o** and **ä > ö** before the -i- pluralizer:

kirsikka	kirsikol|ta	cherry
kynttilä	kynttilöl|tä	candle
peruna	perunol|ta	potato
kitara	kitarol|ta	curl
lukija	lukijol|ta	reader

4 *otherwise*, you use **-A**. The only thing to watch for then is that the -i- pluralizer changes to -j- whenever it winds up between two vowels (as in **tyttöjä** and **sanoja**):

poika	poikl|la	boy
juna	junl|la	train
linkki	linkkel|jä	(internet) link
järvi *e*	järvl|lä	lake
opettaja	opettajl|la	teacher
tyttö	tyttöl|jä	girl
sana	sanol|jla	word

Exercise 4 Put these phrases into the plural partitive. If you're not sure of the meaning (or the stem!) of a word, check in the glossary at the back of this book.

1 uusi talo

2 halpa takki
3 vapaa kansa
4 hyvä ystävä
5 nuori opiskelija
6 vanha opettaja

Direct object roundup: the forms of the accusative

You've already met with the several different ways Finnish has of marking the direct object of a sentence, but it'll be a good idea to round them up now and have a look at them all at once.

Actually, it all boils down to two possibilities, the partitive and the accusative. The partitive is used to mark 'incomplete' or negated direct objects, the accusative to mark 'complete' direct objects.

The main difficulty about the accusative case is that it has no one dedicated suffix. Instead, it 'borrows' the suffixes of various other cases. There are three basic scenarios:

1 For numerals, the accusative is the same as the nominative. Compare:

Tässä on *kolme* voileipää.
Here are *three* sandwiches. (**kolme** = subject)

Mä syön *kolme* voileipää.
I'll eat three sandwiches. (**kolme** = direct object)

Words like **pari** 'pair, a couple of' act like numerals in this connection:

Mä ostan *pari* pulloa viiniä.
I'll buy a couple of bottles of wine.

As mentioned in the previous section, nouns in the plural behave the same way: their accusative is the same as their nominative (**Tässä on voileivä|t** 'Here are the sandwiches'; **Mä syön voileivä|t** 'I'll eat up the sandwiches').

2 For nouns in the singular, the accusative is the same as the genitive *if the verb has a person suffix* (i.e., first, second, or third person, singular or plural):

Mä syö|n voileivä|n.   I'll eat a/the sandwich.
Ne osta|la lampu|n.   They'll buy a/the lamp.

Milloin sä lähetäIt toIn kirjeeIn?
When are you going to send that letter?

but the accusative is the same as the nominative *if the verb does not have a person marker*: most commonly, this means that the verb is an imperative, infinitive, or indefinite. Examples:

KerroIQ *totuus!*	Tell the *truth!*
AvatIkaa *ikkuna!*	Open the *window!*
Mun pitää syöIdä *voileipä.*	I have to eat *a/the sandwich.*
	(More on this construction in Unit 9)
Me syöIdään *voileipä.*	We'll eat *a/the sandwich.*

Sopimus allekirjoiteItaan Washingtonissa.
A/the treaty is being signed in Washington.

3 The personal pronouns have their own special accusative suffix, **-t**:

Se tunteIe *m(in)uIt.*	(S)he knows *me.*
Sä tunneIt *meidäIt.*	You know *us.*
Me tunneImme *häneIt.*	We know *him/her.*
Hänet **tunneItaan.**	(*S*)*he* is known.
Ne näkeIe *s(in)uIt* **joka päivä.**	They see *you* every day.
Mä näeIn *teidäIt,* **kun mä palaaIn.**	I'll see *you* (formal/plural) when I get back.

Exercise 5 Supply the missing accusative forms of the words given in brackets.

1 I'm going to buy a lamp.   Mä ostan ____. (**lamppu**)
2 Let's eat some sandwiches.   Syödään ____. (**voileipä**)
3 Open the door!   Avaa ____! (**ovi** *e*)
4 Whose car is she driving?   Kenen ____ se ajaa? (**auto**)

Noun phrase agreement

With the exception of the numerals and a few words which do not decline (see below), all modifiers which come before a noun must agree with it in number and case. So a noun phrase such as **tämä uusi talo** 'this new house' is **täIssä uudeIssa taloIssa** in the singular inessive ('in this new house') and **näIiIhin uusIiIin taloIiIhin** in the plural illative ('into these new houses').

Noun phrases which contain a numeral are slightly different. If the phrase is in the nominative or accusative, the noun and any adjectives between the numeral and the noun go into the partitive singular, while any modifier before the numeral goes into the plural, for example

Nämä viisi vanhala kirjala on sinun.
These five old books are yours.

Mä maksan seuraavat kaks kaljala.
I'll pay for the next two beers.

A few words do not decline, i.e. they remain invariable while the rest of the noun phrase takes on various number and case suffixes. The most common are **pikku** 'little', **eri** 'various', **joka** 'each, every', **itse** 'none other than', **ensi** 'next', **viime** 'last (= the most recent)', **koko** 'the whole'. Examples: **viime vaalelilssa** 'in the last elections', **eri sylilstä** 'for various reasons', **kahdellla eri kanavallla** 'on two different channels'.

Dialogue 2

Kauppatori

An open-air (summer) market

Pia and Norman get talking about food as they walk along the Esplanadi, Helsinki's showcase east–west avenue

PIA: Tykkäätsä muuten silakasta?
NORMAN: En oo koskaan maistanu![1] Mutta tykkään kyllä kalasta.
PIA: No sittehän me mennään silakkamarkkinoille!
NORMAN: Missä ne[2] on?
PIA: Tossa kauppatorin rannassa. Silakkamarkkinat on vuosittain tähän aikaan, kun saariston kalastajat tulevat Helsinkiin myymään saalistaan.
NORMAN: Joo mennään vaan sinne ja sit samalla ostetaan vihanneksia ja hedelmiä torilta.
PIA: Illalla syödäänki sitte perunoita ja sinappisilakoita.

PIA: *Do you like silakka, by the way?*
NORMAN: *I've never tried (lit. tasted) it! But I **do** like fish.*
PIA: *Well then, we're going to the silakka-market!*
NORMAN: *Where is it?[2]*

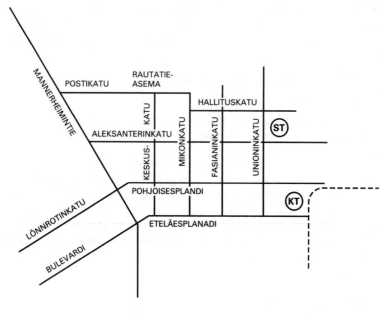

PIA: *(There) on the edge/shore of the kauppatori. There's a silakka-market every year at this time, when the fishermen from the archipelago come to Helsinki to sell their catch.*

NORMAN: *OK, let's go (there) and (at the same time let's) buy some vegetables and fruits (from the market).*

PIA: *And tonight let's eat potatoes and mustard-herring.*

1 **En oo koskaan maistanu** 'I've never tasted (any).' You'll learn about these verb forms in Unit 7.

2 The plural pronoun **ne** is used because **markkinalt** 'market' is plural in Finnish.

Vocabulary

hedelmä	fruit, pP **hedelmiä**	**myylmälän**	(in order) to sell
kalalstalja	fisherman	**no**	well, ...
—ki(n)	and, also, as well	**peruna**	potato
koskaan	(in negative contexts) never	**saaliX**	catch, booty
maistanu →		**saarlisto**	archipelago (**saari** *e* island)
maistalnut		**silakka**	Baltic (smaller) herring
muuten	by the way; otherwise		

sinappi	mustard	**tori**	market
sinne	(to) there	**tossa** →	
sittehän →		**tuolssa**	
sittenlhän		**tykkäX-**	likes
syödäänki →		**vihannes** *kse*	vegetable
syödäänkin		**vuosittain**	every year,
tähän aikaan	at this time		yearly

Language points

On the telephone (puhelimessa)

'Telephone' is **puhelin**, stem: **puhelime-**. Its partitive is **puhelinlta**, so 'May I use the telephone?' is **Saanko käyttää puhelinlta?**

'To call' someone is **soitta-**, the same verb used to refer to the playing of musical instruments. You call *to* a person (with the allative **-lle**):

Mä soitan Liisalle.   I'll call Lisa.

but you call *into* a number (with the illative):

Soita mulle tälhän numerolon.   Call me at this number.

Finns answer the phone in a variety of ways: a simple **Haloo**; saying their name; saying the number dialled; or putting the subscriber's surname into the adessive, e.g. **Lehtosella** 'at Lehtonen('s residence)'. 'Lauri speaking' is **Lauri puhelimelssa**.

When you initiate the call, identify yourself by saying **täällä** (**on/puhuu**) or **tässä** (**on/puhuu**) (lit. 'Here is/speaks . . .') plus your name. If the connection (**yhteys**) is poor, you can say so: **Yhteys on huono**, or simply **Ei kuulu** lit. 'It isn't audible.' Even more than usually, you may want to ask the other person to speak more slowly (**hitaammin**) or more loudly (**kovempaa**).

You can ask whether someone is available to come to the phone by saying **Onko X tavattavissa?** If they're not, you can always leave a message (**Voinko jättälä sanan?**) or call back later (**Soitan uudelleen**). You won't get through at all, of course, if the number is engaged (**varattu**), doesn't answer (**ei vastaa**), or is wrong (**väärä**).

On the phone, 'goodbye' is **kuulemiin** lit. 'until hearing', from **kuule-** 'hears'.

Dialogue 3 ⬚

Here are four quick exchanges which take place over the phone:

Puhelimessa

On the phone 1

First, Liisa wants to reach Lassi; but Matti, his brother, answers, so

MATTI: Matti Rantanen!
LIISA: Täällä puhuu Liisa Lehtisalo. Onkohan[1] Lassi tavattavissa?
MATTI: Kyllä on. Hetkinen.
LIISA: Kiitos.

MATTI: (answering) *Matti Rantanen.*
LIISA: *This is Liisa Lehtisalo. Could I speak with Lassi?*
MATTI: *Of course. Just one moment.*
LIISA: *Thank you.*

1 **Onko|han** Both Liisa and Marja in the next dialogue use the extremely frequent clitic —**hAn** to solicit cooperation/agreement from their collocutors.

On the phone 2

Marja fails to reach Juhani on her first try, so she says she'll ring back

KAISA: Kaisa Hakulinen!
MARJA: Täällä puhuu Marja Koponen. Onkohan[1] Juhani Karjalainen tavattavissa (paikalla)?
KAISA: Hän ei ole nyt täällä. Hän tulee takaisin vasta kello neljä.
MARJA: Kiitos. Soitan uudelleen. Kuulemiin.
KAISA: Kuulemiin.

KAISA: *Kaisa Hakulinen!*
MARJA: *It's Marja Koponen. Is Juhani Karjalainen there?*
KAISA: *He isn't here right now. He won't be coming back until (lit. comes back not-until) four o'clock.*
MARJA: *Thank you. I'll ring back later (lit. I'll ring again). Goodbye.*
KAISA: *Goodbye.*

On the phone 3

Pentti wants to reach a certain Hämäläinen (who happens to be a composer), but Hämäläinen is not in, so Pentti leaves a message.

RITVA: Hämäläisellä. Ritva Nurminen puhelimessa.
PENTTI: Täällä puhuu Pentti Olavinen. Onkohan saveltäjä Hämäläinen tavattavissa?
RITVA: Ei ole. Hän on jo lähtenyt ulos; minä en tiedä varmasti, mihin aikaan hän tulee takaisin.
PENTTI: Voinko jättää sanan?
RITVA: Olkaa hyvää.
PENTTI: Voisitteko pyytää, että hän soittaa minulle? Numero on 45 22 75.
RITVA: Minä sanon.
PENTTI: Kiitos. Kuulemiin.
RITVA: Kuulemiin.

RITVA: *Hämäläinen residence, Ritva Nurminen speaking (lit. in the phone).*
PENTTI: *This is Pentti Olavinen. Is Mr(s)/Ms (lit. composer) Hämäläinen there?*
RITVA: *Not just now. (S)he has gone out already; I don't know exactly when (s)he'll be coming back.*
PENTTI: *May I leave a message?*
RITVA: *Go right ahead.*
PENTTI: *Could you ask (him/her) to call me? (My) number is 45 22 75.*
RITVA: *I'll tell (him/her).*
PENTTI: *Thank you. Goodbye.*
RITVA: *Goodbye.*

On the phone 4

Jouni tries to reach Mika, but Mika has gone out to basketball practice. Jouni leaves a message. **Rva** *stands for* **rouva** *'Mrs'*

RVA. LEHTONEN: Lehtosella.
JOUNI: Täss on Jouni Matikainen hei, onks Mika kotona?
RVA. LEHTONEN: Hei Jouni! Mika ei ole nyt kotona. Se lähti koripalloharjoituksiin.
JOUNI: Ai. Koska se tulee kotiin?

Rva. Lehtonen: Joskus kahdeksan jälkeen. Jätänkö viestin?
Jouni: Joo. Jos se vois soittaa mulle vielä tänään.
Rva. Lehtonen: Selvä, kerron terveisiä.
Jouni: Kiitti. Hei!
Rva. Lehtonen: Hei vaan!

Rva. Lehtonen: *Lehtonen residence.*
Jouni: *Hi, it's Jouni Matikainen. Is Mika home?*
Rva. Lehtonen: *Hi, Jouni! Mika's not home right now. He's gone to basketball practice.*
Jouni: *Oh. When's he coming home?*
Rva. Lehtonen: *Sometime after eight. Should I give him (lit. leave) a message?*
Jouni: *Yea. If he could ring me sometime today.*
Rva. Lehtonen: *OK. I'll tell him you called.*
Jouni: *Ta. 'Bye!*
Rva. Lehtonen: *'Bye!*

Vocabulary

että	that (conjunction)	**mihin aikaan**	at what time?
harjoituksli|in	to practice (sessions) pILL	**mulle →** minu|lle	
hei!	hi!	**numero**	number
X|n jälkeen	after X	**onko|han**	is ... at all?
jättä-	leaves (something somewhere)	**paika|lla**	there, on the spot
		puhelime|ssa	(speaking) on the phone
jos	if		
jos|kus	some time, sometimes	**pyytä-**	requests, asks someone to do something
kello	clock, watch; o'clock		
kerto-	tells, recounts, talks about	**sana**	word
		saveltäljä	composer
kiitti → kiitos		**se läht|i**	(s)he left
kori|pallo	basketball	**se on lähte|nyt**	(s)he has left
koska	when?	**selvä**	clear; OK
kotiin	(coming, going) home	**soitta|a**	calls, rings, plays (instrument)
kotona	(at) home	**täällä**	here
kuulemiin	(on telephone) Goodbye	**takaisin**	back (from where one has gone)
kyllä	yes, indeed	**tänään**	today

täss → **tässä**		**varmasti**	certainly, for certain
tavattav|i|ssa	reachable	**vasta**	not until
terveis|i|ä	greetings	**vielä**	still
tietä-	knows	**vielä tänään**	while it is still today,
ulos	(coming or going)		i.e. before
	out		tomorrow
uudelleen	again	**viesti**	message, bit of
vaan	(expresses		information
	agreement,		
	encouragement)		

Exercise 6 Make up your own short (successful and unsuccessful) telephone dialogues. Phone friends and relative strangers in order to practise your skills with **s(in)ä** and **te**.

Language points

More noun types: stems in =iME and =UKsE

Many Finnish nouns which denote machines, tools, or instruments are built with the suffix **=iME** (for the significance of capital letters in such forms, see the Nuts and bolts section, pages 7 and 8). The citation form ends in **n**:

puhelin	telephone (cf. **puhu-** 'speaks')
avain	key (cf. **avaX-** 'opens')
soitin	musical instrument (cf. **soitta-** 'plays')
elin	organ (of the body; cf. **elä-** 'lives')

but the stem's final **ime** is clear in case forms such as inessive **puhelime\|ssa**. Compression rules apply as usual, e.g. compressed **t** in **soitin** and decompressed **tt** in genitive singular **soittime\|n**. The partitive is a bit unexpected: **iME**-stems behave like **lumi** 'snow', e.g. **puhelin\|ta**, **avain\|ta**, **soitin\|ta**.

You will also often meet with words built with the suffixes **=UKsE** and **=mUKsE**. Finnish uses these to build nouns, usually from verbs. The citation form ends in **s**, for example:

avaus	opening (cf. **avaX-** 'opens')
vastaus	answer (cf. **vastaX-** 'answers')
kirjoitus	essay, document (cf. **kirjoitta-** 'writes')
sopimus	treaty, agreement (cf. **sopi-** 'fits in well, is OK')
kysymys	question (cf. **kysy-** 'asks')

rakennus	building (cf. **rakenta-** 'builds')
hakemus	application(-form) (cf. **hake-** 'fetches')
uudistus	innovation, reform (cf. **uudista-** 'makes new' and **uusi** *te* 'new')
hallitus	government (cf. **halliTSE-** 'rules')

and the partitive also has only **s**, i.e. these nouns behave like dental stems:

Mulla on kolme kysymys|tä.	I have three questions.
Se etsii vastaus|ta.	(S)he is looking for an answer.

but all other case forms have the **ks**, e.g.

rakennukse|n toisella puolella	on the other side of the buiding
Ne allekirjoittaa sopimukse|n.	They will sign the treaty.
Hakemukse|ssa ei ole nimeä.	There's no name on the application.

6 Mennääks kiskalle!

Let's go to the kiosk!

In this unit you will:

- learn more about shopping
- learn about Independence Day in Finland
- go on a visit to Granny's
- learn how to form and use the past tense
- learn another way to link verbs: the third infinitive
- learn how to make adverbs

Dialogue 1 ▣

Leipomossa

At the baker's

MYYJÄ:	Päivää, mitä teille saisi olla?
ROUVA LEHTONEN:	Ovatko nuo lakkaviinerit tuoreita?
MYYJÄ:	Kyllä, tänä aamuna leivottuja.
ROUVA LEHTONEN:	Ottaisin niitä neljä.
MYYJÄ:	Ja muuta?
ROUVA LEHTONEN:	Onkos teillä perunalimppua?
MYYJÄ:	On kyllä. Montako saisi olla?
ROUVA LEHTONEN:	Yksi riittää, kiitos.

ASSISTANT:	*(Good) day. What would you (like to) have?*
MRS LEHTONEN:	*Are those arctic cloudberry danish fresh?*
ASSISTANT:	*Yes (indeed), (they're) baked this morning.*
MRS LEHTONEN:	*I'll take (lit. I would take) four of them.*
ASSISTANT:	*And (anything) else?*
MRS LEHTONEN:	*Do you have any potato loaves?*

ASSISTANT: *Certainly. How many would you like?*
MRS LEHTONEN: *One will be enough, thanks.*

Vocabulary

lakka	arctic cloudberry	**myy-**	sells
leipomo	bakery	**niitä**	of them (pP of **se**)
leivo|ttu	baked	**nuo**	those (pN of **tuo**)
limppu	(round) loaf	**otta|isi|n**	I would take
mon|ta|ko	how much?	**tä|nä aamu|na**	this morning
muu	other, else	**tuoreQ**	fresh
myy|jä	seller	**viineri**	Danish pastry

Language Points

More on pronouns: plural forms of demonstratives

So far you have met various forms of the demonstrative pronouns **tämä** 'this', **tuo** 'that' and **se** 'it'. Here are the full paradigms of these three little words. Notice that the plural forms (**nämä**, **nuo**, and **ne**) all begin with **n**; their differences are therefore all the more important to study so that you don't mix them up.

The asterisked forms are provided to whet your appetite; you'll learn them in later lessons.

	'this'	*'that yonder'*	*'that, it'*
sN	**tämä**	**tuo**	**se**
sG	**tämä|n**	**tuo|n**	**se|n**
sP	**tä|tä**	**tuo|ta**	**si|tä**
sELA	**tä|stä**	**tuo|sta**	**sii|tä** (!)
sINE	**tä|ssä**	**tuo|ssa**	**sii|nä** (!)
sILL	**tä|hän**	**tuo|hon**	**sii|hen**
sABL	**tä|ltä**	**tuo|lta**	**si|ltä**
sADE	**tä|llä**	**tuo|lla**	**si|llä**
sALL	**tä|lle**	**tuo|lle**	**si|lle**
sESS	**tä|nä**	**tuo|na**	**si|nä**
sTRA	**tä|ksi***	**tuo|ksi***	**si|ksi***

	'these'	'those yonder'	'those, they'
pN	nämä	nuo	ne
pG	näi|den*	no|i|den*	ni|i|den*
pP	nä|i|tä	no|i|ta	ni|i|tä
pELA	nä|i|stä	no|i|sta	ni|i|stä
pINE	nä|i|ssä	no|i|ssa	ni|i|ssä
pILL	nä|i|hin	no|i|hin	ni|i|hin
pABL	nä|i|ltä	no|i|lta	ni|i|ltä
pADE	nä|i|llä	no|i|lla	ni|i|llä
pALL	nä|i|lle	no|i|lle	ni|i|lle
pESS	nä|i|nä	no|i|na	ni|i|nä
pTRA	nä|i|ksi*	no|i|ksi*	ni|i|ksi*

Here are some examples of the demonstrative pronouns in action:

Ota kaks no\|i\|ta suur\|i\|a leip\|i\|ä!
Take two of those large loaves. (pP)

Mä otan viis ni\|i\|tä.
I'll take five of them. (pP)

Suomessa nä\|i\|tä kiel\|i\|ä ei opiskella.
These languages aren't studied in Finland. (pP)

Kerro jotain ni\|i\|stä!
Say something about them! (pELA)

Onks se sii\|nä paika\|ssa?
Is it in that place? (sINE)

Adverbs of place and of manner

Adverbs of place

Finnish is rich in little words which indicate where, whence, and whither. Corresponding to the simple English word 'here', for example, is any of four different forms, depending on whether or not motion is implied and on the relative size of the space meant. Study this little chart, which summarizes the forms. Which forms are identical with those of **se** and **tämä**? (You can check your memory by peeking back at the previous section.)

```
┌─────────────────────────────────────────────────────┐
│                                                       │
│         nearer speaker ↔ further from speaker         │
│                                                       │
└─────────────────────────────────────────────────────┘
```

smaller area	**tä|ssä**	**sii|nä**	**tuo|ssa**	stationary
	tä|hän	**sii|hen**	**tuo|hon**	moving towards
	tä|stä	**sii|tä**	**tuo|sta**	moving away

larger area	**tää|llä**	**sie|llä**	**tuo|lla**	stationary
	tä|nne	**si|nne**	**tuo|nne**	moving towards
	tää|ltä	**sie|ltä**	**tuo|lta**	moving away

Examples:

Se kutsui m(in)ut *tänne.*	(S)he invited me (*to*) *here.*
Kai *tähän* **saa istua?**	Might one sit (*to*) *here*, perhaps?
Kirjoita nimesi *tähän.*	Write your name (*to*) *here.*
Me mennään *sinne* **museoon.**	Were going (*to there*) to the museum.
Tässä **on majoneesia.**	Here's some mayonnaise.
Etkö tunne ketään *täällä?*	Don't you know anyone *here?*
Käy *tuonne* **sohvalle.**	Go (lie down) on(to) the sofa (to) *over there.*

Adverbs of manner

These are most commonly formed from adjectives; the suffix used in this derivation is =**sti**, added directly to the stem. To the left of this tight-lid suffix, Q and X are read as #, as usual. Examples:

Adjective	Adverb	English
huono	**huono|sti**	badly
hieno	**hieno|sti**	finely
hirveä	**hirveä|sti**	frightfully
kaunis	**kaunii|sti**	beautifully (stem: **kauniX**)
äänekäs	**äänekkää|sti**	vociferously (stem: **äänekkäX**)
lämmin	**lämpimä|sti**	warmly (stem: **lämpimä**; more on this stem type in Unit 8)

A few of the most common adverbs are formed with =**in**:

hyvä	**hyv|in**	well (**hyvä|sti** means 'farewell')
usea	**use|in**	frequently

Examples: **Se laulaa hyvin** '(S)he sings well', **Me käydään usein Ruotsissa** 'We go to Sweden often.'

It is useful to distinguish such adverbs of manner, which modify verbs, from adverbs of intensity, which modify adjectives. To form these, you simply put the first, intensifying, adjective into the genitive:

hirveä|n kaunis	frightfully beautiful
poikkeuksellise|n tylsä	exceptionally stupid (**poikkeuksellinen** 'exceptional')

Introduction to participles: past and present, passive and active

Participles are simply special kinds of adjectives made from verbs, like English 'broken' (from 'break') in 'This glass is broken' or 'broken promises'.

Finnish has four participles, two with past, or completed, meanings, and two with present (better: non-past), incompleted, meanings. So, for example, the form **leivottu\|j\|a** in the dialogue on page 91 is the partitive plural of the past passive participle, **leivo\|ttu** 'baked', from the verb **leipo-** 'bakes'. We might paraphrase and say that **leivottu** means something like '(that) which has been baked'; you'll learn how to form and use this kind of participle in the next unit. Alongside a past passive participle like **leivottu**, Finnish also has a past *active* participle, e.g. **leiponut**. Paraphrasing again, we could say that this form means something like '(s)he who has baked, that which has baked'. This form is most commonly used together with other verb forms, in compound tenses. For example:

Mä olen leipo\|nut kaks leipää tänään.
I've baked two loaves today.

There will be more on this use of **nUt**-forms like **leiponut** (perfect tense) in the next unit, and you will meet it again later in this unit, in connection with the *negative past*. But first, some more shopping.

Dialogue 2 ▩

Kioskit

Kiosks

Kiosks are the Finns' way of picking up small items out of normal business hours. A colloquial variant of **kioski** *is* **kiska**

Kioskille

(Going) to the kiosk

OSKARI: Hei Pekka, mennääks kiskalle. Mä sain mun viikkorahan.
PEKKA: Joo, mennään vaan. Isä pyyski mua hakee[1] *Iltasanomat*.
OSKARI: Mun tekee hirveesti mieli Valion suklaatuuttia.
PEKKA: Mäkin saan ostaa jotain hyvää.

OSKARI: *Hey Pekka, let's go to the kiosk. I've (just) got my allowance.*
PEKKA: *OK, let's go. My father asked me to get an* Iltasanomat, *anyway.*
OSKARI: *I could really go for a Valio chocolate cone.*
PEKKA: *I'm going to buy something good, too.*

1 **pyyski mua hakee** → **pyysikin minua hakemaan** 'asked me to fetch'. You will learn about i-dropping (**pyysi ~ pyys**) and the third infinitive (**hakemaan ~ hakee**) later on in this unit.

Kioskilla

At the kiosk

MYYJÄ: Mitäs pojille sais olla?
PEKKA: Iltasanomat ja kymmenen noita irtomerkkareita ja yks kingis-puikko.
MYYJÄ: Noin ole hyvä ja se tekee yhdeksän markkaa. Ja mitäs sulle sais olla? (*kääntyy Oskarin puoleen*)
OSKARI: Yks suklaatuutti, kiitos.
MYYJÄ: Tossa, kuus markkaa.
POJAT: Kiitti hei!

ASSISTANT: *What'll (you) boys have?*
PEKKA: *An* Iltasanomat *and ten of those loose sweets, and a kingis-pop.*

ASSISTANT: *All right, here you are; that makes nine marks, then.*
And what will **you** *have?* (turns towards Oskari)
OSKARI: *One chocolate cone, thanks.*
ASSISTANT: *There (you are); six marks.*
THE BOYS: *Thanks. 'Bye!*

Vocabulary

hake-	fetches	**noin**	roughly; so
hei!	Hi, Hey	**noｌilta**	of those (pP)
hirveäｌsti	frightfully	**pojaｌt**	boys pN
hirveesti →		**pojｌiｌlle**	to (the) boys
hirveäｌsti			pALL
Iltasanomat	*Evening Paper*	**Xｌn puoleｌen**	to(wards) X
irtomerkkareita	type of loose	**pyysｌki** →	asked, too
	(penny-)candies	**pyysｌiｌkin**	
isä	father	**saaｌn**	I'm going to
joｌtaｌin	something	**saｌiｌn**	I've got
kingis-puikko	type of ice lolly	**suklaaｌtuutti**	chocolate cone
kiska → **kioski**		**tekeｌe mieli X**	could really go for
kuus → **kuusi**	six		an X
käänty-	turns	**tossa** → **tuoｌssa**	there
mäｌkin	I, too	**Valio**	(brand name)
markka	(Finnish) mark	**viikkoｌraha**	(weekly) pocket
mennääks →			money
mennäänkö		**yks** → **yksi**	

Language points

Colloquial forms

You may have noticed that demonstratives have special shortened forms which occur in colloquial contexts, e.g. **tossa** for **tuossa** in the dialogue above. In particular, note:

more formal:	**tuo**	**nuo**	**tämä**	**nämä**
more colloquial:	**toi**	**noi**	**tää**	**nää**

Exercise 1 Practise your knowledge of demonstratives (and revise the accusative) by putting these into Finnish:

1 What do you want, these or (**vai**) those?
2 What do you want, ice cream (**jäätelö**) or cake?
3 Do you want wine, beer, or juice?
4 I'll eat these sandwiches.
5 Here's a chocolate cone.

Dialogue 3 ▨

Mummolaan

Going to Granny's

Lähtö

Setting out

ÄITI:	Joko[1] kaikki on valmiina? Nyt pitäis jo[1] lähtee mummon luo.
ISÄ:	Onks kukat mukana?
MAIJA:	Ne on jo autossa.[2]
ÄITI:	Sit mennään!
ISÄ:	Ja Matti muistaa sitten[3] ettei ota enempää kuin kaks palaa täytekakkua.
MATTI:	Mut ku[4] mummon täytekakku on niin hyvää.
ÄITI:	Ja nyt kyllä mentiin!

MOTHER:	*Is everything ready? We ought to be leaving for Granny's now.*
FATHER:	*Got the flowers?*
MAIJA:	*They're in the car.*
MOTHER:	*Let's go, then!*
FATHER:	*And Matti will remember not to take more than two pieces of (filled) cake, won't he?*
MATTI:	*But Granny's filled cake is so good!*
MOTHER:	*Right, let's get going!*

1 **Joko**: the little word **jo** is often more an indication of diminishing patience, rather than the equivalent of English 'already'.

2 **autossa**: most foreign words, acronyms, and slang are susceptible only to quantitative consonant compression (tt > t, etc.; Unit 1). Thus **t** remains **t** in **autossa** and **Natossa** 'in NATO', **k** remains **k** in **hetekalla** 'on the sofabed', and **p** remains **p** in **mopolla** 'on (her) motor scooter'.

3 **sitten**: this word often merely indicates earnestness.

4 **ku(n)** 'when, since' here points to an omitted clause like 'it's so difficult for me to restrain myself'

Mummon luona

At Granny's

MUMMO: Tervetuloa! Olipa hauska[1] että tulitte.
MATTI: Me tuotiin mummolle kukkia.
MUMMO: No kiitos. Tulkaa peremmälle. Mitä teille kuuluu?
ÄITI: Kiitos ihan hyvää. Entä itsellesi?
MUMMO: Hyvää vaan. Kahvi onkin ihan valmista. Istutaan pöytään!
MATTI: Mummo, saiskos palan kakkua?
MUMMO: Sitä vartenhan se on tehty. Annahan lautasesi Matti!
ÄITI: Isä ojennahan kuppisi niin kaadan kahvia.
MAIJA: Sunnuntait on aina kivoja, ku tullaan mummolaan!

GRANNY: *Welcome! You've come at just the right time.*
MATTI: *We brought Granny flowers.*
GRANNY: *Well, thank you! Come through! How are you all?*
MOTHER: *Quite well, thanks. And you?*
GRANNY: *Fine, fine. The coffee's just ready, as well. Let's sit down (to table)!*
MATTI: *Granny, can I have a piece of cake?*
GRANNY: *That's what it's made for! Give me your plate, Matti.*
MOTHER: *Pass your cup, Father, and I'll pour the (lit. some) coffee.*
MAIJA: *Sundays, when we come to Granny's, are always wonderful!*

1 **Oli|pa hauska** 'how nice ...' The past tense is sometimes used, particularly with —**pA**, to express enthusiasm or sudden discovery.

Vocabulary

aina	always	**ihan**	quite, rather
auto	car	**istu-**	sits
enempä|ä	more sP	**itse|si**	yourself
entä	and (what about ...?)	**jo|ko**	yet (in questions)
ett|ei = että + ei		**kaata-**	pours
hauska	pleasant, nice; fun	**kaikki** *e*	all, every

kakku	cake	**mut → mutta**	
kiva	great, lovely	**ojenta-**	extends, offers,
ku(n)	when, since, because		passes
kuin	than; as, like	**pala**	piece
kukka	flower	**perelmmälle**	(to) further in
kuppilsi	your cup	**pitäis → pitäisi**	
lautaselsi	your plate	**pöytälän**	(sitting down) to
Xln luo	to X's place		table
Xln luona	at X's place	**tehlty**	made
lähtee → lähteä		**tulliltte**	you (plural/
lähtö	departure		formal) came
menltiin	(it's time) we went	**tuoltiin**	(we) brought
muista-	remembers	**täytelkakku**	filled cake
mukalna	along (with one)	**valmililna**	ready (pESS)
mummo	grandma, Granny	**valmislta**	ready sP
Mummola	Granny's place	**XlTA varten**	for X

Language points

The simple past tense

The Finnish simple past tense corresponds to two past tenses in English. These are the English simple past ('I said', 'you took', 'she went', 'they bought)', and the imperfect ('I was saying', 'you were taking', 'she was going', 'they were buying').

The suffix is **-i-**, attached directly to the verb stem. To the *right* of this **-i-** you put the same endings as those of the present tense, except that there is no lengthening of the vowel in the third person. Contrast:

s3 present: **se sanolo** (s)he/it says
s3 past: **se sanoli** (s)he/it said/was saying

To the *left* of the past-tense **-i-**, certain vowel changes occur. (*Tip:* Since many of these vowel changes – but not all! – are the same as those you learned in connection with the pluralizer **-i-** in the previous unit, a comparison with those rules will be well repaid.)

Here's a summary, which you should have a look through now and use as a reference later. To the left of the **-i-** of the past tense Class III verbs lose their final **e**:

mä menliln I went/was going (stem: **mene-**)

sä tul|i|t	you came/were coming (stem: **tule-**)
se ol|i	(s)he/it was (stem: **ole-**)
sä pääs|i|t	you managed to go/come (stem: **pääse-**)

Class IV verbs reduce their long vowel or diphthong. This means:

aa > a	**uo > o**
ää > ä	**yö > ö**
oi > o	**ie > e**

mä sa|i|n	I received/was receiving (stem: **saa-**)
sä to|i|t	you brought/were bringing (stem: **tuo-**)
he sö|i|vät	they ate/were eating (stem: **syö-**)
ne reago|i	they reacted (stem: **reagoi-**)

In class II verbs, **X** is read as **s**, **XE** as **n**, and **TSE** as **ts**:

mä huomas|i|n	I noticed/was noticing (stem: **huomaX-**)
pimen|i	it got/was getting dark (stem: **pimeXE-**, from **pimeä** dark)
sä mainits|i|t	you mentioned/were mentioning (stem: **mainiTSE-**)

Class I verbs are a bit more complicated. We may summarize their changes as follows:

Stem-final **i**, **e**, **ä** are deleted:

mä ets|i|n	I searched/was searching (stem: **etsi-**)
sä lu|i|t	you read/were reading (stem: **luke-**)
se kest|i	it lasted/was lasting (stem: **kestä-**)

In bisyllabic stems, final **a** changes to **o** if the first (or only) vowel of the first syllable is unrounded (**i**, **e**, **a**; see page 4):

mä auto|i|n	I helped/was helping (stem: **autta-**)
sä anno|i|t	you gave/were giving (stem: **anta-**)
se alko|i	(s)he/it began/was beginning (stem: **alka-**)
hän virkko|i	(s)he uttered/was uttering (stem: **virkka-**)

Otherwise, the final **a** is deleted. This deletion of **a** therefore occurs in bisyllabic stems whose first (or only) vowel of the first syllable is rounded, for example:

mä muut|i|n	I moved house (stem: **muutta-**)
sä ost|i|t	you bought (stem: **osta-**)

and in all stems that are more than two syllables long:

mä tarkastl**i**l**n**	I checked (stem: **tarkasta**-, cf. **tarkka** exact)
mä nukahdl**i**l**n**	I fell asleep (stem: **nukahta**-, cf. **nukku**-sleeps)
sä opetl**i**l**t**	you taught (stem: **opetta**-, cf. **opiskele**-studies)
se tuijottl**i**	(s)he/it stared (stem: **tuijotta**-)

One last rule: a single **t**, if preceded by a vowel, **n**, **l**, or **r**, usually changes to **s** if it is to the left of a stem-final **A** (**a** or **ä**) which is deleted by the **-i-** of the past tense. Examples:

mä pyysl**i**l**n**	I requested (stem: **pyytä**-)
mä tiesl**i**l**n**	I knew (stem: **tietä**-)
sä löysl**i**l**t**	you found (stem: **löytä**-)
sä kielsl**i**l**t**	you forbade (stem: **kieltä**-)
se huusl**i**	(s)he/it shouted (stem: **huuta**-)
se lensl**i**	(s)he/it flew (stem: **lentä**-, cf. **lent**=o+**kenttä** airport)

The most frequently used verbs which are exceptions to this **t** > **s** rule are **pitä**- 'holds' (**mä pid**l**i**l**n**), **vetä**- 'pulls' (**mä ved**l**i**l**n**), **souta**- 'rows' (**mä soud**l**i**l**n**), and **nouta**- 'fetches' (**mä noud**l**i**l**n**).

Note on consonant compression: past-tense forms compress exactly as their corresponding present-tense forms. Notice the parallels:

	anta-	*luke-*	*tapaX-*	*tarkeXE-*	stem
present	**anna**l**t**	**lue**l**n**	**tapaa**l**n**	**tarkene**l**t**	
past	**anno**l**i**l**t**	**lu**l**i**l**n**	**tapas**l**i**l**n**	**tarken**l**i**l**t**	
	yes		no		compressed

Here are the full past-tense paradigms of four verbs, **otta**- 'takes', **huomaX**- 'notices', **mene**- 'goes', and **jää**- 'remains, stays'. The more formal first person plural forms (with **-mme**) are given here; for the usual colloquial indefinite forms, see later on in this unit.

	otta-	huomaX-	mene-	jää-
s1	ot|i|n	huomas|i|n	men|i|n	jä|i|n
s2	ot|i|t	huomas|i|t	men|i|t	jä|i|t
s3	se ott|i	se huomas|i	se men|i	se jä|i
p1	ot|i|mme[1]	huomas|i|mme[1]	men|i|mme[1]	jä|i|mme[1]
p2	ot|i|tte	huomas|i|tte	men|i|tte	jä|i|tte
p3	ne ott|i[2]	ne huomas|i[2]	ne men|i[2]	ne jä|i[2]

1 In more colloquial contexts, the past indefinite is used: see the section later in this unit.

2 In more formal contexts: **he ott\|i\|vat, he huomas\|i\|vat, he men\|i\|vät, he jä\|i\|vät.**

Exercise 2 Change these verb phrases from present to past, or vice versa.

Model: **mä lennän > mä lensin**

1 sä ostit
2 he sanovat
3 te osaatte
4 me halusimme
5 mä voin
6 hän muutti
7 ne saapuu
8 mä tarvitsen
9 se juo
10 me huudamme

Exercise 3 Translate the following sentences into Finnish. In every case, the simple past tense will work.

1 Where were you?
2 What did she say?
3 The cat ate the mouse (**hiiri** e).
4 I helped a little.
5 Did you see him?
6 They took it away.
7 Where did you put (**pistä-**) it?
8 Who mentioned it?
9 Who did you give it to?
10 Where did you find it?

The negative past

The negative past is made of two parts: the negative verb and the *past active participle*. Compare these positive and negative forms:

positive:	**mä sano|i|n**	I said
negative:	**mä en sano|nut**	I didn't say
positive:	**lu|i|tteko te**	did you read?
negative:	**ettekö luke|neet**	didn't you read?

You build the past active participle by attaching the suffix **-nUt** (singular)/**-nee\|t** (plural) to the verb stem. Attaching it is quite straightforward: you simply add it to the stems of class I and IV verbs:

luke|nut	read
sano|nut	said
kieltä|nyt	prohibited
saa|nut	got

The chunks (**X, TSE, XE**) at the end of class II verbs assimilate to the **n**:

huoman|nut	noticed (stem: **huomaX-**)
mainin|nut	mentioned (stem: **mainiTSE-**)
paen|nut	escaped (stem: **pakeXE-**)

Dental stems (class III) behave in the opposite way: they lose their final **e**, and the **n** of **-nUt** assimilates to their last consonant:

tul|lut	come (stem: **tule-**)
men|nyt	gone (stem: **mene-**)
pääs|syt	managed to go/come (stem: **pääse-**)
pur|rut	bitten (stem: **pure-**)

The two stems **näke-** and **teke-** are idiosyncratic:

näh|nyt	seen (stem: **näke-**)
teh|nyt	done (stem: **teke-**)

(You have already met this behaviour in their indefinite forms: **näh\|dään, teh\|dään**).

Exercise 4 Change positive to negative, and vice versa.

1 Se ei mennyt.
2 Ne tuli.

3 Mä en istunut tässä.
4 He eivät sanoneet.
5 Näitkö sen?
6 Mä en lukenut sitä.
7 Me emme ostaneet uutta autoa.
8 Me tapasimme.
9 Hän sai kirjeen Tanjalta.
10 Ne ei lähettäneet rahaa.

Dialogue 4 🞀🞂

Itsenäisyyspäivä (6.12)

Finland's Independence Day, 6 December

(Suomi itsenäistyi Venäjästä 1917)

At university

ARTO: Oliver, olet sä kuullut, että yliopistolla on itsenäisyyspäiväjuhla ens viikolla, itsenäisyyspäivänä.

OLIVER: Ai jaa? Onks sinne kutsuttu kaikki opiskelijatkin?

ARTO: Joo on, mutta liput on kyllä aika kalliit; 50 (viiskyt) markkaa.

OLIVER: Siinä tapauksessa mä taidan jättää ne juhlat väliin. Miten muuten suomalaiset viettävät itsenäisyyspäivää?

ARTO: Aika perinteisesti. Kello kuus illalla sytytetään ikkunalle kaksi kynttilää, joita poltetaan kahdeksaan asti.

OLIVER: Se on varmaan tosi kauniinnäköistä. Mitä ihmiset sitten tekee sinä aikana?

ARTO: Monet katsovat presidentinlinnan tanssiaisia TV:stä. Siellä voi nähdä kaikki Suomen julkkikset. Kutsua linnan tanssiaisiin pidetään kunnia-asiana.

OLIVER: Minusta tuntuu, että minäkin aion viettää itsenäisyyspäivää perinteisesti, sytyttämällä kynttilät ja katsomalla tanssiaisia!

(Finland became independent of Russia in 1917)

ARTO: *Oliver, have you heard? There's going to be an Independence Day celebration at university next week.*

OLIVER: *Oh yes? And are all students invited to it?*

ARTO: *Yes, they are. But the tickets are pretty expensive, to be sure: 50 marks.*

OLIVER: *In that case I'll probably give that celebration a miss. How do Finns celebrate Independence Day, anyway?*

ARTO: *Pretty traditionally. At six o'clock in the evening they light two candles in the window, and burn them (lit. which they burn) until eight.*

OLIVER: *That must be really beautiful-looking. What do people do during that time?*

ARTO: *Many watch the dancing at the Presidential Palace on TV. You can see all of Finland's celebrities there. An invitation to the Palace Ball is considered a great honour.*

OLIVER: *Seems to me I'll be spending Independence Day traditionally, as well, lighting candles and watching the dancing!*

Vocabulary

ai!	Oh!
aika	fairly, pretty
aiko-	intends
ens → ensi	next
ihmiset	people
itsenäisty-	becomes independent
itsenäisyys *te*	independence
jaa	yeah, yes
jolilta	which pP (relative pronoun)
juhla	celebration
julkkis	(stem: julkkikse; NB no compression) celebrity
jättälä seln välilin	gives it a miss
kalliX	beautiful
katso-	looks at, watches
katsolmallla	by watching
kunnia-asia	matter of honour
kutsu	invitation
kutsu-	invites
kutsulttu	invited
kuulllut	heard
kymppi → kymmenen	
kymppii → kymppilä sP	
kynttilä	candle
linna	palace, castle, fortress
lippu	ticket; flag
miten	how?
monelt	many
musta → minusta	in my opinion
muuten	by the way; otherwise
perinteiselsti	traditionally
pitä-	holds, considers
poltta-	burns
presidentti	president
silnä aikalna	during/at that time
sytyttä-	lights, ignites
sytyttälmälllä	by lighting
tanssiaiselt	dance, ball
tapaus *kse*	case
tosi	really
tuntu-	seems

varma⎮an	certainly	**X⎮#n asti**	until X
viettä-	spends (time); celebrates	**X⎮n⎮näköinen**	X-looking, looking like X
voi	one can	**yliopisto**	university

Language points

The third infinitive

We'll skip the second infinitive here and go straight to the third infinitive, because it's a much more useful form to know when you're starting Finnish.

You form it by adding =**mA** to the verb stem; any **X** at the end of the stem gets read as **A**. Here are examples from each verb class, with illative, elative, and inessive endings:

Stem	Third infinitive	Illative	Elative	Inessive
hake-	**hake⎮ma**	**hake⎮ma⎮an**	**hake⎮ma⎮sta**	**hake⎮ma⎮ssa**
tapaX-	**tapaa⎮ma**	**tapaa⎮ma⎮an**	**tapaa⎮ma⎮sta**	**tapaa⎮ma⎮ssa**
opiskele-	**opiskele⎮ma**	**opiskele⎮ma⎮an**	**opiskele⎮ma⎮sta**	**opiskele⎮ma⎮ssa**
käy-	**käy⎮mä**	**käy⎮mä⎮än**	**käy⎮mä⎮stä**	**käy⎮mä⎮ssä**

The most common use of the third infinitive is as a continuation or an accompaniment to some other verb. It then stands in some case form; this is the *illative* in goal-like situations:

Mä tulen hake⎮ma⎮an liput.	I'll come and fetch the tickets.
Mennään hiihtä⎮mä⎮än!	Let's go skiing!
Se tuli käy⎮mä⎮än.	(S)he came to visit.
Se hakee opiskele⎮ma⎮an yliopistoon.	(S)he is applying to study at university.
Se kumartui nosta⎮ma⎮an sitä.	(S)he bent down to pick it up.
Se pyysi mua hake⎮ma⎮an sen.	(S)he asked me to fetch it.
Ne pakotti mut teke⎮mä⎮än sen.	They forced me to do it.

Verbs which are common with this sort of construction include **pakotta-** 'forces', **saa-** 'gets', **autta-** 'helps', **pyytä-** 'asks', and **käske-** 'orders, commands'.

The *elative* is used to convey the notion of source or of distancing:

Me tullaan hiihtä|mä|stä.
We're (just) coming from skiing.

Hän esti minua lähte|mä|stä.
(S)he kept me from leaving.

Lääkäri kielsi sitä tupakoi|ma|sta.
The doctor ordered her/him not to smoke. (lit. prohibited her/him from smoking)

The *inessive* applies to simultaneity or duration:

Se oli Suomessa teke|mä|ssä elokuvaa.
(S)he was in Finland making a film.

Se ero on koko ajan häviä|mä|ssä.
That distinction is disappearing all the time. (häviX- disappears, vanishes)

The *adessive* is frequently used to convey means or method:

sytyttä|mä|llä kynttilät
by lighting the candles

Se haluaa auttaa tarjoa|ma|lla työtä.
(S)he wants to help by offering work.

Finally, the *abessive* (**-ttA**) indicates that something did *not* happen; any subject of such a verb form is put into the genitive.

Se lähti Pekan huomaamatta.
(S)he left without Pekka's noticing.

Exercise 5 It follows from what you have just read in the section above that you can say *Sit down and wait!* by combining the imperative of 'sit' (formal **istukaa**, intimate **istuQ**) with the illative of the third infinitive of 'wait' (**odotta|ma|an**). Practise this model by putting these into Finnish; use both formal and intimate forms of the imperative:

1 Come (plural) home and eat!
2 Run (singular intimate) over there (**tuonne**) and have a look (**katso-**)!
3 Go (singular intimate) swimming (**ui-**)!
4 Go (plural; use **lähte-**) for a walk (**kävele-**)!

The past indefinite

Forming the past indefinite of a verb is easy if you know its present indefinite; if you feel shaky about forming those, you might want to revise now (Unit 5).

The procedure is this: if the present indefinite ends in vowel plus **tAAn**, change the **tAAn** to **ttiin**:

present indefinite: **anneItaan**   **haluItaan**   **tarviItaan**
past indefinite: **anneIttiin**   **haluIttiin**   **tarviIttiin**

Otherwise, change **dAAn**, **nAAn**, **rAAn**, **tAAn** or **lAAn** to **tiin**:

present indefinite: **saaIdaan** **purIraan** **pääsItään** **opiskelIlaan**
past indefinite: **saaItiin**   **purItiin**   **pääsItiin**   **opiskelItiin**

Exercise 6 Change present to past, and vice versa.

1 Me mennään hiihtämään.
2 Me katsottiin televisiota.
3 Mitä me syöttiin?
4 Me halutaan rauhaa (peace).

More on colloquial forms

Earlier in this unit, colloquial variants such as **tossa** (for **tuossa**) were mentioned. Three more types of pronunciation characteristic of colloquial speech are (1) omission of final **i** after **s** as in **isä pyys** for **isä pyysi** 'father asked (me)', (2) levelling of vowel sequences such as **iä, eä, ua** into **ii, ee, uu**: **kymppii** for **kymppiä**, **hirveesti** for **hirveästi**, **kossuu** for **kossua**, and (3) the omission of the -**mA**- of the third infinitive illative of verbs class I and III, i.e. just -**#n** instead of -**mA-#n**, e.g. **hakeen** instead of **hakemaan**, **tuleen** instead of **tulemaan**. In casual speech this final **n** is usually simply nasality, or even dropped; more in Unit 7.

When you speak, you should practise using both types of pronunciation, the more formal and the more colloquial.

Exercise 7 Here are some colloquial forms. Guess at the forms in more formal Finnish, then check your answers in the back of this book.

1 tärkee
2 oikeestaan

3 hulluks
4 puhuun
5 pitäis

Emphasis and word order

To lend special emphasis to a part of a sentence, you can simply say that part more loudly, e.g. **Mä tilasin** *kahvin* 'I ordered a *coffee*.' But Finns also emphasize by moving the subject or the object away from its normal position. Thus another way to emphasize that it's coffee that you ordered is to say: ***Kahvin* mä tilasin.** 'It's a *coffee* I ordered.' Similarly, you can emphasize the subject by saying **Kahvin tilasin** *minä* 'It's I who ordered the coffee.' Notice that in both these examples, the emphasized words are either last or first in the sentence.

And that is the basic rule. There are three fine points which you will also find useful to know:

1 When the emphasized word is at the beginning of the sentence, the verb comes last, e.g. ***Kahvin* mä sulle tilasin** 'It's *coffee* I ordered for you', ***Minä* kahvin sulle tilasin** 'It's *I* who ordered you coffee.'
2 To emphasize the verb, put it first in the sentence. Finns often add the clitic–**pA(s)**, e.g. **Tilasinpa(s) sulle kahvin!** 'I *did* order you a coffee!'
3 To emphasize something which is being negated, sandwich it between the negative verb and the connegative, and say the emphasized word more loudly, e.g. **En** *minä* **kahvia tilannut** 'It wasn't *I* who ordered coffee' or **En minä** *kahvia* **tilannut** 'It wasn't *coffee* I ordered'.

7 Eiks ookki ihana päästä kotiin joulunviettoon!

Isn't it great to get home for Christmas!

In this unit you will learn:

- about Finnish banknotes, and who is on them
- about number words like 'tenner', 'trio', 'triplets', and 'triangle'
- taxi talk
- more about food, particularly Christmas specialities
- how to form and use the perfect tense and its associated participles

Dialogue 1 ⬛

Seteleitä

Finnish Banknotes

PAUL: Hei kuka tässä kahden kympin setelissä on?

MATTI: Väinö Linna, hyvin tunnettu kirjailija. Se on kirjoittanut kaks tosi hyvää teosta, joista molemmista on tehty myös filmi: *Täällä pohjan tähden alla* ja *Tuntematon sotilas*.

PAUL: Kulttuurihenkilö siis. Meillä USA:ssa seteleissä on presidenttejä.

MATTI: No niin oli meilläkin aikaisemmin, mut nyt on sitten suomalaisia kulttuurivaikuttajia.

PAUL: Kenen muun kuvia on suomalaisissa seteleissä?

MATTI: Viiskymppisessä on Alvar Aalto, varmaan kuuluisin Suomen arkkitehdeistä, satasessa on Jean Sibelius, sanooks nimi sulle jotain?

PAUL: Sibeliuksesta mä oon kuullu. Mä olin jopa kesällä konsertissa, jossa soitettiin enimmäkseen Sibeliusta, mm. (muummuassa) Finlandia hymni.

MATTI: Viissatasessa on Elias Lönnroth, Kalevalan kokoaja ja tonnissa on Antti Chydenius, 1800-luvun liberaali taloustieteilijä ja pappi.

PAUL: *Say, who's this on (lit. in) the ten(-mark) note?*

MATTI: *Väinö Linna, a well-known writer. He wrote two really good works, both of which have been made into films:* Here beneath the Northern Star, *and* The Unknown Soldier.

PAUL: *A culture-hero (lit. culture-person), then. In the States we have presidents on our banknotes.*

MATTI: *Well, we did, too, formerly, but now we have Finns who have had cultural influence.*

PAUL: *Who else's picture's on Finnish banknotes?*

MATTI: *Alvar Aalto, surely the most famous Finnish architect, is on the 50(-mark note). Jean Sibelius is on the hundred; does the name ring a bell (lit. say anything to you)?*

PAUL: *Sibelius I've heard about. I was even at a concert (last) summer where they played mostly Sibelius, including Finlandia Hymn.*

MATTI: *On the 500 note is Elias Lönnroth, the compiler of the Kalevala; and on the thousand is Antti Chydenius, the nineteenth-century liberal economist and clergyman.*

Vocabulary

X|n alla	under X	kirjoitta|nut	written
aikaisemmin	earlier	kokoa|ja	collector, compiler
arkkitehti	architect	konsertti	concert
enimmäkseen	for the most part	kulttuuri	culture
filmi	film	kuullu → kuul|lut	heard
henkilö	person	kuuluis|in	the most famous
hymni	hymn	kuva	picture
hyvin	well; very	liberaali	liberal
jo|i|sta	from which	1800-luku	nineteenth century
jopa	even	mm. muu|n	*inter alia*
jossa	in which	mua|ssa	
kene|n	whose?	(muummuassa)	
kirjailija	writer	molemm|i|sta	from both

oon → ole|n		**tieteilijä**	scientist; scholar
pappi	minister, pastor, parson	**tonni**	one grand; 1,000 marks
pohja	bottom, basis; north	**tunne|ttu**	known
presidentti	president	**tunte|ma|ton**	unknown
satanen	100-er (100-mark note)	**tähti** *te*	star
seteli	banknote	**vaikutta|ja**	one who influences
siis	then, so	**varmaan**	certainly, surely
sotilaX	soldier	**viiskymppinen**	50-er (50-mark note)
talous *te*	economy	**viissatanen**	500-er (500-mark note)
teos *kse*	work (of art)		

Language points

Nouns from numbers

You have already met the simple numerals in Unit 2. Here you make the acquaintance of some of the more common nouns derived from these.

In addition to words like **viisi|kymppi|nen** '50-mark note', **sata|nen** '100-mark note', which are derived simply by the addition of =**nen**, there are also derivates built, somewhat capriciously, with =**Onen** and =**ikkO**. These refer to anything with a number written on it, a door, for example, or a bus; or even to the figure of the number itself:

1	ykkönen	7	seiska
2	kakkonen	8	kasi
3	kolmonen	9	ysi
4	nelonen	10	kymppi
5	viitonen	100	satanen
6	kuutonen		

So **kasi** can mean 'figure 8' or 'the number 8 bus' or 'room number 8', depending on the context. (Another way to refer to the bus is **bussi numero kahdeksan**.)

Another flock of useful vocabulary is made from numerals plus =**iO**:

yksiö	bedsit	**neliö**	square
kaksio	two-room flat	**kuutio**	cube
kolmio	triangle		

Notice also **kulmio**, from **kulma** 'corner', which forms words like **viisi|kulmio** 'pentagon', **kuusi|kulmio** 'hexagon', and **kahdeksan| kulmio** 'octagon'.

Kaksose|t are 'twins'; **kolmose|t** are 'triplets'.

There are also =**isen** forms of numerals, which give approximate quantities: **nelisen kilo|a** 'about 4 kilos', **viitisensataa markka|a** 'about 500 marks'.

Unknown and helpless: ways of saying 'without'

You have already seen that one way to say 'without sugar' is to use **ilman** 'without' with the noun for 'sugar' in the partitive: **ilman sokeri|a**. Another way uses the suffix =**ttOmA**. This suffix is called the 'privative' because it deprives us of whatever the stem we add it to is offering. Added to nouns, it means something like 'X-less' or 'X-free'.

raha	money	**raha|ton**	moneyless
uni *e*	sleep, dream	**une|ton**	sleepless
hammas	tooth (stem: **hampaX**)	**hampaa|ton**	toothless

You add it to the third infinitive of verbs. The result is an adjective meaning something like 'which hasn't been X'd', or 'which doesn't X', for example:

odotta|ma|ton	unexpected (**odotta-** 'waits; expects')
liikku|ma|ton	unmoving (**liikku-** 'moves')
tunte|ma|ton	unknown (**tunte-** 'knows')
sopi|ma|ton	inappropriate, unsuitable (**sopi-** 'fits in well, is appropriate')

As you can see, the **mA** at the end of the privative suffix comes out as **n** in the citation form; this **n** duly acts as a tight lid, compressing the **tt** to its left to **t**.

But the double **tt** hasn't gone away. You can tell that it is still there because even though it looks and sounds like a single **t**, it compresses consonants to *its* left:

apu	help	**a***v***uton**	helpless
paita	shirt	**pai***d***aton**	shirtless
ja*l***ka**	foot, leg	**ja***l***aton**	without feet, without legs
lanka	wire	**la***ng***aton**	wireless

The double **tt** is there to see and hear plainly in most case forms, where the **m** is followed by a vowel and so there is no compression:

uusi versio Tunte|ma|ttoma|sta sotilaa|sta
a new version of *The Unknown Soldier* sELA

une|ttom|i|a ö|i|tä
sleepless nights pP

The **mA** changes to **n** also in the partitive singular, e.g. **veroton|ta öljy|ä** 'tax-free oil'; compare **iME**-stems (Unit 5).

For revision and reference, here are the full paradigms of **langaton** 'wireless' and **puhelin** 'telephone':

	lanka=ttoMA		puhel=iME	
	Singular	*Plural*	*Singular*	*Plural*
N	langaton	langattoma|t	puhelin	puhelime|t
G	langattoma|n	langattom|i|en	puhelime|n	puhelim|i|en
P	langaton|ta	langattom|i|a	puhelin|ta	puhelim|i|a
ELA	langattoma|sta	langattom|i|sta	puhelime|sta	puhelim|i|sta
INE	langattoma|ssa	langattom|i|ssa	puhelime|ssa	puhelim|i|ssa
ILL	langattoma|an	langattom|i|in	puhelime|en	puhelim|i|in
ABL	langattoma|lta	langattom|i|lta	puhelime|lta	puhelim|i|lta
ADE	langattoma|lla	langattom|i|lla	puhelime|lla	puhelim|i|lla
ALL	langattoma|lle	langattom|i|lle	puhelime|lle	puhelim|i|lle
ESS	langattoma|na	langattom|i|na	puhelime|na	puhelim|i|na
TRA	langattoma|ksi	langattom|i|ksi	puhelime|ksi	puhelim|i|ksi

Exercise 1 Here are some nouns. What are their privatives?

1 loppu 'end'
2 kenkä 'shoe'
3 työ 'work'
4 polku 'path'
5 hammas 'tooth'

6 maku 'taste'
7 muoto 'shape, form'
8 lumi 'snow'
9 aurinko 'sun'
10 virheQ 'mistake'

Exercise 2 Guess the English equivalents of these privatives built from verbs:

1 olematon
2 kirjoittamaton
3 pesemätön

4 leipomaton
5 syömätön
6 asumaton

Past passive participle

Me ei *menty* **sinne.**	We didn't go there.
Kirjettä ei *annettu* **takaisin.**	They didn't give the letter back/ The letter wasn't returned.

As you can see from these examples, the past tense of the negative indefinite is formed with the negative form **ei** plus a verb form ending in -(t)tU. This is one of the most common uses of this form, but there are several others, as well. You learn how to build this form (which is called the past passive participle) and more about using it in this section.

The past passive participle is really just an adjective made from verbs; it corresponds to the English 'written' and 'falsified' of 'written instructions' and 'falsified ID', but it is much more widely used in Finnish. For transitive verbs, a mechanical translation would go something like 'which has been X'd'; for intransitive verbs, something like 'which has X'd'. You will learn one very common use of this participle later in this unit; but first let's see how to form it.

You form the past passive participle as follows:

Add -tU to verbs of classes III and IV (notice that class III verbs lose their final **e**):

opiskel|tu	(stem: **opiskele-** 'studies')
pes|ty	(stem: **pese-** 'washes')
men|ty	(stem: **mene-** 'goes')
saa|tu	(stem: **saa-** 'gets')
syö|ty	(stem: **syö-** 'eats')

Add -ttU to verbs of class I. Stem-final **A** > **e**:

sano|ttu	(stem: **sano-** 'says')
etsi|tty	(stem: **etsi-** 'searches for')
lue|ttu	(stem: **luke-** 'reads')
kanne|ttu	(stem: **kanta-** 'carries')
kielle|tty	(stem: **kieltä-** 'forbids, prohibits')

Class II verbs also take -ttU, and they lose their final chunks **X**, **TSE**, **XE**, as well:

huoma|ttu	(stem: **huomaX-** 'notices')
tarvi|ttu	(stem: **tarviTSE-** 'needs')
vaie|ttu	(stem: **vaikeXE-** 'falls/is silent')

The past passive participles of the verbs of knowing **tietä-** and **tunte-** deserve special attention. From **tietä-** is formed, alongside the regular **tiede|tty**, the irregular past passive participle **tietty**; this latter is common in the meaning not only of '(well-)known' but also of 'certain (specific)' as in **tiety|i|ssä tapauks|i|ssa** 'in certain cases'. From **tunte-**, the regularly formed **tunne|ttu** means 'well-known, famous'; 'known' in the sense of 'familiar' is **tuttu**.

Note on compression. As with the privative suffix, consonants which have been compressed by the past passive participle suffix remain compressed, regardless of any compression which that suffix itself may undergo. Thus the genitive singular of **käyte|tty** '(which has been) used' (stem: käyttä-) is **käytety|n**, and the genitive singular of **unohdettu** '(which has been) forgotten' (stem: **unohta-**) is **unohdetu|n**.

For your studying pleasure and for later reference, here's a table of the full paradigms of the past passive participles of **käyte|tty** 'used' (from **käyttä-** 'uses') and **saatu** 'received, acquired'. Look closely and you'll see that there's nothing so terribly new here; these are just adjectives, and as such they inflect like **reilu** 'upright, straightforward' or **juttu** 'story, affair, thing'. The paradigm for the latter is placed alongside for the sake of comparison.

	Singular	Plural	Singular	Plural	Singular	Plural
N	**käytetty**	**käytety|t**	**saatu**	**saadu|t**	**juttu**	**jutu|t**
G	**käytety|n**	**käytetty|j|en**	**saadu|n**	**saatu|j|en**	**jutu|n**	**juttu|j|en**
P	**käytetty|ä**	**käytetty|j|ä**	**saatu|a**	**saatu|j|a**	**juttu|a**	**juttu|j|a**
ELA	**käytety|stä**	**käytety|i|stä**	**saadu|sta**	**saadu|i|sta**	**jutu|sta**	**jutu|i|sta**
INE	**käytety|ssä**	**käytety|i|ssä**	**saadu|ssa**	**saadu|i|ssa**	**jutu|ssa**	**jutu|i|ssa**
ILL	**käytetty|yn**	**käytetty|i|hin**	**saatu|un**	**saatu|i|hin**	**juttu|un**	**juttu|i|hin**
ABL	**käytety|ltä**	**käytety|i|ltä**	**saadu|lta**	**saadu|i|lta**	**jutu|lta**	**jutu|i|lta**
ADE	**käytety|llä**	**käytety|i|llä**	**saadu|lla**	**saadu|i|lla**	**jutu|lla**	**jutu|i|lla**
ALL	**käytety|lle**	**käytety|i|lle**	**saadu|lle**	**saadu|i|lle**	**jutu|lle**	**jutu|i|lle**
ESS	**käytetty|nä**	**käytetty|i|nä**	**saatu|na**	**saatu|i|na**	**juttu|na**	**juttu|i|na**
TRA	**käytety|ksi**	**käytety|i|ksi**	**saadu|ksi**	**saadu|i|ksi**	**jutu|ksi**	**jutu|i|ksi**

The past passive participle is used as an adjective most often in written Finnish. Have a look at these rather formal examples of the past passive participle in action:

kive|ty|llä kadu|lla
on a paved street (stem: **kiveX**- 'paves', cf. **kivi** *e* 'stone')

kielle|ty|n kirja|n nimi
the title of the banned book

viime kevää|nä ava|tu|ssa panki|ssa
in the bank (which was) opened last spring

edellämainittu|i|hin ryhm|i|in
into the above-mentioned groups (**ryhmä** 'group')

niin sanottu|j|en normaal|i|en ihmis|t|en maailma|ssa
in the world of so-called normal people

Exercise 3 In this exercise you revise the privative and practise your past passive participles by converting one to the other and vice versa. The verb roots are **rakenta**- 'builds', **käyttä**- 'uses', **maalaX**- 'paints', **keittä**- 'cooks' and **kuori**- 'peels'.

Example: **pesemätön** 'unwashed' > **pesty** 'washed'.

1 rakentamaton
2 käytetty
3 maalattu

4 syömätön
5 keittämätön
6 kuorittu

The perfect tense

The Finnish perfect tense means very much the same as the English perfect ('I have written to him', 'she has come back'). In speech, its main function is to refer to things that happened in the past but which still have relevance today.

Finnish often uses its perfect where English does just as well with a simple past. For example, in the dialogue above we have **Se on kirjoittanut kaks tosi hyvää teosta** 'He wrote two really good works.' Finnish uses the perfect tense here because it is the fact that the works still exist and can be enjoyed that is important, not merely the fact that Väinö Linna sat down at some time in the past and wrote them.

The way the perfect is formed differs from the English perfect in one important way. Unlike in English, where you use forms of the verb 'has' ('he has written'), in Finnish you use forms of the verb 'is', **ole**-. Have a look at these examples:

Olen kirjoittanut sille. I have written to him. (lit. 'I am . . .')

Se on tullut takaisin.   She has come back. (lit. 'She is . . .')

The other part of the perfect is built from the main verb (here: 'write', 'come') in a form you have already learned. This is the past active participle, built with the suffix **-nUt** (singular), **-nee|t** (plural) which you met in Unit 6. The singular-vs.-plural distinction is vital in second person forms; notice the difference between the following examples:

Te olette tul*lut* takaisin.
You (singular, formal) have come back.

Te olette tul*leet* takaisin.
You (plural, possibly formal) have come back.

Here are some more examples of the perfect in action:

Mä oon aina unelmoi|nut elämästä teatterissa.
I've always dreamt of a life in the theatre. (**unelmoi-** 'dreams')

On lakan|nut satamasta.
It has stopped raining. (**lakkaX-** 'desists', **sata-** 'rains')

Hän on autta|nut minua monin tavoin.
(S)he has helped me in many ways.

Olen hake|nut kahteen eri yliopistoon.
I've applied to two different universities.

Oletteko te asu|neet Helsingissä kauan?
Have you (plural/formal) lived in Helsinki long?

Note that the past active participle is not the exact equivalent of English passive participles such as 'written'. For example, you do not say 'written instructions' and the like with **kirjoittanut**; contrast the past passive participle. (In a later unit we'll revise all the participles together.)

There is one further detail. Since in colloquial Finnish the first person plural is normally expressed by means of the indefinite, you must know how to form and recognize the perfect indefinite. Its makeup is, rather logically, (1) the indefinite of the verb **ole-** 'is' (**ollaan**), plus (2) the past passive participle. Examples:

Me ollaan jo puhu|ttu tästä.   We've already talked about this.
Me ollaan juo|tu kaikki oluet.   We've drunk all the beers.

Here is the full perfect-tense paradigm of **osta-** 'buys':

Singular	Plural
1 (mä) oon ostanut	me ollaan ostettu[1]
2 (sä) oot ostanut[2]	(te) olette ostaneet[2]
3 se on ostanut	ne on ostanut[3]

1 In more formal Finnish, **me olemme ostaneet**.

2 To address one person with politeness (and more formality), you say **te olette ostanut**.

3 In more formal Finnish, **he ovat ostaneet**.

The *negative perfect* is formed with the appropriate negative forms of the verb **ole-**:

Singular	Plural
1 mä en ole ostanut	me ei olla ostettu[1]
2 sä et ole ostanut	te ette ole ostaneet
3 se ei ole ostanut	ne ei ole ostanut[2]

1 In more formal Finnish, **me emme ole ostaneet**.

2 In more formal Finnish, **he eivät ole ostaneet**.

Here are some examples of the perfect tense in action. Note that omission (or assimilation, written here with superscript letters) of the final **t** is common.

Se on kertonu[k] kaiken poliisille.	(S)he has told the police everything.
Ootsä koskaan lukenut tätä romaania?	Have you ever read this novel?
Mä oon soittanut taksin.	I've called (for) a taxi.
Me ollaan soitettu taksi.	We've called (for) a taxi.
Me ei olla oltu yhteydessä.	We haven't been in touch.
En ole[n] nähny[m] mitään.	I haven't seen anything.
Ettekö ole[s] saaneet lippuja?	Haven't you (plural) got the tickets?
Ootsä aina asunut täällä?	Have you always lived here?
Mä en ole[v] vielä päässyt ulos koko päivänä.	I haven't (yet) been able to get out all day.
Se ei ole[k] koskaan tehnyt muuta.	(S)he's never done anything else.

Tämä ei ole mitenkään helpottanut asiaa.	This hasn't made the matter any easier.

Exercise 4 Change the verb forms in these snippets into the perfect tense, then translate into English.

1 mä tulen
2 se hakee
3 ne saapuu
4 Ootsä Hesassa?
5 mä avaan ikkunan

6 me avataan ikkuna
7 me tullaan
8 hän tarvitsee apua
9 Mistä se saa rahan?
10 se pakenee

Exercise 5 Change affirmative to negative and vice versa. Remember to change accusative/partitive, something/nothing (**jotain/ mitään**), yet/already (**vielä/jo**) as appropriate.

Example: Ootsä lähettänyt kirjeen? Etsä ole[l] lähettänyt kirjettä?

1 Se on lähtenyt.
2 Mä olen huomannut sen.
3 Ne ei ole[s] sanonut mitään.

4 En mä ole[v] vielä nähnyt sitä.
5 Me ollaan jo puhuttu siitä.
6 Mä en ole tavannut häntä.

Dialogue 2 ▄▄

Taksissa

A ride in a taxi

To revise some of the grammar and vocabulary you've learned so far, ride with Juuso as he takes a taxi from Helsinki Station to Haukilahti ('Pike Bay'). Notice the use of the genitive (**taksi|n**) in **Taksin|kuljetta|ja** 'taxi driver'.

Juuso takes a taxi from Helsinki Railway Station

JUUSO:	*(taksinkuljettajalle)* Oletteko vapaa?
TAKSINKULJETTAJA:	Kyllä. Mihin mennään?
JUUSO:	Haukilahteen, kiitos.
TAKSINKULJETTAJA:	Mihin päin Haukilahtea?
JUUSO:	Kuhatie neljään.
TAKSINKULJETTAJA:	Osaatteko neuvoa Länsiväylältä? Olen ajanut niin vähän Espoossa, etten ole aivan varma siitä missä päin Haukilahtea Kuhatie on.

JUUSO:	Kyllä osaan. Paljonko se tulee maksamaan?
TAKSINKULJETTAJA:	Siinä[1] 7–8 (seitsemän kahdeksan) kymppiä.
JUUSO:	*(to the taxi driver) Are you (formal) free?*
TAKSINKULJETTAJA:	*Yes. Where shall we go?*
JUUSO:	*To Haukilahti, thanks.*
TAKSINKULJETTAJA:	*(To) where (abouts) in Haukilahti?*
JUUSO:	*To 4 Kuhatie ('Pike-perch Road').*
TAKSINKULJETTAJA:	*Can you advise me from Länsiväylä (on)? I've driven so little in Espoo that I'm not quite sure (of it) where (abouts) Kuhatie is.*
JUUSO:	*Sure, I can (advise you). How much will it come to (to cost)?*
TAKSINKULJETTAJA:	*About 70 or 80 (marks).*

1 **siinä** 'about' (lit. 'in it').

Vocabulary

aivan	quite	**neuvo-**	advises
aja-	drives	**päin**	towards, about
asema	station	**rauta|tie**	railway
ett|en = että e|n		**taksi**	taxi
kuljetta-	drives	**vähän**	(a) little

Exercise 6 Make up your own taxi dialogue. Tell the driver where you want to go, say where that is, ask how much it'll cost and how long it'll take. Here's some vocabulary to get you started:

taksi\|mittari   taxi metre   **taksi\|asema**   taxi rank

Paljonko maksu on kilometri\|ltä?
How much is the charge per kilometre? (**tunni\|lta** 'per hour')

Kauanko sinne kestää ajaa?
How long does it take to drive there?

Voi(si)tteko viedä minut tähän osoittee\|seen?
Could you take me to this address?

Don't forget to use imperatives to get the driver to stop (**pysähty-**), keep going (**jatka-**), slow down (**hidasta-**), or wait (**odotta-**). When you get there, say:

Tässä on hyvä, kiitos.	Here is fine, thanks.
Pitäkää lopu|t!	Keep the change.

Dialogue 3 ▣

Listen to Tanja and Raija as they anticipate returning to Finland
for Christmas.

Jouluherkkuja

Yuletide treats

On a plane about to take off for Finland

RAIJA: Eiks ookki ihana päästä kotiin joulunviettoon.
TANJA: Nii. Tässä ei ookkaan vielä päässy jouluntunnelmaan.
RAIJA: Mä meen jouluks mummolaan. Entäs sä?
TANJA: Mä oon vaan kotona ja meinaan syödä paljon kinkkua.
RAIJA: Mun tekee tosi paljon mieli äidin imellettyä perunalaa-
tikkoa.
TANJA: Teettekste ite lanttu- ja porkkanalaatikonki?
RAIJA: Joo. Me tehdään kotona kaikki jouluruuat, sillit, silakat,
lipeäkala, rosolli ja jopa joulusinappi.
TANJA: Tykkäätsä todella lipeäkalasta?
RAIJA: No en, mut se kuuluu traditioon.
TANJA: Meillä leivotaan vaan piparit ja joulutortut ite.

RAIJA: *Isn't it great to be able to get home for Christmas!*
TANJA: *Yes. I haven't been able to get into a Christmasy mood here.*
RAIJA: *I'm going to my grandmother's for Christmas. What about
you?*
TANJA: *I'll just be staying home, and I intend to eat a lot of ham.*
RAIJA: *I really could go for some of my mother's malted-potato
casserole.*
TANJA: *Do you make your own swede casserole and carrot casse-
role, as well?*
RAIJA: *Sure. We make all the Christmas dishes at (our) house:
herring, Baltic herring, slippery cod, rosolli, and even
Christmas mustard.*
TANJA: *Do you actually **like** slippery cod?*
RAIJA: *Well, no, but it's part of the tradition.*
TANJA: *At our house the only things we bake ourselves are ginger-
snaps and Christmas cake.*

Vocabulary

herkku	gourmet item	**oon** → **ole**|**n**	
ihana	wonderful, lovely	**pipari**|**t**	gingersnaps
imelle|**tty**	malted	**porkkana**	carrot
ite → **itse**	self	**rosolli**	salad of salted
joulu	Christmas		herring,
joulu|**ks** →	for Christmas		beetroot,
joulu|**ksi**			carrots, etc.
joulusinappi	Christmas mustard	**ruua**|**t**	! pN of **ruoka**
kinkku	ham		'food, dish'
kuulu-	belongs	**silli**	herring
laatikko	box; casserole	**teettekste** →	
lanttu	swede, rutabaga	**teettekö te**	
lento|**koneQ**	aeroplane	**tode**|**lla**	really, trully
lipeäkala	slippery cod, cod	**torttu**	cake
	soaked in lye	**traditio**	tradition
meen → **mene**|**n**		**tunnelma**	feeling, mood
meinaX-	intends, means to	**vaan** → **vain**	only, just
nii → **niin**		**vietto**	celebration
ookkaan →			(**viettä-** 'spends,
olekaan			celebrates')
ookki → **olekin**			

Language points

Colloquial pronunciation: three more fine points

1 In colloquial contexts like that of the dialogue above, most Finns usually pronounce the common verbs **ole-**, **tule-**, **mene-**, and **pane-** 'puts' in a shortened way, namely as **oo-**, **tuu-**, **mee-**, and **paa-**. Here are examples of the forms in question:

more formal: **ole**\|**n ei ole**\|**Q tule**\|**t mene**\|**t pane**\|**tte mene**\|*s* **sinne!**
more colloquial: **oo**\|**n ei o(o)**\|**Q tuu**\|**t mee**\|**t paa**\|**tte mee**\|*s* **sinne!**

The -**Q** suffix of the imperative and connegative (as in **ei o**) means that following consonants will sound long; this lengthening is reflected in spellings such as **ookkaan** (formal **olekaan**).

2 Notice also that final **n** (but not the **n** of the genitive, or of the first person singular of verbs) is often merely nasality, or even

dropped: to indicate this, we will write **ku** instead of **kun**, **ookki** instead of **ookkin** (formal: **olekin**).

3 Many Finns pronounce **tt** (or even **t**) instead of **ts** in certain common words such as **itse** 'self' at least when they are in colloquial mode. Other examples are **kattoo** (> **katso|a** 'looks at, watches') and **seittemän** (> **seitsemän**).

Extra reading

Imelletty perunalaatikko

A recipe for malted potato casserole

There's a translation of this recipe at the back of the book (see exercise 7); but try not to peek until you've given it an honest try with the help of the vocabulary given here.

Imelletty perunalaatikko

2 kg perunoita	2–3 rkl voisulaa
1 dl vehnäjauhoja	2 tl suolaa
4–5 dl maitoa	muskottipähkinää

Keitä perunat kypsiksi ja kuori ne heti höyryttämisen jälkeen. Survo perunat ja ripota jauhot joukkoon. Anna seoksen imeltyä muutama tunti tai vaikka seuraavaan päivään. Sekoita pari kertaa. Lisää maito, voi ja mausteet. Kaada seos voideltuun uunivuokaan ja kypsennä 150 asteessa noin kaksi tuntia.

Vocabulary

anna X|n Y|TAQ	let X Y	**joukko**	mass, bulk, heap
		kaata-	pours
asteQ	degree	**keittä-**	cooks, boils
dl (deka|litra)	decalitre	**kg (kilo|gramma)**	kg
heti	at once, right away	**kuori-**	peels
höyryttäminen	allowing to steam	**kypsentä-**	ripens, roasts
imelle|tty	malted	**kyps|i|ksi**	'until they are ready' (**kypsä pTRA**)
imelty-	malts, becomes malted		
jauho|t	flour, meal	**lisäX-**	adds

mausteQ	spice	**survo-**	crushes, mashes, grinds
muskotti|pähkinä	nutmeg		
muutama	a few	**tai**	or
pari kerta|a	a few times	**tl (tee|lusikka)**	teaspoon
ripotta-	sprinkles	**tunti**	hour
rkl	tablespoon	**uuni**	oven
(ruoka|lusikka)		**vaikka**	or even
sekoitta-	mixes, stirs, shuffles	**vehnä**	wheat
		voi	butter
seos *kse*	mixture	**voi|sula|a**	melted butter
seuraava	next, following	**voidel|tu**	buttered
suola	salt	**vuoka**	mould, dish

Exercise 7 Write out an English translation of the recipe above, then compare it with that given at the back of this book.

Exercise 8 Make the casserole!

8 Huonosta vielä huonommaksi

From bad to worse

In this unit you will learn:

* how to say how you're feeling; vocabulary of medicine and illness
* how to form and use the comparative and superlative
* about entering and being in states (the translative and essive cases)
* a little about Finnish sport
* about the stem-type **talous** 'economy'

Dialogue 1 ▦

Sairaana

Feeling ill

Matthew hasn't been feeling very well for the last few days, so he asks Mikko for advice

(Tapaavat yliopistolla)

MATTHEW: Kuule Mikko, voisit sä neuvoa mua yhdessä asiassa. Mulla on ollu jo kaks päivää yskä ja kurkkuki on aika kipee. Pitäskö mun mennä lääkäriin?

MIKKO: Mee nyt ihmeessä! Se voi tulla pahemmaks jos viivyttelet.

MATTHEW: Minne mun pitäis mennä?

MIKKO: Lähimpään terveyskeskukseen. Niihin ei tartte varata aikaa. Meet vaan päivystykseen oottamaan. Joskus voi kyllä joutua odottamaan pariki tuntia. Lähin terveyskeskus on ihan tässä yliopiston vieressä Yliopistokadulla.

MATTHEW: Kiitti sulle mä lähenki tästä heti sinne.

(At university)

MATTHEW: *Listen, Mikko, could you give me some advice on something (lit. a matter). I've had a cough for two days now and (my) throat is pretty sore, too. Should I go to (see) the doctor?*

MIKKO: *Go now, for goodness' sake! It can get worse if you hang about.*

MATTHEW: *Where should I go?*

MIKKO: *To the nearest health centre. You don't have to make an appointment (there). You just go and wait your turn to see the GP on duty. Of course sometimes you may wind up waiting as much as a few hours. The nearest health centre is right here next to the university, in Yliopistokatu.*

MATTHEW: *Thanks! I'm going to go there right now.*

Vocabulary

asia	matter, affair	**pahempi**	worse
ihan tässä	just here	**pitäskö** →	
ihmeQ	wonder	**pitäisikö**	
joutu-	winds up, ends up (used with 3rd infinitive)	**sinne**	(to) there
		tapaX-	meets
		tartte → **tarvitse**	
keskus *kse*	centre	**tarviTSE-**	is necessary; needs
kipee → **kipeä**	sore; ill		
kurkku	throat	**terveys** *te*	health
lähen → **lähdeln**		**varaX-**	books, reserves, orders
lähimpään	illative of **lähin**		
lähin	nearest	**viivyttele-**	delays, hangs about
minne	(to) where?		
oottamaan →		**Xln vierelssä**	next to X
odottalmalan		**yhdelssä**	together; at the same time
pahemmaks	sTRA of **pahempi**		
		yskä	cough
päivystys *kse*	day rota		

Language points

Forming the comparative

This is the English '-er' of 'bigger', 'smaller', or the 'more' of 'more beautiful'. In Finnish you add the suffix of the comparative to the adjective stem; the suffix is **-mpA**.

There are just two complications. One is that in the nominative singular this suffix comes out as **mpi**. So we have:

iso|mpi	bigger (**iso**)
piene|mpi	smaller (**pieni** *e*)
korkea|mpi	higher (**korkea**)
matala|mpi	lower (**matala**)
kirkkaa|mpi	brighter (**kirkkaX**)
tuoree|mpi	fresher (**tuoreQ**)
suomalaise|mpi	more Finnish (**suomalainen**; stem: **suomalaise-**)

The other complication is this: bisyllabic roots which end in single **A** change this vowel to **e**. Thus we have:

kove|mpi	harder (**kova** 'hard')
syve|mpi	deeper (**syvä** 'deep')
vanhe|mpi	older (**vanha** 'old'; note **se|n vanhe|mma|t** 'his/her parents')

Finally, as in English, a few of the most frequent forms are irregular:

good	**hyvä**
better	**parempi**
best	**paras** (stem: **par*h*aX**, so sG is **parhaa|n**)
long	**pitkä**
longer	**pitempi**

Note: the Finnish words **kumpi** 'which? (of two), **kumpikin** 'both', and **jompikumpi** 'either (of two)' all contain the comparative suffix (**jompikumpi** has it twice: its partitive singular is **jompaakumpaa**):

Kumpi on kalliimpaa, viini vai viina?
Which is more expensive, wine or spirits?

Kummatkin vanhemmat jäävät kotiin.
Both parents are staying home.

Mitä saisi olla, kahvia vai teetä?
What'll you have, coffee or tea?

Jompaakumpaa, kumpaa vaan.
One or the other, it doesn't matter.

Even more common than **jompikumpi** is **kumpi tahansa** or **kumpi vaan** 'whichever (of the two)', as in the last example.

Here are the full paradigms of three adjectives, **paksu** 'thick, fat', **ohut** (stem: ohuTe) 'thin', and **puhdas** (stem: puhtaX) 'clean', in their comparative form:

	paksu	*ohuTe*	*puhtax*
sN	paksu|mpi	ohue|mpi	puhtaa|mpi
sG	paksu|mma|n	ohue|mma|n	puhtaa|mma|n
sP	paksu|mpa|a	ohue|mpa|a	puhtaa|mpa|a
sELA	paksu|mma|sta	ohue|mma|sta	puhtaa|mma|sta
sINE	paksu|mma|ssa	ohue|mma|ssa	puhtaa|mma|ssa
sILL	paksu|mpa|an	ohue|mpa|an	puhtaa|mpa|an
sABL	paksu|mma|lta	ohue|mma|lta	puhtaa|mma|lta
sADE	paksu|mma|lla	ohue|mma|lla	puhtaa|mma|lla
sALL	paksu|mma|lle	ohue|mma|lle	puhtaa|mma|lle
sESS	paksu|mpa|na	ohue|mpa|na	puhtaa|mpa|na
sTRA	paksu|mma|ksi	ohue|mma|ksi	puhtaa|mma|ksi
pN	paksu|mma|t	ohue|mma|t	puhtaa|mma|t
pG	paksu|mp|i|en	ohue|mp|i|en	puhtaa|mp|i|en
pP	paksu|mp|i|a	ohue|mp|i|a	puhtaa|mp|i|a
pELA	paksu|mm|i|sta	ohue|mm|i|sta	puhtaa|mm|i|sta
pINE	paksu|mm|i|ssa	ohue|mm|i|ssa	puhtaa|mm|i|ssa
pILL	paksu|mp|i|in	ohue|mp|i|in	puhtaa|mp|i|in
pABL	paksu|mm|i|lta	ohue|mm|i|lta	puhtaa|mm|i|lta
pADE	paksu|mm|i|lla	ohue|mm|i|lla	puhtaa|mm|i|lla
pALL	paksu|mm|i|lle	ohue|mm|i|lle	puhtaa|mm|i|lle
pESS	paksu|mp|i|na	ohue|mp|i|na	puhtaa|mp|i|na
pTRA	paksu|mm|i|ksi	ohue|mm|i|ksi	puhtaa|mm|i|ksi

Here are a few more examples of comparative forms in action:

nuore\|mma\|n sukupolve\|n tilanne
the situation of the younger generation

varme\|mma\|lla pohja\|lla   on a firmer basis

piene\|mp\|i\|en ma\|i\|den taloude\|t
the economies of smaller countries

Using the comparative

If you want to say that A is bigger than B, you have a choice. Typical of more formal Finnish is to put B into the partitive:

Helsinki on Turkua suurempi.
Helsinki is bigger than Turku.

(Notice the word order of this construction.)
The more colloquial option is to use **kuin**:

Helsinki on isompi kuin Turku.

To say 'more and more X', 'Xer and Xer', you use **yhä**: **yhä useammat suomalaiset** 'more and more Finns', **yhä sitkeämpi vastarinta** 'tougher and tougher resistance'.

Note: to compare equals, you use **yhtä** (**niin** with adverbs) A **kuin** B (with no comparative suffix, as in English):

yhtä kevyt kuin höyhen.	as light as a feather
Toinen on yhtä hyvä kuin toinenkin.	One is as good as the other.
niin usein kuin mahdollista	as often as possible

Exercise 1 Put these adjectives into the comparative.

Example: **iso > isompi**

1 **nopea** 'fast'	6 **pieni** e 'little'
2 **selvä** 'clear'	7 **paksu** 'fat, thick'
3 **mukava** 'comfortable, pleasant'	8 **ohut** 'thin'
4 **kiltti** 'nice, kind, well-behaved'	9 **punainen** 'red'
5 **voimakkaX** 'powerful'	10 **terveQ** 'healthy'

Exercise 2 Practise using the comparative by writing Finnish comparative sentences with the following sets of nouns and adjectives:

Example: **Tanska, Suomi, iso > Suomi on isompi ku(i)n Tanska**

1 Sä, mä, nuori
2 pihvi, keitto, kallis
3 Espanja, Portugali, iso
4 lääkäri, lapsi, vanha
5 paperi, kulta, kevyt ('light'; stem: **kevyTe-**)

Exercise 3 Practise looking for things that are bigger, better, smaller, and more comfortable. Remember to use the partial (partitive) direct-object form.

Example: parempi sanakirja > Mä etsin parempaa sanakirjaa 'I'm looking for a better dictionary.'

1 kuiva (dry), viini (wine)
2 halpa (cheap), vihko (notebook)
3 pieni, laukku
4 yksinkertainen (simple), vastaus (answer; stem: **vastaukse**)
5 makea (sweet), mehu (juice)

Exercise 4 Now say that you've found what you were looking for in the previous exercise. You'll need to use the complete-object form (accusative = genitive).

Example: **Mä oon löytänyt paremman sanakirjan.** 'I've found a better dictionary.'

Se tulee pahemmaksi (it gets worse): the translative

The translative suffix is **-ksi**, pronounced colloquially without the **i**, of course. This case indicates, among other things, entrance into a state or mode of being. It is therefore often used with verbs such as **muutta-** 'changes (transitive)', **muuttu-** 'changes (intransitive)', **tule-** 'becomes'. Examples:

Se muutti saunan olohuonee|ks.
(S)he turned the sauna into a living room.

Asia muuttuu vaikea|ks.
The matter becomes difficult.

Rikkaat tulee rikkaamm|i|ks.
The rich get richer.

Se tulee yhä vaikea|mma|ksi.
It gets more and more difficult.

On tullut tava|ksi.
It has become a custom.

Se tuli tunnetu|ksi.
It became known.

Mä kirjoitan sen puhtaalksi.
I'll make a clean copy of it.

The translative is also often used to express the capacity in which something is used; the most common example is **esimerkilksi** 'for example'. Further examples are:

Jälkiruualksi oli mansikoita.
There were strawberries *for dessert.*

Mä sain sen lahjalks.
I got it *as a gift.*

Dialogue 2 ▣

Doctors are forever giving orders, so this is a good opportunity to revise the forms of the imperative (Unit 3).

Lääkärissä

At the doctor's

Matthew waits at the health centre until it's his turn. Then

LÄÄKÄRI: *(pyytää ovelta)* Matthew Smith, olkaa hyvä.
Matthew menee lääkärin perässä sisään.
Ja mikäs teitä vaivaa?
MATTHEW: Mulla on ollu yskä jo pari päivää, eikä se tunnu oikein menevän ohi[1]. Kurkku on myös aika kipee.
LÄÄKÄRI: Ja kuumetta?
MATTHEW: Ei oo.
LÄÄKÄRI: Katsotaanpa kurkkuun ja kuunnellaan keuhkoja. *(Hän kuuntelee ja katsoo.)* Näyttää siltä että kyse ei ole mistään vakavasta tulehduksesta. Levätkää kotona pari päivää ja juokaa runsaasti kuumaa juotavaa. Flunssa- ja särkylääkkeitä voitte ottaa tarpeen mukaan. Ne helpottavat oloa. Jos olo huononee tulkaa uudelleen.

DOCTOR: (calls from the doorway) *Matthew Smith, please.*
Matthew goes in after the doctor.
DOCTOR: *And what is troubling you?*
MATTHEW: *I've had a cough for a couple of days now, and it doesn't*

really seem to be going away. (My) throat is also pretty sore.

DOCTOR: *And (do you have) any fever?*

MATTHEW: *No.*

DOCTOR: *Let's have a look into (your) throat and listen to (your) lungs.* (S)he listens and looks). *It looks as though it isn't a question of any serious inflammation. Rest at home for a few days and drink plenty of hot beverages. You can take 'flu and pain medicines as necessary. They'll help you to feel better (lit. they'll ease the being/condition). If it gets worse, come again.*

1 **eikä se tunnu oikein mene|vä|n ohi** 'and it doesn't really seem to going away'; you'll learn about this construction in Unit 12.

Vocabulary

flunssa	'flu	**ohi**	(adv.) past, by, over
helpotta-	eases, relieves	**ol|o**	condition, the way
huonoXE-	worsens, gets worse		X is
juo-	drinks	**X|n perä|ssä**	behind X
juo|tava	to be drunk, potable	**pyytä-**	asks, requests
keuhko	lung	**runsaasti**	in generous
kuuma	hot, warm		quantities
kuumeQ	fever	**sisä|än**	(to) inside
kuuntele-	listens	**särky**	pain
kyseQ	question, matter	**tarpeQ**	need
lepäX-	rests	**tulehdus** kse	inflammation (**tuli** e
lääkkeQ	medicine		'fire')
X|n mukaan	according to	**uudelleen**	again
myös	also	**vaiva-**	troubles
X|ltA näyttä-	seems X	**vakava**	serious

Exercise 5 Pick out the imperative forms in the two dialogues above, then convert them from formal to informal or vice versa, as appropriate.

Additional vocabulary

Whether you're feeling ill or not, some basic anatomical vocabulary is always handy, so have a good look at these items:

tukka	head hair	**rinta**	breast
otsa	forehead	**käsivarsi** *te*	arm
silmä	eye	**kyynärpää**	elbow
nenä	nose	**sormi** *e*	finger
suu	mouth	**peukalo**	thumb
kieli *e*	tongue	**lanteelt**	hips
huuli *e*	lip	**reisi** *te*	thigh
leuka	chin	**polvi** *e*	knee
korva	ear	**sääri** *e*	leg
poski *e*	cheek	**jalka**	foot, leg
kaula	neck	**varpaX**	toe

Dialogue 3 ▣

Jorma raukka!

Poor Jorma!

Anna and Sanna are colleagues. At work, they discuss Jorma's health

SANNA: Hei Anna!
ANNA: Hei. Mitä kuuluu?
SANNA: Kiitos hyvää. Entäs sulle?
ANNA: Hyvää. Mitä perheelles kuuluu?
SANNA: Siinähän se menee . . .
ANNA: Kuinka Jorma voi? Se näytti vähän väsyneeltä eilen illalla.
SANNA: Nii, se on kai vähän vilustunut. Se sanoo ettei sitä mikään vaivaa, mutta tänä aamuna mä huomasin, että se yski koko ajan kun se pani takkia päälleen.
ANNA: Ei sen pitäis sitten mennä töihin, sen pitäis jäädä kotiin lepäämään. Onks sillä kuumetta?
SANNA: En mä tiedä. Se ei antanu mun mitata sitä.[1] Se sano, ettei se oo mitään ja et se menee nopeasti ohi.
ANNA: No, toivotaan niin.

SANNA: *Hello, Anna.*
ANNA: *Hi. How are things?*
SANNA: *Fine, thanks. And you?*
ANNA: *Fine. How's your family?*
SANNA: *They're all right . . .*
ANNA: *How is Jorma feeling? He looked a bit done in last night.*
SANNA: *Yes; he may have caught a cold. He says there's nothing*

wrong with him, but I noticed this morning that he was coughing all the time he was putting his coat on.

ANNA: He shouldn't be going to work, he should be staying home and getting some rest. Does he have a fever?

SANNA: I don't know. He wouldn't let me take his temperature. He said it's nothing, that it'll soon pass.

ANNA: Well, let's hope so.

1 **Se ei antanu mun mitata sitä** 'He didn't let me measure it.'

Vocabulary

aja|n: koko ajan	all the time	mittaX-	measures
eilen	yesterday	nii → niin	
et → että		nopea|sti	quickly
jää-	stays	pää|lle|en	onto her/himself
koko	(the) whole, entire; size	sano → sano|i	
		takki	jacket
kuinka	how?	toivo-	hopes
mi|kä|län: ei mikään	nothing (sN)	väsy-	becomes tired
		vilustu-	catches cold
mi|tä|län: ei mitään	nothing (sP)	yskä-	coughs

Dialogue 4 🔲

Urheilua Suomessa

On sport in Finland

Jeremy asks his friend Jyri about the kinds of sport Finns go in for

JEREMY: Mitkä urheilulajit kiinnostaa suomalaisia?

JYRI: Luulisin että jääkiekko on suosituin, mut jalkapallo on myös todella suosittu.

JEREMY: Näyttää siltä että jalkapallo on kansainvälisesti suosittua.

JYRI: Suomen erikoisuus on kuitenki pesäpallo. Sitä vois pitää Suomen kansallisurheiluna.

JEREMY: Miten sitä pelataan?

JYRI: Vähän niin ku amerikkalaista basebollia, mut siinä on takaraja lyönneissä ja se on enemmän joukkuepeli.

JEREMY: *What types of sport interest Finns?*
JYRI: *I would think that ice hockey is the favourite. But football is really liked a lot, as well.*
JEREMY: *It seems that football is a favourite internationally.*
JYRI: *In any case, a Finnish speciality is* **pesäpallo**. *You could think of it as Finland's national sport.*
JEREMY: *How is it played?*
JYRI: *A little like American baseball, but there's a back limit to hits, and it's more of a team sport.*

Vocabulary

basebolli	baseball	**pelaX-**	plays (game)
enemmän	more (adv.)	**pesis → pesälpallo**	
erikoisluus	speciality	**pesälpallo**	(Finnish ball
jalkalpallo	football		game)
joukkuelpeli	team sport	**pitä-**	holds; considers
jäälkiekko	ice hockey		to be X
kansainlvälselsti	internationally	**suosilttu**	favoured
kansallislurheilu	national sport	**suositulin**	most favoured,
kiinnosta-	interests		favourite
kuitenki →	anyway	**takalraja**	back boundary,
kuitenkin			limit
luullisiln	I should/would	**urheilullaji**	type of sport
	think	**volis → volisi**	one could
lyönti	hit, strike		

Exercise 6 If you're interested in sport (**kiinnostunut urheilusta**), make up your own dialogue, in which friends discuss their favourites. You'll find the following vocabulary useful: The verb **kilpaile-** is 'competes' and **kilpa(ilu)** is 'competition'; so **kilpa-auto** is 'racing car', **kilpalsoutu** is 'competitive racing', and **kilpalpurjehdus** is 'competitive (regatta) sailing'; 'Amateur' is **harrastelija**, 'professional' **ammattilainen**.

tennis *kse*	tennis
käsilpallo	handball
nurmilpallo	hockey
hiihtolurheilu	skiing (for sport)
pyöräily	cycling
kelkkailu	bobsleighing, tobogganing

korkeus|hyppy	high jump
pituus|hyppy	long jump
keihään|heitto	throwing the javelin (stem: **keihäX**)
uinti	swimming (**ui-** 'swims')
joukkueQ	team, side

You may also want to have them argue about the difference between a sport and a game (**peli**). If so, you'll need **šakki** 'chess', and **tammi** *e* 'draughts, checkers'. You can also talk about playing (**pelaX-**) cards (**kortti\|a**) or bridge (**bridge\|ä**).

Language points

The superlative

This is the '-st' of English 'the biggest', 'the smallest', and the 'most' of 'the most unusual'. In Finnish, you add the suffix =**impA**. There are two complications. First, the suffix =**impA** comes out as -**in** in the nominative singular. Thus we have:

stem:	**iso**	**reilu**
superlative:	**iso|in**	**reilu|in**
	'the biggest'	'the most reliable, the most straightforward'

The shape **in** also occurs in the partitive singular, as in:

Kirjan kolmas luku käsittelee Grönlanti\|a, maailman iso\|in\|ta saar\|ta.

The book's third chapter treats Greenland, the world's largest island.

The **mpA** (with compression: **mmA**) of the superlative suffix is clear from forms such as:

iso|impa|an pullo|on	into the largest bottle
iso|imma|ssa pullo|ssa	in the largest bottle

The second complication is this. The **i** initial in this suffix causes changes in the end of the stem to which it is attached. Here are examples of the main types:

halpa	cheap	**halv|in**	the cheapest	(**a** > zero)
korkea	high	**korke|in**	highest	(**a** > zero)
herkkä	sensitive	**herk|in**	the most sensitive	(**ä** > zero)

tavallinen	usual, common (stem: **tavallise-**)	**tavallis|in**	the most common	(**e** > zero)
siisti	clean	**siiste|in**	the most clean	(**i** > **e**)
tuoreQ	fresh	**tuore|in**	the freshest	(**Q** > zero)
rikas	rich (stem: **rikkaX**)	**rikka|in**	richest	(**X** > zero)
kaunis	beautiful (stem: **kaunix**)	**kaune|in**	the most beautiful	(**X** > zero, **i** > **e**)

Note on compression. As forms like **halv\|in** and **herk\|in** show, attaching the superlative suffix compresses consonants to the left; but as you already know from studying the plural partitive (Unit 5), compression does not take place if a deleted item (either **A** or **X**, as above in **korkein**, **rikkain**) would have been part of a long vowel or diphthong. Thus we have compressed **d** and **t** in the superlatives

outo	strange, eerie	**oudo|in**	the strangest
suosittu	favoured, liked	**suositu|in**	the most liked, the favourite

but uncompressed **k** in

korke\|in   'the highest', with strong **rk**, from **korkea\|impA**

and uncompressed **kk** in

rikka\|in   'the richest', with strong **kk**, from **rikkaX\|impA**

Here are the full paradigms of two adjectives, **halpa** 'cheap' and **rikas** 'rich':

	halpa		rikar	
	Singular	*Plural*	*Singular*	*Plural*
N	**halvin**	**halvimma|t**	**rikkain**	**rikkaimma|t**
G	**halvimma|n**	**halvimp|i|en**[1]	**rikkaimma|n**	**rikkaimp|i|en**[1]
P	**halvin|ta**	**halvimp|i|a**	**rikkain|ta**	**rikkaimp|i|a**
ELA	**halvimma|sta**	**halvimm|i|sta**	**rikkaimma|sta**	**rikkaimm|i|sta**
INE	**halvimma|ssa**	**halvimm|i|ssa**	**rikkaimma|ssa**	**rikkaimm|i|ssa**
ILL	**halvimpa|an**	**halvimp|i|in**	**rikkaimpa|an**	**rikkaimp|i|in**
ABL	**halvimma|lta**	**halvimm|i|lta**	**rikkaimma|lta**	**rikkaimm|i|lta**
ADE	**halvimma|lla**	**halvimm|i|lla**	**rikkaimma|lla**	**rikkaimm|i|lla**
ALL	**halvimma|lle**	**halvimm|i|lle**	**rikkaimma|lle**	**rikkaimm|i|lle**
ESS	**halvimpa|na**	**halvimp|i|na**	**rikkaimpa|na**	**rikkaimp|i|na**
TRA	**halvimma|ksi**	**halvimm|i|ksi**	**rikkaimma|ksi**	**rikkaimm|i|ksi**

1 You will also come across genitive plurals such as **halvinten**, **rikkainten**, built with a **t**-suffix. You will learn how to form the genitive plural in the next unit.

Notice that in many cases the only difference between the forms of the superlative and the comparative is the **i** to the left of the **mm**:

syve|mmä|t the deeper ones   **syv|immä|t** the deepest ones

For adjective stems whose last vowel is **i**, you must look to the **i** > **e** change mentioned above to help you spot the superlative:

comparative: **siisti|mmä|ssä huonee|ssa** in a cleaner room
superlative: **siiste|immä|ssä huonee|ssa** in the cleanest room

Finally, as in English, a few of the most frequently used superlatives are irregular:

hyvä	good	**paras**	best
pitkä	long	**pisin**	longest
paljo|n	lots, much	**enin**	greatest, sG: **enimmä|n**

Tip. They're not superlatives, but the words for 'left' (**vasen**) and 'warm' (**lämmin**) have stems which look and behave the same way: **vasempa-** and **lämpimä-**.

Exercise 7 To check you have learnt how to form it, put the following adjective forms into the superlative. (model: **huonon** > **huonoimman**)

1	ujolta	6	suuret
2	tumma	7	nuorissa
3	kylmempi	8	terve
4	kovasta	9	iloinen
5	isoon	10	pitkälle

Using the superlative

Much as in English, the superlative in Finnish is used to single out the egregious, isolated case. The genitive and the inessive are common markers for the field in which the superlative excels:

Iso-Saimaa on Suomen suurin järvi.
Iso-Saimaa is Finland's largest lake.

Tukholma on suurin kaupunki Ruotsissa.
Stockholm is the largest city in Sweden.

If selection from a plurality is meant, the plural elative is used:

Sä oot ahkerin niistä.
You are the most diligent of the lot (lit. 'out of them').

Se on vanhin tytöistä.
She is the oldest (out) of the girls.

You can mitigate your enthusiasm by using the partitive plural of the superlative:

München on Saksan suurimpia kaupunkeja.
Munich is one of Germany's largest cities.

You say 'at his/her/its X-est' by putting the superlative adjective in the plural adessive and slapping on the suffix **-#n**. For example:

huono|imm|i|lla|an	at his worst
parha|imm|i|lla|an	at her best
syv|imm|i|llä|än	at its deepest

You'll find out more about superlative (and comparative) adverbs in Unit 11, and more on the suffix **-#n** in Unit 10.

Exercise 8 Translate into Finnish:

1 She is the youngest in the class.
2 Denmark is Europe's oldest monarchy (**kuningaskunta**).
3 This bag is heavier than mine, but yours is the heaviest.
4 The fastest one wins (**voitta-**), but the slowest one is best.

The essive

This case is the static cousin of the translative: it indicates states and modes of being in which things and people are or were. Contrast the two sentences:

sESS	**Se oli sairaa|na.**	(S)he was ill.
sTRA	**Se tuli sairaa|ksi.**	(S)he became ill.

Here are some more examples:

Pidä kahvi kuuma\|na!
Keep the coffee hot!

Ne on asiakkaita nyt, ja ne pysyykin asiakka\|i\|na.
They're customers now, and they'll remain customers.
   (**asiakkaX** customer)

Mä opin sen nuore|na.
I learned it when I was young (lit. as a young [one]).

Se oppi lukemaan aika piene|nä.
(S)he learned to read when fairly little.

Hän oli nuorempa|na unelmoinut elämästä teatterissa.
When younger, (s)he had dreamt of a life in the theatre.

Väinämöistä pidetään historiallise|na henkilö|nä.
Väinämöinen is held to be a historical person.

Seisoimme liikkumattom|i|na.
We stood motionless.

Minulla oli valhe valmii|na.
I had a lie ready.

The essive has two other common uses which you will learn in the next unit.

Stems made with =(U)UTE

Finnish abounds in abstract nouns like **terveys** 'health', **erikoisuus** 'speciality', and **talous** 'economy'. These are all made with the derivational suffix =(U)UTE, most commonly from adjectives, but also from some nouns and even pronouns. Study these examples, noting the meanings and changes in the stems:

helppo	easy	**emäntä**	mistress of the house; hostess
helppo|us	ease, facility		
terveQ	healthy	**emänn|yys**	household management
terve|ys	health		
vanha	old	**alempi**	lower, inferior
vanh|uus	old age	**alemm|uus**	inferiority
lapsi *e*	child	**ohut**	thin
laps|uus	childhood	**oh|uus**	thinness
erikoinen	special	**naapuri**	neighbour
erikois|uus	speciality	**naapur|uus**	neighbourhood
mahd|ollinen	possible		
mahdollis|uus	possibility		

Note the unmotivated compression of consonants in forms built from comparative stems (like **alemmuus**) and in forms like **emän-nyys**. Notice also the especially striking **pituus** 'length, height' from **pitkä** 'long, tall'.

In the singular and in the nominative plural, these stems take case suffixes just like **käsi** (Unit 1, *dental stems*), except that they have no **i** at the end of their citation form:

sN	sG	sILL	pN	
käs*i*	**käde|n**	**käte|en**	**käde|t**	hand
talou*s*	**taloude|n**	**taloute|en**	**taloude|t**	economy

In the other forms of the plural, these stems switch over to being =**UKsE** stems (Unit 5), so we have, for example, **talo|uks|i|ssa** as the plural inessive of **talous**, **mahdollisuuks|i|in** as the plural illative of **mahdollisuus**.

9 Aika ja tila

Time and space

In this unit you will learn:

- about time expressions
- about prepositions and postpositions
- how to form the genitive plural
- about going to the country, and about the sauna

Dialogue 1 ▭

Apteekissa

At the chemist's

Pasi goes to the chemist's to get kitted out for a trip to the country

APTEEKKARI: Päivää, kuinka voin auttaa?
PASI: Onks teillä jotain tehokasta hyttysenpuremiin?
APTEEKKARI: Kokeile Pantysonia. Se laskee turvotusta ja lievittää kutinaa.
PASI: Hyvä, mä otan sitä ja sitte vielä laastareita, pullo desinfiointiainetta ja kyypakkaus.
APTEEKKARI: Taidat olla mökille menossa!

CHEMIST: *(Good) day, how can I help (you)?*
PASI: *Do you have anything effective against mosquito bites?*
CHEMIST: *Try Pantyson. It reduces swelling and relieves itching.*
PASI: *Fine, I'll take some and (then also) (there'll be) some plasters, a bottle of disinfectant and a snakebite kit.*
CHEMIST: *You must be on (your) way to (your summer) cabin!*

Vocabulary

aineQ	matter, stuff	**laske-**	lowers, reduces;
apteekkari	chemist, pharmacist		drops
apteekki	chemist's/pharmacist's	**lievittä-**	relieves, alleviates
	shop	**meno**	going, departure
desinfiointi	disinfection	**meno|ssa**	en route
hyttynen	gnat, midge;	**mökki**	(summer) cabin
	mosquito	**pakkaus** *kse*	pack, kit
kokeile-	tries	**pullo**	bottle
kutina	itch	**pure|ma**	bite
kyy	venomous snake	**tehokas**	effective (stem:
laastari	sticking plaster,		**tehokkaX**)
	bandage	**turvotus** *kse*	swelling

Dialogue 2 🔲

Kutsu maalle

An invitation to the country

Pasi is not the only one who is headed to the countryside for the weekend. Steve, like many a lucky foreigner in Finland, has been invited by his hosts to their summer cabin. He asks his friend Sami what sorts of things are in store for him, particularly regarding the sauna

STEVE: Kuule Sami, mut on kutsuttu ens viikonloppuna Aaltosten mökille saunomaan. Kerro jotain saunomisesta.

SAMI: Sauna on perussuomalainen juttu. Suomalaiset ei oikein osaa olla ilman saunaa.

STEVE: Mikä siinä on nyt sit niin erikoista.

SAMI: Kuuman löylyn jälkeen juostaan yleensä talvella lumihankeen ja kesällä järveen. Sen jälkeen on tosi hyvä olo.

STEVE: Mikä se vihta oikein on?

SAMI: Se on kimppu koivun oksia ja sillä sitte vihdotaan löylyssä toinen toista. Se vilkastuttaa verenkiertoa.

STEVE: Saunan jälkeenkö syödään sitte lenkkimakkaraa ja juodaan saunakaljat?

SAMI: Joo. Sulla tulee oleen kiva viikonloppu.

STEVE: *Listen, Sami, I've been invited to the sauna (lit. to use the sauna) at the Aaltonens' summer cabin next weekend. Tell me something about sauna'ing.*

SAMI: *The sauna is a very basic Finnish thing. Finns really don't know how to be without it.*

STEVE: *So what's so special about it, then?*

SAMI: *After the superheated steam you generally run out into a snowbank or, in summer, into the lake. After that it really feels good.*

STEVE: *(And) what is this 'vihta', actually?*

SAMI: *It's a bunch of birch twigs, and people hit each other with it in the superheated steam. It stimulates the blood circulation.*

STEVE: *Is it after the sauna that people eat sausages and drink beer, then?*

SAMI: *Yep. You're going to have a great weekend.*

Vocabulary

Aaltosten	pG of surname Aaltonen	**löyly**	superheated steam
		mökki	summer cabin
ens → ensi		**oksa**	twig, branch
erikoinen	special	**oleen** →	
hanki *e*	drift, bank	**ole|ma|an**	
juokse-	runs	**osaX-**	knows how
juos|taan ind		**perus+**	basic, fundamental
juokse-		**sauno-**	uses the sauna
juttu	story, thing	**toinen**	one/other of two
järvi *e*	lake	**veren|kierto**	blood circulation
kimppu	bunch	**vihta**	see dialogue!
koivu	birch	**vihto-**	uses **vihta**
kutsu-	invites, calls	**viikon|loppu**	weekend
lenkki	ring/link of sausage	**vilkastutta-**	livens, stimulates
makkara	sausage	**yleensä**	generally
lumi *e*	snow (sP **lun|ta**)		

Language points

The genitive plural

This corresponds to the English plural 'children's' as opposed to singular 'child's'. For most English words, the placement of the apostrophe is vital: 'boy's' is singular, 'boys'' is plural.

The Finnish genitive plural has a great variety of forms, and many nominals have at least two forms to choose from. You will keep your bearings if you remember that for most nouns, the genitive plural is analogous to the partitive plural: if the pP has -**tA**, the pG will be -**den**, and if the pP has -**A**, the pG will be -**en**. Study these parallel forms:

stem	yö	huoneQ	hampaX	asema	talo
pP	öli|tä	huone|i|ta	hampa|i|ta	asem|i|a	talo|j|a
pG	öli|den	huone|i|den	hampa|i|den	asem|i|en	talo|j|en
	'night'	'room'	'tooth'	'station'	'house'

The suffix -**den** has an alternative form -**tten**, so you will also see and hear **öli|tten**, **huone|i|tten**, and **hampa|i|tten**.

There are two kinds of nominal that upset this neat parallelism. First, many polysyllabic nouns ending in **i** which form their pP with -**tA** take -**en** in the pG. In such cases, the stem-final vowel vanishes without a trace. For example:

stem	paperi	sipuli	dekkari	kolari	apteekkari
pP	papere|i|ta	sipule|i|ta	dekkare|i|ta	kolare|i|ta	apteekkare|i|ta
pG	paper|i|en	sipul|i|en	dekkar|i|en	kolar|i|en	apteekkar|i|en
	'paper'	'onion'	'detective novel'	'car crash'	'chemist/ druggist'

Second, **e**-stems form their pG more often with -**ten** than with -**en**. So you will usually come across, e.g.,

stem	kiele	naise	puheliME	kysymykse
pP	kiel|i|ä	nais|i|a	puhelim|i|a	kysymyks|i|ä
pG	kiel|ten	nais|ten	puhelin|ten	kysymys|ten
	'language'	'woman'	'telephone'	'question'

You have already met the consonant changes **m > n** (in **puhelin|ten**) and **k > 0** (in **kysymys|ten**), and **p > 0** (**lapsi** *e* 'child', pG **las|ten**) in connection with the partitive singulars of these words.

Finally, notice that nominals which end in **A** have an extra form in simple **-i-n** which is used in certain fixed or formal expressions and in poetry, e.g. alongside normal **kanso|j|en** there is also **kansa|i|n** 'of nations', as in **kansainvälinen** 'international'.

Exercise 1 Practise forming the genitive plural by translating these phrases into Finnish:

1 the boys' father
2 the girls' names
3 the prices of the larger radios
4 the numbers of the rooms
5 the laws (**laki**) of many other countries

Time expressions

It is helpful to distinguish words which refer to specific periods of time such as 'Monday', 'August', 'Spring', and 'evening' from words which refer to time-spans, such as 'minute', 'hour', 'century'. These two types are discussed in (a) and (b) below. Section (c) lists some very common miscellaneous phrases.

(a) We look first at specific time-words: the days of the week, the months of the year, the seasons, and the various times of the 24-hour cycle.

viiko|n päivä|t 'the days of the week'

Monday	**maanantai**	**maanantai|na**
Tuesday	**tiistai**	**tiistai|na**
Wednesday	**keskiviikko**	**keskiviikko|na**
Thursday	**torstai**	**torstai|na**
Friday	**perjantai**	**perjantai|na**
Saturday	**lauantai**	**lauantai|na**
Sunday	**sunnuntai**	**sunnuntai|na**

Note that in Finnish the names of the days are not capitalized. 'On Sunday', 'on Monday', etc. are expressed by the essive (Unit 8). Examples: **keskiviikko|na** 'on Wednesday', **tä|nä tortstai|na** 'this Thursday', **viime perjantai|na** 'last Friday', **ensi lauantai|na** 'next Saturday'. The names of holidays are also in the essive: **joulu|na** 'on Christmas day', **vappu|na** 'on May Day', **juhannukse|na** 'on Midsummer's Day', **juhannusaatto|na** 'on Midsummer's Eve'. 'Every Sunday' is **joka sunnuntai|na**; there is also a suffix =**sin**, as in **sunnuntai|sin** 'Sundays; every Sunday (as a rule)'.

vuode|n kuukaude|t 'the months of the year'

January	**tammikuu**	July	**heinäkuu**
Febuary	**helmikuu**	August	**elokuu**
March	**maaliskuu**	September	**syyskuu**
April	**huhtikuu**	October	**lokakuu**
May	**toukokuu**	November	**marraskuu**
June	**kesäkuu**	December	**joulukuu**

All the month-names end with the word **kuu** 'moon; month'; again, note that they are not capitalized in Finnish. 'In January', 'in February', etc. are expressed by the inessive case, e.g. **syyskuu|ssa** 'in September'. More examples: **seuraava|ssa helmikuu|ssa** '(in) the following February', **tämä|n vuode|n lokakuu|ssa** 'in October of this year'.

Dates are expressed just as in English by means of ordinal numerals ('fifth', 'twenty-second', etc.; you'll learn how to form these in Unit 11). You either put the ordinal numeral first, in which case the the month-name goes into the partitive, e.g. **kuudes (päivä) elokuu|ta** 'the sixth (day) of August', or you place the ordinal second, in which case the month-name is in the genitive, e.g. **elokuu|n kuudes**.

vuode|n+aja|t 'the seasons'

kevät (stem: **kevää-** !)	**kevää|llä**	Spring
kesä	**kesä|llä**	Summer
syksy	**syksy|llä**	Autumn
talvi *e*	**talve|lla**	Winter

As you can see from the examples above, 'in Spring', etc. is expressed by the adessive case; to single out one season in particular, however, you put the entire expression in the essive: **tuleva|na kesä|nä** 'in the coming Summer', **viime kevää|nä** 'last Spring', **edelli|se|nä syksy|nä** 'the previous Autumn'.

Alongside **kesä** there is also a special word for 'Summer' which you will hear most often in poetry and song: **suvi** e.

Words for parts of the day include

aamu	morning	**yö**	night
ilta	evening	**aamu|päivä**	forenoon
päivä	day, daytime	**ilta|päivä**	afternoon

These words take the same cases as the seasons: adessive if used alone, essive if modified. Here are some examples:

aamu|lla	in the morning
tä|nä aamu|na	this morning
erää|nä joulukuu|n aamu|na	(on) one December morning
kahte|na perättäise|nä aamu|na	(on) two consecutive mornings
yö|llä	at night
perjantai|n ja lauantai|n	during the night between
välise|nä yö|nä	Friday and Saturday
tä|nä ilta|na	this evening
yhte|nä syksy|n ilta|na	(on) one Autumn evening
seuraava|na iltapäivä|nä	(on) the following afternoon
maanantai-iltapäivä|nä	(on) Monday afternoon

(b) Here are the more common words that refer to time-spans:

sekunti	second	**kuukausi** *te*	month
minuutti	minute	**vuosi** *te*	year
tunti	hour	**vuosikymmen**	decade (NB!)
päivä	day	**vuosisata**	century
vuorokausi *te*	24-hour period	**vuosituhat** *nte*	millennium
viikko	week	**hetki**, **tuokio**	instant, flash

You will recognize the second components of 'century' and 'millennium' as the Finnish words for 100 and 1,000. The word for 'decade', however, is built with **kymmen** (stem: **kymmene-**), not **kymmenen**. Note the **te**-stems: **vuosi vuote-** 'year' and **kausi kaute-** 'time-period'.

Just like English, Finnish uses time-span words most commonly to express duration. English usually expresses duration with the preposition 'for', as in the sentences 'I lived there for a year', 'I haven't seen them for a year', and 'I'm going to Finland for a year.' In Finnish, however, these are seen as quite different sets of circumstances and are expressed by three different case suffixes: (1) the time something actually lasted, as in 'I lived there for a year', is put in the accusative, e.g. **Mä asuin siellä vuode\|n**; (2) the time during which something didn't happen ('I haven't seen them for a year') goes into the illative, e.g. **En ole nähnyt niitä vuote\|en**; (3) the amount of time something is supposed/intended to last ('I'm going to Finland for a year') is expressed by the translative (Unit 8), e.g. **Mä menen Suomeen vuode\|ksi**.

The translative is also used to express the point of time by which something will happen or be ready, e.g. **Mä tuun sun luoksesi kello viide\|ksi** 'I'll come to your place by five o'clock.'

Colloquial Finnish is also available in the form of a course pack (ISBN 0-415-11390-3), containing this book and two cassettes, recorded by native speakers of Finnish, and are an invaluable aid to improving your language skills.

If you have been unable to obtain the course pack, the double cassette (ISBN 0-415-11390-3) can be ordered separately through your bookseller or, in case of difficulty, send payment with order to Routledge Ltd, ITPS, Cheriton House, North Way, Andover, Hants SP10 5BE, or to Routledge Inc., 29 West 35th Street, New York, NY 10001, USA.

The publishers reserve the right to change prices without notice.

CASSETTES ORDER FORM

Please supply one/two/ .... double cassette(s) of

Colloquial Finnish, Abondolo.
ISBN 0-415-11390-3

Price   £14.99* incl. VAT
         $22.95*

* The publishers reserve the right to change prices without notice.

☐ I enclose payment with order.
☐ Please debit my Access/Mastercharge/Mastercard/Visa/American Express. Account number:

Expiry date ....

Name ....

Address ....

....

Date ....

Signature ....

Order from your bookseller or from:

ROUTLEDGE LTD
ITPS
Cheriton House
North Way
Andover
Hants
SP10 5BE
ENGLAND

ROUTLEDGE INC.
29 West 35th Street
New York
NY 10001
USA

Finally, the time-span during which something happens or is accomplished is expressed by means of the inessive, e.g.

puolelssa tunnilssa	in a half hour
muutamalssa tunnilssa	in a few hours
vajaalssa tunnilssa	in less than an hour
runsaalssa tunnilssa	in a good hour, in an hour and then some
kerraln tai pari viikolssa	once or twice a week

(c) Finnish is rich in miscellaneous time expressions. In this section we look at some of the most useful.

aina	always
uselin	often (**usea** 'frequent')
joskus	sometimes (**jos** 'if')
harvolin	seldom (**harva** 'rare')
kerraln	once
taas, uudellelen	again
kerraln vielä	one more time, once again
ei vielä	not yet
ei enälä	not any more
ei koskaan	never
ei koskaan enälä	never again
nyt	now
nykyisin	nowadays
ennen	previously
nyttemmin	lately
äskettäin	recently
äsken	just now
pian, kohta	soon
heti	straight away, at once
tänään	today
huomenna	tomorrow
ylihuomenna	the day after tomorrow
eilen	yesterday
toissapäivänä	the day before yesterday
pari päivälä sitten	a few days ago
pariln päiväln kuluttula	after a few days, a few days later
koko päiväln	all day (long)
joka toinen päivä	every other day

si**ll**ä aika**l**a	during that time, meanwhile
tä**ll**ä kerta**l**a	this time, on this occasion
sii**l**hen aika**l**an	at that time
sama**l**an aika**l**an	at the same time

Exercise 2 **Mihin aikaan?** expects an answer with clock time. Practise using clock time by giving or making up answers to these questions:

1 Mihin aikaan sä heräät?
2 Mihin aikaan sä lähdet kotoa töihin?
3 Mihin aikaan sä syöt illallista?
4 Mihin aikaan sä meet nukkumaan?
5 Mihin aikaan juna lähtee?
6 Mihin aikaan juna on perillä?
7 Mihin aikaan bussi saapuu Helsinkiin?

Exercise 3 As you have seen above, the question **Montako kertaa?** asks how many times (per X) something happens; X goes into the inessive. Fill in the blanks in the following sentences, supplying either the missing number of times, or the time-frame.

1 Eeva harjoittelee soittamaan pianoa joka päivä. Se harjoittelee siis _____ viikossa.
2 Sanna juo kahvia vain aamiaisen aikaan. Se juo kahvia siis kerran _____.
3 Me mennään saunaan tiistaina ja lauantaina. Me mennään saunaan siis _____ viikossa.
4 Se käy kylässä naapurin luona vain jouluna ja juhannuksena. Se käy siellä siis kaksi kertaa _____.

Dialogue 3 🔊

Saunanlämmityspuuhissa

Sauna preparations in the country

STEVE: Mikä tän järven nimi on?
JUHA: Pielisjärvi. Se on yks Suomen suurimpia järviä.
STEVE: Täällä on kyllä tosi vihreetä ja puhdasta.
JUHA: Eiköhän aleta[1] heti saunanlämmityspuuhiin, ku se vie kuitenki aika paljon aikaa.

TIMO: Steve, sä voisit mennä hakeen koivuhalkoja saunan takaa pinosta. Mä ja Juha ruvetaan kantaa vettä järvestä.

JUHA: Sytytetään sitte yhdessä tuli kiukaan alle.

TIMO: Mä käyn vaan laittamassa ruuat ja kaljat kylmään.

STEVE: *What's this lake's name?*

JUHA: *Pielisjärvi. It's one of Finland's largest lakes.*

STEVE: *It really is green and clean here.*

JUHA: *Perhaps we ought to get started warming up the sauna. It always takes quite a bit of time.*

TIMO: *Steve, you could go fetch some birch logs from the pile at the back of the sauna. Juha and I'll start bringing water from the lake.*

JUHA: *Then we'll light the fire together under the **kiuas**.*

TIMO: *I'll just go and put the food and the beers in a cool place.*

1 **Eiköhän aleta** roughly, 'perhaps we ought to begin'; grammatically, we have here the negative (**ei**) interrogative (-**kö**) indefinite (**aletaan/ei aleta**), with mitigation via the clitic –**hän**.

Vocabulary

X|n al|le	to underneath X	pino	pile, heap
hakeen → hake|ma|an		puhtaX	clean, pure (sN: **puhdas**)
halko	(short) log	puuha	chore, job
kantaan → kanta|ma|an		rupeX-	starts (used with 3rd infinitive)
käy-	goes, comes, passes	X|n taka|a	from behind X
kiuas	(stem: **kiukaX**)	tän → tämä|n	
kylmä	cold	vie-	takes (away)
laitta-	prepares, sets up	vihreä	green
lämmitys *kse*	heating, warming	vo|is|it	you could, you might

Culture point

Going to the sauna (**sauno|minen**) is one of the most Finnish things one can do. The Finnish sauna is a survival of a practice once widespread in Central and Eastern Europe. Nowadays the Finnish sauna has evolved into several different varieties; the oldest form is best preserved in the smoke sauna, **savusauna**. (The word **sauna** is connected etymologically with **savu** 'smoke'.)

In cities, saunas are cunningly integrated as modern facilities into homes, blocks of flats, and the premises of larger companies. But the roots of the sauna are in the countryside: here, the sauna is a building traditionally made of logs (**hirre|t**) and with a turf roof (**turve|katto**). It is usually built near a shore, something which is very easy to do since Finland has over 40,000 lakes. In one typical arrangement the sauna consists of three rooms: the steam (or sweat) room (**löylyhuone**), the washroom (**pesu|huone**), and a room for relaxing in away from the heat, (**takka|huone**).

After showering in the **pesuhuone**, one proceeds to the **löylyhuone**, where there are benches (**lautee|t**) arranged stair-fashion around the 'stove'. This 'stove' is actually a pile of stones (**kiuas**, stem: **kiukaX**) set over a heat-source which is traditionally wood-burning, but which may also, especially in cities, be powered by electricity (**sähkö|llä**) or, more rarely, gas (**kaasu|lla**) or oil (**öljy|llä**).

The **lauteet** are made of wood, a material which is slow to conduct heat and quick to absorb moisture. Sitting-places set at different heights provide a maximum of choice – the higher one sits, the hotter it will be. The floor is the best place for children and beginners: temperatures normally range from 80 to 100 C.

Such high temperatures are bearable because the sauna is a very dry place. The intense heat comes not from hot water or even hot water vapour, but from superheated steam, **löyly**, which is produced by the judicious pouring of warm water over the stones of the **kiuas**. This work, **heittä- löyly|ä** (lit. 'throws *löyly*') is normally carried out by the host or the guest of honour.

Language points

Prepositions and postpositions

You have already met the words **ennen** 'before' and **jälkeen** 'after'. Whereas **ennen** precedes the word it goes with and thus is much like an English *pre*position, **jälkeen** comes after its word. It and others like it are therefore called *post*positions.

Most Finnish prepositions are like **ennen** in that they take the partitive, e.g. **ennen helmikuulta** 'before February', **ilman sinula** 'without you'.

Most postpositions are like **jälkeen** in that they take the genitive, e.g. **koululn jälkeen** 'after school', **kirkoln ohi** 'past the church'.

Many prepositions and postpositions which refer to spatial and temporal relations come in three varieties, depending on whether movement from or to, or simple location is meant. Thus 'in front of' occurs in the three **s**-cases: the inessive, elative, and illative, as **edelssä**, **edelstä**, or **etelen**:

Ne odottaa kirkon *edelssä*.
They're waiting *in front* of the church.

Ne tuli kirkon *edelstä*.
They came *from in front* of the church.

Me mentiin kirkon *etelen*.
We went (*to*) *in front of* the church.

If *both* items are in motion (as in a race), the corresponding **l**-cases are used:

Se pysyy kilpailijan edelllä.
(S)he keeps ahead of her/his rival.

L-cases are also used for non-spatial meanings such as **edellä mainittu** 'before-mentioned'.

'At the back of' or 'behind' is **takalna**, **takala**, or **taalkseQ**:

Saa nähdä, mitä sanojen takalna on.
We'll have to see what is behind the words.

Se kävelee kädet selän takalna.
(S)he walks with (his/her) hands behind (his/her) back.

Kuva on otettu selän takala.
The picture has been taken from behind (his) back.

Mä menin näyttämön taalkse.
I went (to) behind (the) stage.

Temporal uses of **takala** and **taalkseQ** are also frequent:

Se viha juontaa satojen vuosien takala.
This hatred stems from hundreds of years back.

Se ulottuu yli tuhannen vuoden taalkse.
It stretches back over a thousand years.

If both items are in motion, **perälssä** is common:

Se juoksee merkkien perälssä.
(S)he runs after brand names.

'Under' is **allla, allta, allle**:

Ne asuu saman katon allla.
They live under the same roof.

Mä en etsinyt sitä sängyn allta.
I didn't look for it (from) under the bed.

Koira juoksi penkin allle.
The dog ran (to) under the bench.

'Over' is **yläpuolellla, yläpuolellta, yläpuolellle**, 'outside' is **ulkopuolellla, ulkopuolellta, ulkopuolellle**, for example:

Sängyn yläpuolella riippuu kolme kuvaa.
Above the bed hang three pictures.

Suomen ulkopuolella ei sitä kovin paljon opiskella.
Outside Finland it isn't studied much.

'On top of' is expressed by the adessive, ablative, and allative of **pää** 'head': **päälllä, päälltä, päällle**. Examples:

Kissa nukkuu pianon päälllä.
The cat is sleeping on the piano.

Mä löysin sen kaapin päälltä.
I found it on the cabinet.

Pistä se takaisin television päällle!
Put it back on top of the television!

The same word with **s**-forms refers to the remove at which something is located (or going to, or coming from):

Ne asuu parin korttelin pää|ssä.
They live a few blocks away.

Pysäkki siirrettiin 200 (kahdensadan) metrin pää|hän.
The bus stop was moved (to a place) 200 metres away.

Tie alkaa noin kymmenen kilometrin pää|stä.
The road begins (from) about 10 kilometres away (from there/here).

But **päästä** is most often used in time expressions such as **tunni|n päästä** 'an hour having passed, after an hour'.
'Between' is **väli** in one of the local cases, as in:

Puhelin oli pöydällä sänkyjen väli|ssä.
The telephone was on a table between the beds.

Timon ja Juhan väli|llä oli riita.
There was a dispute between Timo and Juha.

Moraalisoinnin ja moraalin väli|llä on ero.
There is a difference between morality and moralizing.

'Next to' is most commonly **viere|ssä, viere|stä, viere|en**:

Tohvelit on tolla (more colloquial: **tossa**) *seinän viere*|ssä.
The slippers are over there *next to the wall.*

Se pysäköi auton *tien viere|en.*
(S)he parked the car *at the side of the road.*

Lompakko löytyi eteisestä, *oven viere|stä.*
The wallet was found in the entrance hall, *next to the door.*

Case forms of **ääri** *e* 'edge' (**ääre|ssä, ääre|stä, ääre|en**) are used to express location near something which one uses in certain normal ways: **pöydä|n ääre|ssä** is not simply 'next to the table', it is 'at table (in order to have a meal)'. Similarly: **piano|n ääre|ssä** 'at the piano', **brandy|n ääre|ssä** 'over (= while having) brandy'.
'At' is **luo|na, luo|ta, luo** (with possessive suffixes: **luokse-**) if someone's home is meant, as in:

Se vierailee *Juuso|n luona* **pari päivää.**
(S)he's visiting at Juuso's for a couple of days.

He tulivat *meidän luoksemme.*
They came to our place.

But 'at the doctor's' and similar expressions involving professions are made with the inessive, e.g. **lääkäri|ssä**.

'Through' is **halki** or **läpi**, and 'across' is **poikki** or **yli**, as in

Me käveltiin kotiin *puisto|n halki*.
We walked home *through the park*.

Me ajettiin *kaupungi|n läpi*.
We drove *through the city*.

Kettu juoksi *tie|n poikki*.
The fox ran *across the road*.

Kissa hyppäsi *aida|n yli*.
The cat jumped *over the fence*.

The cause or reason for something is usually expressed by **takia** 'on account of', or **vuoksi** 'for the sake of', e.g. **Mä myöhästyin *su|n takia|si*** 'I was late *because of you*', **huvi|n vuoksi** 'for fun', **varmuude|n vuoksi** 'for the sake of security (= to be safe)'.

'With' is normally **kanssa**; but you will also come across **kera**, especially in connection with food and drink:

Ne odottaa *matkalaukku|j|en kanssa* terminaalin ulkopuolella.
They're waiting outside the terminal *with (their) bags*.

suola|n ja pippuri|n kera
with salt and pepper

Few postpositions take the partitive. The most important are **vastapäätä** 'opposite', **varten** 'for', **pitkin** 'along', and **kohti** 'towards':

Kirkko on *pankki|a vastapäätä*.
The church is *opposite the bank*.

Se osti sen *me|i|tä varten*.
(S)he bought it *for us*.

Se seurasi m(in)ua *katu|a pitkin*.
(S)he followed me *along the street*.

Se ajoi *Jyväskylä|ä kohti*.
(S)he was driving *towards Jyväskylä*.

Notice also the adverbs **ylös** 'up', **alas** 'down', which are used mainly with the partitive, as in

Bussi kulkee mäke|ä alas. The bus goes down the hill.

Se juoksi porta|i|ta ylös.   (S)he ran up the stairs.

Kautta 'via' and **kesken** 'amidst' both take the genitive, and they are used as both prepositions and postpositions. There are meaning differences, however. Notice these examples:

kautta Euroopa|n	all over Europe
Euroopa|n kautta	via Europe
ystäv|i|en kesken	among friends
kesken vuode|n	in the middle of the year, before the year is over/out

Finally, consider **ympäri**. As a preposition, **ympäri** takes the partitive or genitive and means 'located all around in, moving around in':

Sillä on markkinoita *ympäri Eurooppa\|a*.
It has markets *all over Europe*.

Se kulki puhumassa *ympäri Yhdysvalto\|j\|a*.
(S)he went *around the US* speaking.

Se juoksenteli *ympäri kenttä\|ä*.
(S)he ran around *in the field*.

As a postposition, **ympäri** takes the genitive and refers to the circumference:

Se juoksi *kentä\|n ympäri*.
(S)he ran (once) *around (the perimeter of) the field*.

Mä kävelin *auto\|n ympäri*.
I walked *around the car*.

Exercise 4 Revise some postpositions by translating these sentences into Finnish:

1 He stood in front of the boys.
2 They put the letter back under the lamp.
3 I'd like to go to Stockholm by way of Turku.
4 The church is next to the school.
5 They took us behind the building.

Dialogue 4 🔲

Saunomassa

In the sauna at last

The boys sweat as they sit on the lauteet

TIMO: Heität sä Steve lisää vettä kiukaalle!
STEVE: Mitä, vieläkö lisää? Täällähän on jo yli kahdeksankymmentä astetta.
JUHA: Anna mennä vaan! Näitten löylyjen jälkeen hypätään järveen.
TIMO: Juha, vihdohan ensin mun selkää!
STEVE: Nyt alan ymmärtää miks sauna on niin tärkee suomalaisille. Mulla on jo nyt hyvä olo.
JUHA: Odotas ku päästään juomaan saunakaljat, sitte se olo vasta hyvä on. Nyt mä lasken kolmeen ja sit juostaan järveen kilpaa. Yks, kaks, kolme.
(*Pojat juoksevat ulos löylystä.*)

TIMO: *Would you throw a little more water on kiuas, Steve!*
STEVE: *What, even more? It's already over 80 degrees (in) here.*
JUHA: *Just go ahead (lit. let it go). After the superheated steam(s) we'll jump in the lake.*
TIMO: *Juha, first give my back a good whisk, would you?*
STEVE: *Now I'm beginning to understand why the sauna is so important to Finns. I'm beginning to feel really good now.*
JUHA: *Just wait till we get to drink the beers, you won't feel really great until then. Now I'll count to three and then we'll run a race into the lake. One, two, three.*
(The boys run out of the superheated steam.)

Vocabulary

heittä-	throws	**lauteet**	benches in sauna
hikoile-	sweats	**lisä|ä**	more, additional
hyppäX-	jumps	**löyly**	superheated steam
kilpa	race	**yli**	over
laske-	counts		

10 Mitä tehtäs tänään?

What'll we do today?

In this unit you will learn:

- how to form and use the conditional, and more about modals
- vocabulary and phrases connected with making plans and appointments
- about possessive suffixes
- about the verbal noun
- about Suomenlinna, and about language and religion in Finland

---

Dialogue 1 ⬤⬤

Vuodenajat

The seasons

You can learn something about Finland's climate, and revise the names of the months and seasons, by listening in on this conversation between Peter and Päivi

PETER: Onk se totta, että Suomessa on neljä erilaista vuodenaikaa?
PÄIVI: Joo.
PETER: Kerro jotain niistä! Millaista on talvella?
PÄIVI: Talvikuukaudet ovat joulu-, tammi-, ja helmikuu.[1] Joskus lumi tulee jo marraskuussa tai lokakuun lopulla. Parhaiten talvea voisivat kuvata sanat *lumi, pakkanen, pimeys* ja *hiihto*.
PETER: No entäs kevät?

Päivi: Maaliskuussa päivät pitenee ja lumi alkaa vähitellen sulaa. Leskenlehdet ja hiirenkorvat ovat varma keväänmerkki.

Peter: Kesällä on varmaan kuuma ku aurinko ei kuulemma laske yöksi ollenkaa.

Päivi: (*naurahtaa*) Totta se on, että Lapissa aurinko ei laske keskikesällä ollenkaan, mutta Suomessa kesä on harvoin liian kuuma. Parasta kesässä on mökkielämä ja mansikat.

Peter: Syyskuukaudet on sitte syys-, loka-, ja marraskuu?

Päivi: Alkusyksystä on kaunista ku lehdet vaihtaa väriä. Loppusyksy on yleensä sateista ja harmaata.

Peter: *Is it true that Finland has four different seasons?*

Päivi: *Yes.*

Peter: *(Could you) say something about them? What's it like in the Winter(time)?*

Päivi: *The Winter months are December, January, and February. Sometimes the snow comes as early as (in) November or (at) the end of October. The words that would best describe Winter are 'snow', 'frost', 'darkness', and 'skiing'.*

Peter: *Well and what about Spring?*

Päivi: *In March the days grow longer and the snow begins gradually to melt. 'Widow's leaves' (coltsfoot) and 'mouse's ears' (birch buds) are a sure sign of Spring.*

Peter: *It must be warm in the Summer, when they tell me the sun doesn't set at all all night.*

Päivi: *(laughs) It is true that in Lappi the sun doesn't set at all in midsummer, but Summer is rarely too hot in Finland. The best (thing) in Summer is spending time at one's mökki, and the strawberries.*

Peter: *The Autumn months are September, October, and November, then?*

Päivi: *In early Autumn it's beautiful when the leaves change colour. The end of Autumn is generally rainy and grey.*

1 **joulu-, tammi-, ja helmikuu**: Finns avoid repeating the second member of compounds even more often than we do in English (cf. 'North and South America'). They use a hyphen to mark the missing member (i.e., **joulu-** and **tammi-** are short for **joulu|kuu** and **tammi|kuu**).

Vocabulary

alku	beginning	**elämä**	life
aurinko	sun	**erilainen**	different, distinct

harmaa	grey	millainen	what kind?
hiihto	skiing	naurahta-	bursts out
keski *e*	middle		laughing
kuulemma	they say;	(ei) ollenkaan	(not) at all
	supposedly	pakkanen	frost
kuvaX-	describes	parhaiten	best (adv.)
Lappi	'Lappland'	pimeys *te*	darkness
lehti *e*	leaf	piteXE-	gets longer
leskenlehti	coltsfoot	sateinen	rainy
leski *e*	widow(er)	sula-	melts
liian	too	vaihta-	changes, swops
loppu	end	vähitellen	gradually
mansikka	strawberry	väri	colour

Exercise 1 Check that you know the names of the seasons, the months, and basic climate vocabulary by writing a brief description in Finnish of the seasons where you live.

Dialogue 2 ▣

Kieli ja uskonto

Language and religion

Nick stops by to see Katja, and gets a quick lesson in Finnish demography

KATJA: (*aukaisee oven*) Moi Nick. Kiva kun tulit käymään. Mulla alkokin olla jo pää sekaisin ruotsin pänttäämisestä.[1]

NICK: Sulla on varmaan joku hyvä syy lukea sitä, vai?

KATJA: No on. Huomenna on pakollinen ruotsinkielen tentti, joka pitää läpäistä, ennen kun pääsee yliopistosta.[2] Se vaaditaan kaikilta opiskelijoilta.

NICK: Ai. Miks suomenkielisten pitää suorittaa se?

KATJA: No koska ruotsi on Suomen toinen virallinen kieli, ja kaikkien virkamiesten pitää pystyä hoitamaan asiat kummallakin kielellä. Suomen väestöstä on 6 (kuus) prosenttia ruotsinkielisiä. Lähes loput onki sitte suomenkielisiä, ku Suomessa on tosi vähän ulkomaalaisia. Tosin Lapissa saamen kieli on virallinen kieli.

NICK: Nii, mä olen huomannu, että suomalaiset on kielen ja

uskonnon suhteen aika yhtenäistä porukkaa. Eiks suurin osa suomalaisista ole luterilaista uskonnoltaan?[3]

KATJA: On. Eiköhän se luku ole jotain 86 prosenttia. Ortodoksisia on vain noin 1 prosentti väestöstä ja muitten uskontojen osuus on vielä pienempi.

KATJA: (opens the door) *Hi, Nick. It's great you've come to visit. My head was beginning to spin with this swotting for Swedish.*

NICK: *You must have some good reason to be reading it, right?*

KATJA: *Well, yes. Tomorrow's the compulsory Swedish language exam, which you've got to get through in order to graduate. It's required of all students.*

NICK: *Ouch. Why do Finnish speakers have to sit it?*

KATJA: *Well, it's because Swedish is Finland's other official language, and every official has to be able to carry on business (lit. take care of things) in both languages. About 6 per cent of Finland's population is Swedish-speaking. Nearly (all) the rest are of course Finnish-speaking, since there are really very few foreigners in Finland. Saami (= Lappish) is an official language in Lappi, of course.*

NICK: *Yes, I've noticed that Finns are a pretty homogeneous bunch as regards language and religion. Aren't the greatest part of Finns Lutherans by (their) faith?*

KATJA: *Yes. I think the figure is something like 86 per cent. Orthodox make up only about one per cent of the population, and the proportion of the other religions is even smaller.*

1 **Mu|lla alko(i)|kin olla jo pää sekaisin ruotsi|n pänttää|mise|stä** 'My head was beginning to spin from swotting up Swedish', lit. 'I was beginning to have (my) head mixed up . . .'

2 **joka pitä|ä läpäis|tä, ennen kun pääse|e yliopistosta** 'which one has to get through before one gets out of university'; Katja omits subject pronouns and uses third person singular verb forms to distance herself a bit from the context

3 **uskonno|lta|an** 'by (their) religion'

Vocabulary

ai!	ouch!	**joka**	which (relative pronoun)
alkokin → **alkoi|kin**		**joku**	every
aukaise-	opens	**Xn|kielinen**	X-speaking

kummalla|kin	both (Unit 8)	**sekaisin**	mixed up,
käy-	visits		muddled
lopu|t	(all) the rest,	**X|n suhte|en**	as regards X
	(all) the others	**suhteQ**	relation
luku	figure, number;	**suoritta-**	does, executes
	chapter	**syy**	reason, cause
luterilainen	Lutheran	**tentti**	examination
lähes	nearly	**toinen**	the other (of
läpäise-	passes (exam);		two); second
	penetrates	**tosin**	to be sure;
mu|i|tten	pG of **muu**		granted, ...
ortodoksinen	orthodox	**ulko|maalainen**	foreigner
osa	part	**uskonto**	religion
osuus *te*	(pro)portion	**vaati-**	demands, requires
pakollinen	obligatory,	**vai**	right? (question
	compulsory		tag)
pitä|lä	it is necessary	**virallinen**	official (**virka**
porukka	bunch, gang		'office')
prosentti	per cent	**virkamies**	official (person)
pysty-	is (cap)able	**väestö**	population
pänttäX-	grinds, swots,	**yhtenäinen**	uniform,
	crams		homogeneous
saame[1]	Saami, Lapp		

1 A marginal, but growing, group of nouns have stems ending in **e** but do not change this to **i** in either the citation form or the plural. To this group belong, besides **saame** 'Saam; Lapp', **ale** 'sale; reduced prices in shop', **nukke** 'doll', and **nalle** 'teddy bear', many slang items such as **fade** 'father' and **ope** 'teacher', and all given names ending in **e**, such as **Kalle**, **Rasse**. (There's a good-sized list of Finnish given names in an appendix at the back of this book.)

Language points

Forming and using the conditional mood

This corresponds roughly to English forms made with 'would', or to past-tense forms like 'asked', as in 'If they asked me (=if they were to ask me), I would tell them.' The Finnish conditional is quite easy to form. Its suffix is -**isi**-, which you add directly to the stem of the verb. The only changes which occur at the ends of verb stems are these:

1 The long vowels and diphthongs at the end of class IV verbs are reduced, as in the past tense:

stem	**syö-**	**reagoi-**
present	**syö|n**	**reagoi|n**
past	**söi|i|n**	**reago|i|n**
conditional	**sö|isi|n**	**reago|isi|n**
	'eats'	'reacts'

2 Also as in the past tense, any **e** at the end of a class I or III verb is deleted:

stem	**luke-**	**mene-**
present	**lue|n**	**mene|n**
past	**lu|i|n**	**men|i|n**
conditional	**luk|isi|n**	**men|isi|n**
	'reads'	'goes'

3 The **X** at the end of class II verbs is read as **A**; contrast the past tense, where **X** is read as **s**:

stem	**haluX-**	**kerkiX-**
present	**halua|n**	**kerkiä|n**
past	**halus|i|n**	**kerkis|i|n**
conditional	**halua|isi|n**	**kerkiä|isi|n**
	'wants'	'has time'

As in the past tense, there is no lengthening of the vowel in the third person: **Se sanoisi, jos se haluaisi sitä** '(S)he would say, if (s)he wanted it.'

Negative forms are made with the negative verb plus the conditional connegative. This form looks like the third person singular, but since it has the connegative suffix -**Q** at the end you will hear, and should pronounce, the usual lengthened consonants, for example:

En haluaisi[m] mennä sinne.   I wouldn't want to go there.

To form the indefinite conditional, chop the **U** off the past passive participle and add **Aisiin**:

	Class I	*Class II*	*Class III*	*Class IV*
past passive participle	**anne|ttu**	**maini|ttu**	**men|ty**	**saa|tu**
indefinite conditional	**anne|ttaisiin**	**maini|ttaisiin**	**men|täisiin**	**saa|taisiin**

The corresponding negative forms are **ei annettaisi, ei mainittaisi, ei mentäisi, ei saataisi**.

In colloquial speech, the endings **Aisiin** and **Aisi** are both commonly pronounced **As**, so you will usually hear **annettas, mainittas, mentäs**, and **saatas** in both positive and negative sentences, for example:

Mitä me tehtäs siellä?	What would we do there?
Me ei sanottas mitään.	We wouldn't say anything.

The *past conditional* is simply the verb to be, **ole-**, in the conditional plus the past active participle, for example:

Mä olisin mennyt, jos olisin ehtinyt.
I would have gone if I'd had time.

Sä et olisi saanut istumapaikkaa.
You wouldn't have got a seat.

Jos olisin tiennyt, en olisi sanonut sitä.
If I had known, I wouldn't have said it.

In parallel fashion, the *past indefinite conditional* is simply the negative indefinite conditional of the verb to be (**ei oltas**) plus the past *passive* participle:

Me ei oltas menty sinne kuitenkaan.
We wouldn't have gone there, anyway.

The conditional has three main uses:

1 To mitigate statements which might otherwise seem too brusque, as in **Mä ottalisiln suuremman** 'I would (like to) take the larger one' (rather than the simple present: **Mä otaln suuremman** 'I'll take the larger one').
2 To refer to things that don't (or didn't) really happen, in other words, to the contrary-to-fact. As the name 'conditional' suggests, one such counterfactual is a condition, e.g. **Jos mulla olisi aikaa ...** 'If I had time (but I don't) ...' The conditional also expresses what would happen if the condition were to be met: **... mä lähtisin heti** 'I would leave at once'. Note also the negative **Jos ei sataisi, mä lähtisin heti** 'If it weren't raining, I'd leave at once.'
3 To express fond hopes, e.g. **Jospa mä tietälisiln** 'If I only knew.'

Exercise 2   Change these statements into wishes by putting the verb into the conditional (remember to use **jospa** to entertain hypotheses, **kunpa** to refer to that which is contrary to fact).

1 Minulla on aikaa.
2 Mä tiedän, mitä sä tarkoitat.
3 Sä jäät vähäks aikaa.
4 Me ei tehdä sitä.
5 Me ei menty sinne eilen.

More on modals

Back in Unit 3, you learned how to use modal constructions like that of **Mä haluaisin ostaa kartan** 'I'd like to buy a map.' In such sentences, the subject is in the nominative. Alongside verbs of wanting (**haluX-**) and intending (**aiko-**), many verbs which express different types of ability occur in this type of construction: **voi**- 'is able', **pysty**- 'is capable', **osaX**- and **taita**- 'knows how', **ehti**- and **kerkiX**- 'has time'.

But there is also a second type of modal construction, one in which the subject is less in control, the subject's feelings and intentions are of less importance, or both. Verbs which enter into this type of construction include **pitälä** and **täytyly** 'it is necessary' and the expressions **on pakko** 'it is necessary', **on tärkeä** 'it is important', **on vaikea** 'it is difficult', **on helppo** 'it is easy'. In this second type of modal construction, the subject is demoted: it is put into the genitive, and the verb is always in the third person singular. Any direct-object nominals are put in the nominative and partitive (compare object forms used with the indefinite). Examples:

Muln pitälä soittala kotiin.
I have to phone home.

Häneln täytyly ostala uusi auto.
(S)he has to buy a new car.

Pekaln on helppo poikelta sinne.
It's easy for Pete to drop in there.

Melidän on pakko löytälä hänelt.
We must find him/her.

Sitä muln on vaikea uskola.
That's difficult for me to believe.

Ei meidäln tarvitse lähteä vielä.
We don't have to leave yet.

This kind of modal construction is quite common with the conditional, especially of **pitä-**, which then means something like English 'ought', 'should'. For example:

Ei su|n pitäis sanoa sitä.   You shouldn't say it.
Meidä|n pitäis soittaa sille.   We ought to call him/her.

As in English, the negative of 'must' is not 'mustn't'. Negating the verb **pitä-** gives **ei pidä**, which means 'it isn't necessary'. To say 'one musn't', you use the negative of **saa-** 'one is permitted, one gets to X'.

Exercise 3 Say in Finnish:

1 I have to go home.
2 Irma might know about that.
3 They don't feel like coming with us.
4 Where are you thinking of going this evening?
5 She ended up writing the whole letter.
6 It's important for me to exercise (**voimistele-**) at least three times a week.
7 We ought to write to him.
8 You don't have to answer.
9 You mustn't answer.

Exercise 4 Write out Finnish translations for the following English sentences; if you get stuck, raid the dialogue on language and religion earlier in this unit. (You may have to change or omit a word here and there.)

1 You must have a good reason for doing it, right?
2 It's required of all students.
3 Swedish is Finland's other official language.
4 Don't the majority of Finns also know Swedish?
5 In France all officials have to know French.

More on possession: the personal (possessive) suffixes

m(in)u|n vihko   my notebook (colloquial)
vihko|ni   my notebook (more formal)

As you learned in Unit 1, Finnish has personal suffixes for its verbs, such as first person singular **-n** in **Mä soita|n sulle** 'I'll call you' and second person plural -**tte** in **Voi**|**tte**|**ko auttaa minua?** 'Can you help me?'

But Finnish nouns can also take personal suffixes. You will sometimes encounter them in colloquial Finnish, and far more frequently in more formal Finnish. They most usually indicate possession, so we'll call them *possessive suffixes* from now on. Study the forms:

	Singular	*Plural*
1	-**ni**	-**mme**
2	-**si**	-**nne**
3	-**nsA**/-**#n**	

You will see that only one of these suffixes is identical to its verbal analogue: the first person plural -**mme**.

There is another important difference: despite their appearance, the suffixes -**mme**, -**nne**, and -**nsA** are not tight lids, so they don't compress consonants to their left. For example, the **t** of **koti** and **katu** remain uncompressed in **koti**|**mme** 'our home', and **katu**|**nne** 'your (plural/formal) street'.

In the third person, the same suffix is used for both singular and plural; the distinction is maintained by the genitive form of the appropriate personal pronoun, **häne**|**n** 'his/her' or **heidä**|**n** 'their': so **hänen kirja**|**nsa** is 'her/his book', but **heidän kirja**|**nsa** is 'their book'. This pronoun is *not* used, however, if the possessor is the same person as the subject of the sentence. For example, **Anne ei halunnut sanoa nime**|**ä**|**än** means 'Anne didn't want to say her (own) name', but in the sentence **Anne ei halunnut sanoa *hänen* nime**|**ä**|**än**, Anne is protecting someone else's identity: **hänen** refers to some person *other* than Anne.

As for the difference between the variants (-**nsA** vs. -**#n**) of this suffix: the -**nsA** variant is always used in the nominative, genitive, and illative, both singular and plural. In the other cases, it is a matter of style: you will come across forms built with -**nsA**, but -**#n** is much more common.

The possessive suffixes always come *after* any case suffix, but *before* any of the enclitics --**kin**/--**kAAn**, --**kO**, --**pA**, --**hAn**, --**s**. For example:

huonee|**ssa**|*mme*|**ko**	in our room?
ystäv|**i**|**stä**|*si*|**hän**	about your friends, you know . . .

sELA	**Vihko löydettiin heidän huonee**|**sta**|**an.**
	The notebook was found in their room.

pELA   **Mä puhuin hänen ystäv|i|stä|än.**
I was talking about her friends.

sP   **En mä nyt muista hänen nime|ä|än.**
I don't remember his name now.

If a case suffix ends in a consonant, this consonant is obliterated without a trace when a possessive suffix follows. This means that the forms of the nominative and genitive singular and of the nominative plural all look and sound alike when followed by possessives. Have a look at these examples:

	Plain	*Possessed*
		(third person singular)
sN	**käsi**	**(hänen) käte|nsä**
sG	**käde|n**	**(hänen) käte|nsä**
pN	**käde|t**	**(hänen) käte|nsä**

Nouns which have genitives plural in both **-den** and **-tten** (Unit 9) use only the latter form when a possessive suffix is attached: thus we have **hampa|i|den/hampa|i|tten** but only **hänen hampa|i|tte|nsa** 'his/her teeth'.

Possessive suffixes are also attached to postpositions which take the genitive; the rules are the same as with ordinary nouns. Thus we have, for example:

Mä kuulin naisen äänen (meidän) taka|na|mme.
I heard a woman's voice behind us.

Paketti oli avoinna hänen viere|ssä|än penkillä.
The package was open next to him on the bench.

Poika veti tuolin hänen al|ta|nsa.
The boy pulled the chair out from under him/her.

Minun oli pakko nousta vaunuun hänen perä|ssä|än.
I had to get into the (railway) car behind him.

He seisoivat edelleen ede|ssä|ni.
They were still standing in front of me.

Here a few more examples of the possessive suffixes in action:

Mitä te pidätte tästä meidän kaupungi|sta|mme?
What do you think of this town of ours?

Pari päivää sitten minä sain poja|lta|nne šekin.
A couple of days ago I received a cheque from your son.

Heidän riita|nsa kävi yhä kiihkeämmäksi.
Their argument got more and more heated.

Tarvitsen apu|a|nne.
I need your help.

Autoin takin hänen y|ltä|än.
I helped him/her off with his/her coat. (lit. 'I helped the coat off him/her.')

Se vaihtoi paremman puvun pää|lle|en.
(S)he put a better dress/suit on. (lit. 'changed a better dress/suit onto him/her(self).')

Hän katsoi ympäri|lle|en.
(S)he looked around him/her(self).

Finally, you should be aware of the fact that many adverbial expressions which would have no person-marking in English are built with possessive suffixes in Finnish. For example, 'in earnest, seriously' is the plural inessive of **tosi** 'true', **tos|i|ssa**, plus the appropriate possessive suffix: **Sanoitsä sen tos|i|ssa|s(i)?** is 'Did you really mean it?' 'The door is ajar' in Finnish becomes 'The door is on its crack', **Ovi on rao|lla|an**, and 'I'll leave the door ajar' is **Mä jätän oven rao|lle|en** (adessive and allative of **rako** 'crack, slit'). Other examples are:

Adverb	English	Literally
ede|lle|en	still	to its fore
uude|lle|en	again	at its new
uude|sta|an	again	out of its new
kerra|ssa|an	utterly	in its time
kerra|lla|an	at a time	at its time
viimeis|tä|än	at the latest	its last (sP)
tyhj|i|llä|än	vacant	at its empties
oikea|sta|an	actually	out of its correct
enimmä|kse|en	for the most part	to its most (sTRA)[1]
hilja|lle|en	slowly, gradually	to its quiet

1 Notice that the translative suffix **-ksi** becomes **-kse-** before possessive suffixes.

Exercise 5 In colloquial Finnish, possessive suffixes are relatively rare. Instead of **koira|ni** you say **mun koira**, instead of **häne|n ystävä|nsä** you say **se|n ystävä**. Practise both types of construction by converting these sentences into less formal, more colloquial, versions.

1 Juoksin hänen huoneeseensa.
2 Minun oli vaikea ymmärtää hänen puhettaan.
3 Hänen vaimonsa odottaa lasta.
4 Pane sitä minun kuppiini.
5 Nyt on teidän vuoronne.
6 Olen ollut neljä kertaa hänen luonaan.

Exercise 6 Check your understanding of possessive suffixes by translating these sentences into Finnish:

1 He was standing behind us.
2 The keys were found in your (plural/formal) room.
3 She didn't want to introduce her friend.
4 Why are you (informal) shaking (**pudista-**) your head?
5 He drank half (**puole|t**) of his beer.

Vocabulary building: nominals from verbs and vice versa

In this and previous units you have met many nominals which are built from verbs, and many verbs which are built from nominals. In this section we'll round all these up and look at them a little more systematically.

Many nominal/verb pairs differ only in their last vowel, so it is well worth your while to pay close attention to this. For example, in these pairs:

	word	sauna	bread	needle
nominal	**sana**	**sauna**	**leipä**	**neula**
verb	**sano-**	**sauno-**	**leipo-**	**neulo-**
	says	uses sauna	bakes	sews

the verbs all differ from their nominals in that they end in **o**. The following pairs, on the other hand, all have verbs that end in **U** (i.e., **u** or **y**, according to vowel harmony; see below):

	dry	ripe	one	black
nominal	**kuiva**	**kypsä**	**yksi**	**musta**
verb	**kuivu-**	**kypsy-**	**yhty-**	**mustu-**
	dries	ripens	unites	blackens

With the following pairs, it is the *nominals* which end in **U**:

	beginning	laughter	entrance	wash	bill
nominals	**alku**	**nauru**	**pääsy**	**pesu**	**maksu**
verbs	**alka-**	**naura-**	**pääse-**	**pese-**	**maksa-**
	begins	laughs	gets	washes	pays, costs

but the nominals of these pairs end in **O** (i.e., **o** or **ö**, according to vowel harmony; see below):

	departure	skiing	memory	victory	fact	soup
nominals	**lähtö**	**hiihto**	**muisto**	**voitto**	**tieto**	**keitto**
verbs	**lähte-**	**hiihtä-**	**muista-**	**voitta-**	**tietä-**	**keittä-**
	leaves	skis	remembers	wins	knows	cooks

You will notice that the vowel harmony of word-formation differs somewhat from that of inflection. The front-vowel variants of many derivational suffixes, e.g. the **ö** of the suffix **O** and the **y** of the suffix **U**, occur only if an **y**, **ö**, or **ä** occurs earlier in the word. We therefore have **läht|ö** 'departure' but **tiet|o** 'fact'; **pääs|y** 'entrance' but **pes|u** 'wash'.

You have already met four of the most common suffixes which build nouns from verbs. These are the suffix of the verbal noun, =**minen** (Unit 3), the suffix =**iME**, which builds the names of many tools and instruments (Units 5 and 7), and the suffix of the third infinitive (Unit 6), =**mA**. Finally, there is the suffix =**jA**, first introduced in Unit 1, which builds the names of agents. Notice that any stem-final **e** changes to **i** before this suffix, e.g. **luki|ja** 'reader' from **luke-** 'reads'.

Dialogue 3 ▨

Sovitaan tapaaminen

Let's make a date

Two friends quickly arrange a place and time to meet

VILLE: (*huutaa*) Hei Kalle, oota vähän!
KALLE: Moi Ville! Mitäs sulle?
VILLE: Ei mitään ihmeempää. Kuule, me sovittiin poikien kanssa et tavataan 'Häppärissä' kuudelta.
KALLE: Mitä kello on nyt?
VILLE: Puol viis.

KALLE: Mun täytyy hoitaa ensin pari juttuu, mut mä voisin tulla sitte, joskus seitsemän maissa.
VILLE: Tuu sit ku kerkiit, me ootetaan siellä.

VILLE: (shouts) *Hey Kalle, wait a bit!*
KALLE: *Yo, Ville! What's up?*
VILLE: *Nothing special. Listen, me and the boys've decided to meet at the 'Häppäri' at six.*
KALLE: *What time's it now?*
Vile: *Half four.*
KALLE: *I have to sort a few things first, but I could come later, sometime around seven.*
VILLE: *Come when you can, we'll be waiting for you there.*

Vocabulary

hoita-	takes care of, sees to, sorts	**ootetaan → odote**l**taan**	
		puol → puoli	
huuta-	shouts	**sopi-**	agrees (trans)
ei ihmeel**mpä**l**ä**	not bad	**tapaa**l**minen**	from the stem
juttuu → juttul**a**			**tapaX-** meets
kerkiit → kerkiäl**t**		**täyty**l**y**	it is necessary
Xl**n ma**l**i**l**ssa**	at about X(o'clock)	**tuu → tule**	
oota → odota		**X**l**n kanssa**	with X

Dialogue 4 🔲

Suomenlinna

Varpu and Sanna decide to do a day trip to the Suomenlinna, a fortress built by Sweden in 1746. You can read more about Suomenlinna in Unit 14

SANNA: Hei mitä tehtäs[1] tänään?
VARPU: Mä en oo ollu pitkään aikaan Suomenlinnassa. Voitas[1] tehdä päiväretki sinne.
SANNA: Joo. Soitetaan Marille ja pyydetään se mukaan.
VARPU: Sovitaan että tavataan Kauppatorilla Suomenlinnan lauttojen luona vaikka kaheltatoista.
SANNA: Onkohan siellä mitään mielenkiintoista näyttelyä meneillään?

VARPU: Täytyy kattoo Hesarista. Ootsä käyny koskaan siinä sukellusveneessä?

SANNA: Vesikossa vai. En, mut en tiiä[2] kiinnostaaks mua sukel-lusveneet. Mieluummin mä otan sit aurinkoa kallioilla.

VARPU: No katotaan sit siellä mitä tehdään.

SANNA: Marillakin voi olla ideoita. Mä meen nyt soittaa sille.

SANNA: *Hey, what can we do today?*

VARPU: *I haven't been to the Suomenlinna for a long time. We could do a day trip (to) there.*

SANNA: *Yeah. Let's call Mari and ask her along.*

VARPU: *Let's agree to meet in the market, at the ferries, at say twelve (o'clock).*

SANNA: *Is there any interesting exhibit (going) on there, I wonder?*

VARPU: *Have to look in the paper (= **Helsingi\n Sanoma\t**). Have you ever been in the diving boat there?*

SANNA: *(You mean) in the 'mink', right? No, but I don't know whether I'm interested in diving boats. I'd rather just catch some sun on the cliffs.*

VARPU: *Well, let's just see what we'll do (when we get) there.*

SANNA: *Mari might have some ideas, too. I'll go phone her now.*

1 **tehtäs, voitas** are colloquial pronunciations of **tehtäisiin, voitaisiin**.

2 **tiiä** is a colloquial pronunciation of **tiedä**

Vocabulary

(X\n) muka\an	along (with X)	**mielen\kiintoinen**	interesting
Hesari →	Helsinki's (and	**mieluu\mm\in**	rather, for
Helsingi\n	Finland's) leading		preference
Sanoma\t	newspaper	**näyttely**	exhibit(ion)
idea	idea	**päivä\retki**	day trip
kallio	cliff	**sukellus** *kse*	diving
kattoo →		**veneQ**	boat
katso\a		**vesikko**	mink; name of
kiinnosta-	interests		a submarine at
lautta	ferry		Suomenlinna
mene\i\llä(\än)	going on		

Exercise 7 Write out Finnish translations for the following English sentences by raiding the two dialogues above. (You may have to change or omit a word here and there.)

1 I'd rather have some coffee on the balcony.
2 What time is it now? – Three-thirty.
3 Me and the girls've decided to meet on Esplanaadi at eight.
4 Let's see what we'll do when we get there.
5 I have to sort a few things first.

Language points

One further note on vowel harmony

The simple vowel-harmony rule given in Unit 1 works most of the time, but as you have seen in the previous section, there are certain complications. Here we look at one more.

Certain foreign words like **amatööri** 'amateur', **karikatyyri** 'caricature' complicate the picture. These words contain a vowel from the set **u**, **o**, **a**, but they also contain, further along in the body of the word, a vowel from the set **y**, **ö**, **ä** and no further **u**'s, **o**'s, or **a**'s. Usage fluctuates, but more often than not these words also take the **y**, **ö**, **ä** forms of suffixes with **U**, **O**, **A**. So we have **amatööri|llä**, **karikatyyri|ä**. Contrast **asymmetria** 'asymmetry', which, with the sequence **a-y-a**, takes **u**, **o**, **a** forms, e.g. **asymmetria|sta**.

11 Yhä nopeammin

More and more quickly

In this unit you will:

- learn more about Finnish winter festivities
- learn how to form ordinal numerals and fractions
- read about Finnish parliament, and about Senate Square
- learn about comparative and superlative adverbs
- systematize your knowledge of words for 'some', 'every', 'all', 'many', and 'few'

Dialogue 1 ▪▪

Matkatoimistossa

At the travel agent's

Paul goes to a travel agent's to buy air tickets to Stockholm, and finds out where he can change some money. **Toimisto\virkailija** *(lit. 'office official') is something like 'agent'*

PAUL:	Päivää, mitä maksaa lento Helsingistä Tukholmaan?
TOIMISTOVIRKAILIJA:	Katsotaanpa, edestakainenko?
PAUL:	Eiku yhteen suuntaan.
TOIMISTOVIRKAILIJA:	Viis sataa markkaa yhteen suuntaan plus kolmekymmentä markkaa toimistokuluja, joten se tekee viissataa kolmekymmentä markkaa yhteensä.
PAUL:	Onks vielä paikkoja jäljellä huomenna?
TOIMISTOVIRKAILIJA:	Hetkinen, SASilla vai Finnairilla?

PAUL:	Ei sillä ole väliä.[1] Joskus iltapäivällä jos on tilaa.
TOIMISTOVIRKAILIJA:	Viistoista kolmekymmentä Finnairin koneessa on vielä paikkoja.
PAUL:	Varataan se. Voiko täällä maksaa Visalla?
TOIMISTOVIRKAILIJA:	Totta kai.
PAUL:	Mä tarvitsen kruunuja. Missä vois vaihtaa rahaa?
TOIMISTOVIRKAILIJA:	Rahaa voi vaihtaa pankissa kadun toisella puolella.
PAUL:	Sopiiko että tulen noutamaan lipun noin tunnin päästä?
TOIMISTOVIRKAILIJA:	Lippunne on silloin valmiina. Voitte hakea sen tuolta tiskiltä.

1 **Ei sillä (ole) väli**|**ä** 'It doesn't matter.'

Vocabulary

There'll be no more translations of dialogues from now on, since you should be getting the hang of it by now. There's a lot of help with the trickier forms in this vocabulary though; you can look up the stems in the glossary at the back of this book and in the grammatical sections to which they are cross-referenced.

edes|**takainen**	return (trip, ticket)	**nouta-**	fetches
hake-	fetches; applies for	**paikka**	place; seat
		pankki	bank
jälje|**llä**	left (over)	**plus**	plus
joten	(and) so	**puoli** *e*	side, half
katso|**taan**|**pa**	let's see ...	**tila**	space, room
koneQ	machine; plane	**tiski**	counter, desk
kruunu	crown; (Swedish) *krona*	**toimisto**	office
		vaihta-	changes
kulu|**t**	expenses	**vara**X-	books, reserves
lent|**o**	flight	**yhte**|**ensä**	all together
luotto|**kortti**	credit card	**yhte**|**en suunta**|**an**	(into) one direction, i.e. single

Exercise 1 Raid the dialogue above to write your own, in which two friends discuss what flight arrangements they'd like to make, where they'll buy the tickets, where they'll change money, and so on.

Dialogue 2 🔲

Pikkujoulu

Little Christmas

*In the two or three weeks leading up to the real Christmas, Finns usually throw and go to a number of 'Little Christmas' (**pikku\joulu**) parties at clubs, at work, and among various circles of friends. The following dialogue is in two parts: part one is an invitation (**kutsu**) to a **pikkujoulu** celebration; the second part is set at the party itself, where Jane samples some traditional Little Christmas fare, including some mulled wine (**glögi\ä**) and gingersnaps (**piparkakku\j\a, pipare\i\ta**)*

Kutsu:

JANE: Hei Mikko!
MIKKO: Moi Jane, olipa hyvä että tavattiin.[1]
JANE: Ai miks?
MIKKO: Ensi lauantaina mulla on pikkujoulut. Pääset sä tulemaan?
JANE: Mikä se pikkujoulu on?
MIKKO: No, se on semmonen juhla, jota vietetään ystävien ja työtovereiden kanssa ennen joulua. Yleensä niissä juodaan paljon glögiä ja syödään piparkakkuja.
JANE: Ai mitä?
MIKKO: Tuu lauantaina kuudelta niin näet!
JANE: Kiitos, tuun mielelläni.

Pikkujouluissa:

Ovikello soi. Mikko avaa oven.
MIKKO: Moi tuu sisään. Kiva ku tulit.
JANE: *(ojentaa paketin)* Tässä sulle tuliainen.
MIKKO: Kiitos. Ota glögiä! Se on ku kuumaa punaviiniä ja siinä on rusinoita ja manteleita.
JANE: *(maistaa glögiä)* Hyvää!
MIKKO: Ota myös pipareita.
JANE: Leivoit sä ne itse?
MIKKO: No, äiti auttoi vähän. Tule niin esittelen sut muille.

1 **olipa hyvä että tavattiin** 'it's a good thing we've run into one another' (Unit 6).

Vocabulary

ai	oh!	pipari → piparkakku	
esittele-	introduces	piparkakku	gingersnap
glögi	mulled wine	puna|viini	red wine
jota	which (relative	rusina	raisin
	pronoun)	semmonen	sort of a, a kind of
juhla	celebration	soi-	rings
manteli	almond	tuliainen	present given by
miele|llä|ni	gladly		person arriving;
ojenta-	passes		**tuliaise|t** party
ovi|kello	doorbell		given for person
paketti	package		arriving
		työ|toveri	work colleague

Language points

The relative pronouns: jo|ka and mi|kä

This **mi|kä** is the same as the interrogative pronoun first introduced at Unit 3. However, we are *not* talking here about the indeclinable **joka**, which means 'each, every'. *This* **jo|ka** is an entirely different word; you use it to link clauses, analogous to English 'who', 'which', and 'that':

> **Se on mies, *jo|ka* on ollut töissä pankissa.**
> It's a man *who* has worked in a bank.

> **Se on tehtävä, *jo|ka* kysyy aikaa ja vaivaa.**
> It's a task *which* calls for time and hard work.

> **Toi on se poika, *jo|ka* löi ikkunan rikki.**
> That's the boy *that* broke the window.

Unlike English, Finnish can't leave the little link-word out:

> **Tossa on se ikkuna, *jo|n|ka* poika löi rikki.**
> There's the window (*that*) the boy broke.

As you can see from the last example, **jo|ka** declines, i.e. it takes case suffixes: **jo|ka** is the nominative singular, **jo|n|ka** is the genitive singular (indicating the accusative in the example above), and **jo|ta** is the partitive singular, as in:

Tämä on se, *jo*|*ta* etsin.
This is the one (*that*) I was looking for.

Se on asia, *jo*|*ta* mun on vaikea todistaa.
It is a thing *which* it is difficult for me to prove.

As a rule, **jo|ka** is more concrete, and **mi|kä** is more abstract. Here are their full paradigms:

	Singular	Plural	Singular	Plural
N	jo|ka	jo|t|ka	mi|kä	mi|t|kä
G	jo|n|ka	jo|i|den	mi|n|kä	= sG
P	jo|ta	jo|i|ta	mi|tä	= sP
ELA	jo|sta	jo|i|sta	mi|stä	= sELA
INE	jo|ssa	jo|i|ssa	mi|ssä	= sINE
ILL	jo|hon	jo|i|hin	mi|hin	= sILL
ABL	jo|lta	jo|i|lta	mi|ltä	= sABL
ADE	jo|lla	jo|i|lla	mi|llä	= sADE
ALL	jo|lle	jo|i|lle	mi|lle	= sALL
ESS	jo|na	jo|i|na	mi|nä	= sESS
TRA	jo|ksi	jo|i|ksi	mi|ksi	= sTRA

Notice that the forms of **jo|ka** and **mi|kä** run parallel right through to the plural nominative (**jo|t|ka**, **mi|t|kä**). They then part company: other than **mi|t|kä**, the plural forms of **mi|kä** are identical to its singular forms, while **jo|ka** has a plural stem **jo|i**-.

Study these further examples of the relative pronouns in action:

Tarina kertoo suomalaisesta taksikuskista, *jo*|*lla* on italialainen vaimo.
The tale tells of a Finnish taxi driver *who* has an Italian wife.

Pankeissa on paljon väkeä, *jo*|*i*|*lta* nykyaikainen tietotekniikka vie työpaikan.
There are many people in banks *from whom* today's information technology is going to take (their) job.

Hän aina tervehtii minua, *mi*|*kä* on outoa, sillä minä en tunne häntä.
(S)he always greets me, *which* is strange, since I don't know him/her.

Viinistä se sanoi saman, *mi*|n|*kä* se sanoi musiikistakin.
(S)he said the same (thing) about the wine *(that)* (s)he said
about the music.

Mä teen *mi*|n|*kä* pystyn.
I'll do *what* I can.

Exercise 2 Combine the sentences under A and B with the appropriate form of the relative pronoun.

Model: (A) **Kuka toi nainen on** 'Who's that woman?' + (B) **Naisella
on punaiset kengät** 'The woman has red shoes'

Kuka toi nainen on, jo|lla on punaiset kengät?
'Who's that woman who has red shoes?'

A	*B*
Tämä on se huone.	Me puhuttiin siitä.
Noi kirjat on mun.	Ne on ylimmäisellä hyllyllä.
Se sanakirja on parempi.	Mä unohdin sen kotiin.
Uusi opettaja tulee huomenna.	Te ette tunne häntä.

Dialogue 3

Helmikuun juhlista

February festivities

*February may be the shortest month, but in Finland it's crammed
full of special days. In the following three-part dialogue, friends talk
about Runeberg Day, sledding on Shrove Tuesday, and Kalevala
Day*

Runebergin päivä:

ROBERT: Miksi tänään liputetaan?
LIISA: 5. (viides) helmikuuta on Runebergin päivä. Se on
virallinen liputuspäivä.
ROBERT: Kuka on Runeberg?
LIISA: Johan Ludwig Runeberg on Suomen kansalliskirjailija.
Hän on kirjoittanut sanat *Maamme laulu*un, Suomen
kansallislauluun. Hän on myös kirjoittanut kirjan
Vänrikki Stoolin tarinat, joka kertoo Suomensodasta
1808–1809. Tiesitkö että vuonna 1809 Suomesta tuli osa

Venäjän keisarikuntaa? Aikaisemmin Suomi oli osa Ruotsia.

ROBERT: Liittyyks Runebergin päivään erityisiä tapoja?

LIISA: Runebergin vaimo Frederika leipoi sille torttuja. Nykyään niitä kutsutaan Runebergin tortuiksi ja niitä syödään Runebergin päivän tienoilla.

Laskiainen:

ULLA: Läheks pulkkamäkeen?

JOHN: Ai tänäänkö?

ULLA: Eiku huomenna, ku on laskiaistiistai.

JOHN: Ai niin, Eeva kysykin multa sitä viime viikolla.

ULLA: No sitten se varmaan kertokin sulle, että pulkkamäen jälkeen mennään sen luo syömään hernekeittoa ja laski-aispullia.

Kalevalanpäivä (28.2):
(Helsingin Akateemisessa kirjakaupassa.)

KAIJA: Mä olen menossa pääsiäisenä New Yorkiin, Markin perheen luo. Mitä mä voisin viedä sinne tuliaisiksi?

ANNE: Hei osta Kalevala[1]. Senhän saa englanninkielisenä.

KAIJA: Hyvä idea!

ANNE: Muista sitte mainita Elias Lönnrothista ja sen runonkeruu-matkoista ympäri Karjalaa 1800-luvulla.

KAIJA: Niin, Kalevalahan on tärkein suomalainen teos, johon on kerätty vuosisatoja suusta suuhun kulkeneita kansan-tarinoita.

1 Kalevala on Suomen kansalliseepos.

Vocabulary

akateeminen	academic	**kirjaili|ja**	writer, author
eepos *kse*	epic	**kirja|kaupa**	bookshop
erityinen	special	**kulkene|i|ta**	which have gone/
herneQ	pea		travelled
kansallis|	national	**läheks** → **lähdetkö sä**	
kansan|tarina	folk tale	**laskiainen**	Lent
Karjala	Karelia	**laskiais|pulla**	Lent bun
keisari|kunta	empire	**laskiais|tiistai**	Shrove Tuesday
keräX-	collects	**laulu**	song, anthem
kerto|kin	s3 pt of **kerta-**	**liitty-**	is attached, is
keruu	collecting, gathering		associated

liputta-	flies flag (**lippu**)	**pulkka**	(a kind of sled)
1800-luvulla	in the nineteenth	**runo**	poem
	century	**suulsta suulhun**	from mouth to
maa	land, country		mouth
nykyään	nowadays	**tapa**	custom, way
pääsiäinen	Easter	**tarina**	tale
perheQ	family	**vänrikki**	ensign
perinteQ	tradition		

Language points

Comparative and superlative adverbs

Here we have the equivalents of English expressions such as 'more quickly' and 'the most easily'.

To form these, you add =**in**, a tight-lid suffix, to the comparative or superlative stem of the adjective. These stems both end in **MPA**, and =**in** cancels the final **A** and compresses the **MP** to **mm**. For example, 'more quickly' is **nopeammin** (stem: **nopealmpa-**), and 'most quickly' is **nopeimmin** (stem: **nopelimpa-**).

The full set of adjectival and adverbial forms of **nopea** 'quick, fast' looks like this:

	Adjective	*Adverb*
positive	**nopea**	**nopealsti**
comparative	**nopealmpi**	**nopealmmlin**
superlative	**nopelin**	**nopelimmlin**

Notice the forms of these common temporal adverbs:

pian	soon	**aikaislin**	early	**myöhälän**	late
pikemmin	sooner	**aikaiselmmlin**	earlier	**myöhelmmlin**	later
pikimmin	soonest	**aikaislimmlin**	earliest	**myöhlimmlin**	last

Irregular are

paljoln	a lot	**hyvlin**	well	**pialn**	soon
enemmän	more	**parelmmlin**	better	**pikelmmlin**	sooner
eniten	most	**parhaliten**	best	**piklimmlin**	soonest

Examples:

Mä rakastan sua *enemmän* kuin koskaan.
I love you *more* than ever.

Se pitää maalauksesta ja kirjallisuudesta, mutta musiikki kiinnostaa sitä *eniten*.
(S)he likes painting and literature, but music interests him/her *the most*.

Note these constructions, made with **mi|tä** and **se**:

Mitä pikemmin, sen parempi.   The sooner, the better.
mitä pikimmin   as soon as possible

'More and more X-ly' is expressed by **yhä**, as with the comparative adjectve: **Se juoksi yhä nopeammin** '(S)he ran more and more quickly.'

Exercise 3 Put into Finnish:

1 more and more simply
2 most cheaply
3 as soon as possible
4 more deeply
5 (S)he came earlier.

Dialogue 4

Parlamentti

Finnish parliament

TIM: Et auttas mua vähän Petteri? Sähän tiedät hyvin Suomen hallintojärjestelmää.
PETTERI: No se riippuu vähän siitä mitä sä haluut tietää.
TIM: Suomen presidenttihän on Martti Ahtisaari, mut koska siitä tuli presidentti ja kuinka pitkäks aikaa?
PETTERI: Ahtisaari vannoi presidentinvalansa ensimmäinen maaliskuuta 1994 ja Suomessa presidentti istuu kuus vuotta vallassa.
TIM: Istuuko eduskunta sit neljä vai kuus vuotta?
PETTERI: Eduskunta istuu neljä vuotta kerrallaan.
TIM: Paljonko on Suomen eduskunnassa kansanedustajia?
PETTERI: 200 (kakssataa). Viimeiset eduskuntavaalit oli maaliskuussa 1995. Silloin Sosiaalidemokraatit sai 63 paikkaa, Keskustapuolue 44 ja Kokoomuspuolue 39. Ne onkin historiallisestikin Suomen kolme suurinta puoluetta.

TIM: Istuuko eduskunnassa muita puolueita?
PETTERI: Vihreät, Kristillinen puolue, Ruotsalainen kansan-puolue, Maaseudunliitto, Vasemmisto puolue ja pari muuta.
TIM: Sähän tiedät tosi tosi paljon.
PETTERI: Meillä oli viime viikolla kokeet Suomen politiikasta.

Vocabulary

auttas →	cd connegative	**kristillinen**	Christian
auttal**isi**		**liitto**	union, league,
edusl**kunta**	parliament		alliance
ensimmäinen	first	**maa**l**seutu**	rural area
hallinto	administration	**parlamentti** =	
haluut → **haluat**		**eduskunta**	
historiallisesti	historically	**puolueQ**	(political) party
järjestelmä	system	**riippu-**	depends, hangs
kansanl**edustaja**	MP (member of	**silloin**	then, at that time
	parliament)	**vaali**	election
kansanl**puolueQ**	National Party	**vala**	oath
kerrallaan	at a time	**valla**l**ssa**	in power (**valta**)
keskusta	centre	**vanno-**	swears
kokeQ	test	**vasemm**l**isto**	the Left
kokoomus *kse*	coalition	**vihreä**	green

Language points

Ordinal numerals and fractions

'First' is **ensimmäinen** (colloquial: **eka**), and 'second' is **toinen** (**toka**). After that, the formation of ordinal numerals is regular: you add =**NTE** to every stem in the word.

In the nominative singular, =**NTE** is read as **s**. Study these forms:

cardinal	**kolme**	**neljä**	**viisi**	**kuusi**	**seitsemä**l**n**	**kahdeksa**l**n**
ordinal	**kolma**l**s**	**neljä**l**s**	**viide**l**s**	**kuude**l**s**	**seitsemä**l**s**	**kahdeksa**l**s**
	'third'	'fourth'	'fifth'	'sixth'	'seventh'	'eighth'

cardinal	**yhdeksä**l**n**	**kymmene**l**n**	**yksi**l**toista**	**kaksi**l**kymmentä**
ordinal	**yhdeksä**l**s**	**kymmene**l**s**	**yhdes**l**toista**	**kahdes**l**kymmenes**
	'ninth'	'tenth'	'eleventh'	'twentieth'

cardinal	**kolme	kymmentä	neljä**
ordinal	**kolmas	kymmenes	neljäs**
	'thirty-fourth'

cardinal	**kuusisataaviisikymmentäkahdeksa	n**
ordinal	**kuudessadasviideskymmeneskahdeksa	s**
	'558th'

Notice the change **e** > **a** in **kolma|s** 'third', and the fact that the teen-formant **toista** remains unchanged.

In the partitive singular, the **NTE** is read as **t**, so we have **kolma|t|ta, kymmene|t|tä**.

The **nte** (compressed: **nne**) of the ordinal suffix is evident in inflected forms such as **kuude|nte|na, kolma|nne|ssa, kahdeksa| nne|ksi** in:

Se saapui marraskuun *kuude|nte|na*.
(S)he arrived *on the sixth* of November.

Toimistomme on uuden rakennuksen *kolma|nne|ssa* kerrokse|ssa.
Our office is *on the third floor* of the new building.

Sen bruttokansantuote on lännen *kahdeksa|nne|ksi* *suurin*.
Its gross national product is the *eighth largest* in the west.

Notice, in the last example, the use of the translative to express ranking.

To the left of the generic pluralizer **-i-**, **NTE** is **ns**, as in **kolma|ns|i|a**:

Niillä on epäluulo kolmansia puolueita kohtaan.
They have suspicion towards third (political) parties.

In numerals with more than one stem, the ordinal suffix is attached to every stem and inflected equally:

Me juhlitaan mun kuude|t|ta||kymmene|t|tä||kahdeksa|t|ta syntymäpäivä|ä|ni.
We're celebrating my sixty-eighth birthday.

Notice also how the partitive of ordinals is used in these two kinds of time expression:

Mä tykkäsin susta *eka kerta|a* kun mä näin sut.
I liked you *the first time* I saw you.

Mä asun täällä *kolma|t|ta vuot|ta.*
I've been living here for more than two years.

Here is the full paradigm of **kolmas** (stem: kolmante) 'third', placed alongside that of **tuhat** (stem: tuhante) 'thousand' for comparison:

	Singular	Plural	Singular	Plural
N	kolmas	kolmanne|t	tuhat	tuhanne|t
G	kolmanne|n	kolmans|i|en	tuhanne|n	tuhans|i|en
P	kolmat|ta	kolmans|i|a	tuhat|ta	tuhans|i|a
ELA	kolmanne|sta	kolmans|i|sta	tuhanne|sta	tuhans|i|sta
INE	kolmanne|ssa	kolmans|i|ssa	tuhanne|ssa	tuhans|i|ssa
ILL	kolmante|en	kolmans|i|in	tuhante|en	tuhans|i|in
ABL	kolmanne|lta	kolmans|i|lta	tuhanne|lta	tuhans|i|lta
ADE	kolmanne|lla	kolmans|i|lla	tuhanne|lla	tuhans|i|lla
ALL	kolmanne|lle	kolmans|i|lle	tuhanne|lle	tuhans|i|lle
ESS	kolmante|na	kolmans|i|na	tuhante|na	tuhans|i|na
TRA	kolmanne|ksi	kolmans|i|ksi	tuhanne|ksi	tuhans|i|ksi

Notice that the case forms of these two words differ only in the nominative singular: the **NTE** of ordinals is read as **s**, but the **NTE** of 'thousand' is read as **t**.

Fractions

'Half' is **puoli** *e*. The other fractions are made by adding =**KsE** to the stem of the relevant ordinal. In the singular nominative and partitive, this suffix is read as =**s**. So, 'one-third' is **kolmannes** (stem: **kolmannekse-**). Examples:

kolme neljännes|tä	three-quarters
kuusi kahdeksannes|ta	six-eighths
kaksitoista kuudennes|ta||toista	twelve-sixteenths

For fractions whose numerator is one, the use of **osa** 'part' is common, e.g. **kuudes osa** 'one-sixth' (lit. sixth part).

Exercise 4 Say and write out these fractions in Finnish:

1 three-fifths
2 four-sixths
3 seven-eighths
4 two-thirds
5 twenty-two sevenths

Dialogue 5 ▣

Senaatintori

Senate Square

(Turistineuvonnassa, rautatieasemalla)

VIRKAILIJA: Päivää, voisinko jotenkin auttaa?

MR SMITH: Olen juuri saapunut Helsinkiin, enkä[1] oikein tiedä mistä aloittaa. Mikä on Helsingin vanhin kaupunginosa?

VIRKAILIJA: Senaatintori on vanhan Helsingin keskusta. Tori edustaa neoklassista tyylisuuntaa ja on rakennettu vuosina 1818–1852. Helsingistähän tuli pääkaupunki 1812.

MR SMITH: Onko Senaatintorilla se iso valkoinen kirkko, joka on monissa postikorteissa?

VIRKAILIJA: Tuomiokirkko, kyllä. Senaatintorilla on myös Helsingin vanhin kivitalo, Sederholmin talo, joka on rakennettu rokokootyyliin 1700-luvulla (tuhatseitsemänsataa).

MR SMITH: Miten parhaiten pääsen täältä Senaatintorille?

VIRKAILIJA: Menkää pääovesta ulos, sitten kadun ylitettyänne vasemmalle. Käännytte Keskuskadulle ja seuraatte sitä Aleksanterinkadulle. Sitten taas käännytte vasemmalle ja jatkatte Aleksanterinkatua kunnes tulette Senaatin torille. Tässä kartta avuksi.

MR SMITH: Kiitos.

1 e|n|kä 'and I don't' –kA is a little cliuc which links clauses something like English 'and'; it is most often added to the negative verb, as here.

Vocabulary

Aleksanterinkatu	Alexander Street	**juuri**	just
aloitta-	begin, start (something)	**olen juuri saapunut**	I've just arrived
avu|ksi: apu sTRA		**Keskuskatu**	Centre Street
edusta-	represents	**kivi|talo**	stone house
jatka-	continues	**kunnes**	until
jotenkin	in some/any way	**mon|i|ssa**	pINE **moni** *e* 'many'

neoklassinen	neoclassical	**Senaatti**	Senate
neuvonta	advice	**suunta**	direction,
parhaiten	best (adv.)		tendency
posti|kortti	postcard	**Tuomiokirkko**	cathedral
pää|kaupunki	capital	**turisti**	tourist
pää|ovi *e*	main door	**tyyli**	style
rakenne|ttu	built	**valkoinen**	white
rautatie|asema	railway station	**vuos|li|na**	pESS of **vuosi** *te*
rokokoo	rococo	**ylite|tty|ä|nne**	after you have
saapu-	arrives		crossed
Senaatintori	Senate Square		

Language points

'All', 'every', 'many', 'few', 'some'

'All' is **koko** only if 'the whole (thing)' is meant; a more general word is **kaikki** e, which is equivalent not only to 'whole' but also to 'each', 'every', and 'all'. **Koko** is invariable, so any case suffix can go only onto the word that it modifies. Compare **koko aja\|n** = **kaike\|n aika\|a** 'the whole time, all the time'. In the plural nominative and accusative, **kaikki** is unchanged, e.g. **Isä söi kaikki kaku\|t** 'Father ate all the cakes.' Plural forms built with -i- are usually equivalent to English expressions with 'every(one)'. Here are some more examples:

Isä söi *koko kaku\|n*.
Father ate *the whole cake*.

Koko matka\|n aikana* ei vaihdettu sanaakaan.
During the whole journey we didn't exchange a word.

Kaike\|n muu\|n* paitsi lompakon hän laittoi salkkuun.
(S)he put *everything else* but the wallet into the bag.

Uutinen tuli *kaik\|i\|lle* yllätyksenä.
The news came as a surprise *to everyone*.

Notice also the common adjective **kaiken\|lainen**:

Me nähtiin *kaikenlaisia* eläimiä.
We saw *all kinds* of (= many various) animals.

'Every' in the sense of 'each' is usually the invariable **joka**:

Joka tapauksessa **sä soitat mulle, eikö?**
You'll ring me *in any case*, right?

Se tulee käymään *joka toinen päivä.*
(S)he comes to visit *every other day.*

'Few' is often expressed with **harva** (which also means 'rare' and 'sparse'); 'many (a)' is **moni** *e.* Both are frequent in the singular, e.g.

Mä oon *mone|ssa asia|ssa* **samaa mieltä sun kanssasi.**
I agree (lit. 'am of the same mind') with you *on many matters.*

Harva muusikko **soittaa konsertissaan niin** *mon|ta soitin|ta.*
Few musicians (lit. 'rare musician') play so *many instruments* (lit. 'so many an instrument') in their concert.

but **mone|t**, the plural nominative of **moni**, is also common as subject:

Monet **haluavat sämpylät ja kahvileivät ennen seitsemää.**
Many (people) want (their) rolls and coffee and a little something before seven.

Large and small amounts are expressed as **paljo|n** and **vähä|n**:

Mulla on (vähän/paljon) viiniä. I have (a little/lots of) wine.

'Anyone' in the sense 'no matter who' is **ku|ka tahansa** or **kuka vaan**, and similarly 'anywhere' in the sense 'no matter where' is **missä tahansa** or **missä vaan**. Be careful to distinguish such 'any'-words with the words like 'anyone', 'anywhere' which English uses in negative and interrogative contexts such as 'There isn't anyone there', which in Finnish is **Ei siellä ole ketään.**

To refer to a definite but unspecified 'some(thing)' you use **jo|kin**; because of its inherent vagueness, this word is more common in the partitive, **jo|ta|kin**. In colloquial contexts, the **k** of this word is left out to the right of **a**, so we have **jo|ta|in** as in:

Haluaisitko *jo|ta|in* **muu|ta?** Would you like something else?

Further examples:

Ne antoi sen *jo|lle|kin* **toise|lle perhee|lle.**
They gave it *to some* other family.

Se tapahtui *jo|i|takin* **vuosia sitten.**
It happened *some* years ago.

Totuus on kai *jo|ssa|in* sillä välillä.
The truth is perhaps *somewhere* in between.

Jos mä oon *jo|hon|kin* tyytyväinen, mä en muuta sitä.
If I'm satisfied with something (lit. 'into something'), I don't change it.

Notice these common expressions: **jo|sta|in syy|stä** 'for some reason', **jo|lla|in tava|lla** 'in some way', **jo|ssa|in muodo|ssa** 'in some form (or other)', **jo|i|den|kin miele|stä** 'in some people's opinion', **jo|ksi|kin aika|a** 'for a time'.

To refer to a definite but unspecified 'some(one)', you use **jo||ku**. Both parts of this word decline, so the genitive singular is **jo|n||ku|n**, as in **jonkun salkku** 'someone's bag', and the nominative plural is **jo|t||ku|t**, as in **Jotkut ei tykkää teestä** 'Some people don't like tea.'

Here are the full paradigms of **jo|kin** 'something' and **jo||ku** 'someone':

	Singular	Plural	Singular	Plural
N	jo|kin	jo|t|kin	jo||ku	(jo|t||ku|t)
G	jo|n|kin	jo|i|den|kin	(jo|n||ku|n)	(jo|i|den||ku|i|den)
P	jo|ta|(k)in	jo|i|ta|(k)in	(jo|ta||ku|ta)	(jo|i|ta||ku|i|ta)
ELA	jo|sta|(k)in	jo|i|sta|(k)in	(jo|sta||ku|sta)	(jo|i|sta||ku|i|sta)
INE	jo|ssa|(k)in	jo|i|ssa|(k)in	(jo|ssa||kus|ssa)	(jo|i|ssa||ku|i|ssa)
ILL	jo|hon|kin	jo|i|hin|kin	(jo|hon||ku|hun)	(jo|i|hin||ku|i|hin)
ABL	jo|lta|(k)in	jo|i|lta|(k)in	(jo|lta||ku|lta)	(jo|i|lta||ku|i|lta)
ADE	jo|lla|(k)in	jo|i|lla|(k)in	(jo|lla||ku|lla)	(jo|i|lla||ku|i|lla)
ALL	jo|lle|kin	jo|i|lle|kin	(jo|lle|ku|lle)	(jo|i|lle||ku|i|lle)
ESS	jo|na|(k)in	jo|i|na|(k)in	(jo|na||ku|na)	(jo|i|na||ku|i|na)
TRA	jo|ksi|kin	jo|i|ksi|kin	(jo|ksi||ku|ksi)	(jo|i|ksi||ku|i|ksi)

In spoken Finnish, the forms given here in brackets are becoming increasingly rare; instead, people use the corresponding forms on the left.

Exercise 5 Give English equivalents.

1 joku muu
2 jotain muuta
3 jotkut
4 kaikenlaista
5 monet luulee

12 Maton alla tuntuu olevan jotain

There seems to be something under the carpet

In this unit you will learn:

- new ways to join up clauses and link verbs
- about two warmer-weather Finnish holidays, **vappu** and **juhannus**
- about restaurants and Finnish culinary specialities

Dialogue 1 ▣

Ruokakaupassa

Food shopping

*In a food shop, John learns about various Finnish culinary specialities by talking with a very patient salesperson (**myy|jä**)*

JOHN: Anteeksi, voisitteko auttaa. Haluaisin ostaa erilaisia suomalaisia ruokia.

MYYJÄ: Tottakai. Minkälaista ruokaa haluaisitte?

JOHN: Vähän kaikenlaista. Sellaista, mitä suomalaiset itse[1] syövät ja erityisesti sellaista, mitä ei syödä muualla maailmassa.

MYYJÄ: No ruisleipä on ehdottomasti suomalaista. Niitä löytyy täältä leipähyllystä. Samalla voitte ostaa karjalanpiirakoita, ne ovat todella herkullisia.

JOHN: Mistä ne on tehty?

MYYJÄ: Piirakoiden kuori on tehty ruis- ja muista jauhoista ja täytteenä on riisiä, perunaa tai ohraa.

JOHN: Hyvä, otan pussin sekä peruna- että riisipiirakoita.[2]
MYYJÄ: Kala-altaasta löydätte lohta. Se on suomalainen ruoka,
        samoin kuin lihapullat. Niitä voi ostaa valmiina kylmäal-
        taasta, vaikka yleensä niitä tehdäänkin itse jauhelihasta.
JOHN: Onko teillä lakkoja? Olen kuullut, että lakkaa pidetään
        marjojen kuninkaana.
MYYJÄ: Ainakin valmiina hillona sitä on. Voimme vielä tarkistaa
        onko niitä pakastettuna. Suomalaiset syövät paljon
        marjoja. Mustikoita, mansikoita ja vadelmia meillä on
        aina pakastettuina täällä kaupassa.
JOHN: Entäs jotain makeaa? Mitä suomalaiset syövät kahvin
        kanssa?
MYYJÄ: No pullat nyt ainakin kuuluvat kahvipöytään, erityisesti
        korvapuustit.
JOHN: Kiitoksia paljon avustanne.
MYYJÄ: Eipä kestä. Hyvä, että osasin auttaa. Toivottavasti valin-
        tanne olivat onnistuneita.

1 **suomalaiset itse** 'the Finns themselves'.

2 **sekä peruna- että riisipiirakoita**: to say 'both X and Y', use **sekä X että Y**.

Vocabulary

ainakin	at least, anyway	**liha|pulla**	meatball
altaX	basin, pool, tank	**loh|ta**	sP **lohi** e salmon
avu|sta|nne	for your help	**löyty-**	is found
	(**apu**)	**löytä-**	finds
ehdo|ttoma|sti	absolutely,	**maailma**	world
	unconditionally	**makea**	sweet
erityise|sti	particularly	**mansikka**	strawberry
herkullinen	gourmet-style	**marja**	berry
hillo	jam	**minkä|lainen**	what kind?
jauheQ|liha	mince	**mustikka**	bilberry
jauho|t	flour	**muu|a|lla**	elsewhere
jotain	something	**ohra**	barley
korva|puusti	'box on the ear',	**onnistu-**	succeeds
	a kind of pastry	**onnistunut**	successful
kuninkaX	king	**pakasta-**	freezes
kuori e	peel, skin, crust,	**pakaste|ttu**	frozen
	bark	**piirakka**	a kind of pie
kuulu-	belongs	**pussi**	bag

riisi	rice	tarkista-	checks
rukiX	rye	toivolttavalsti	hopefully
samalla	at the same time	täytteQ	filling
samoin	the same as;	vadelma	raspberry
	likewise	valinta	choice
sellainen	a sort of		

Exercise 1 Make up your own short dialogues, in which you ask about things for sale in various shops. Ask what things are made of, whether the shop has larger or smaller (and cheaper and dearer) ones, how much things cost, and whether or not things are especially Finnish.

Dialogue 2 ▨

Vappu

May Day

Learn about vappu, a holiday which Pia, a university student, thinks is the most fun of the year

RUTH: Mikä susta on vuoden paras juhla?

PIA: Parhaasta en tiedä, mutta hauskin on kyllä vappu.

RUTH: Ai miks niin?

PIA: Ku mä olin pieni siman juominen, tippaleivät, serpentiinit ja ilmapallot, oli parasta mitä tiesin.

RUTH: Ja nykyään?

PIA: No nykyään vappu opiskelijoiden juhlana merkitsee paljon. Kello kuus vapun aattona lakitetaan Espalla Manta.[1] Tunnelma on kyllä silloin huipussa.

RUTH: Kai vappuna muutakin tapahtuu?

PIA: No se on kyllä melkein ku karnevaalit. Helsingissä hulinoidaan silloin ihan kunnolla, vähän liiankin kunnolla.

RUTH: Entäs vapunpäivänä?

PIA: Vapunpäivä on vähän rauhallisempi. Silloin perheet menee vapputorille, vappukonserttiin ja jotkut jopa vappumarssille. Opiskelijat kerääntyvät Ullanlinnanmäelle piknikille.

1 **Havis Amandan patsas Helsingin Esplanadilla.**

Vocabulary

aatto	eve	**laki**l**tta-**	puts cap (**lakki**) on X
Espalla →		**liian**	too much,
Esplanadilla			excessively
Esplanadi	a main street in	**marssi**	march
	Helsinki	**merkiTSE-**	means
huippu	peak, summit	**patsaX**	statue
hulinoi-	acts in hooliganish	**piknikki**	picnic
	manner	**rauha**l**linen**	peaceful
ihan	quite, very	**serpentiini**l**t**	streamers
ilmal**pallo**	balloon	**sima**	mead
jopa	even, as much as	**tapahtu-**	happens
juhla	celebration, festival	**tippa**l**leivä**l**t**	crullers (a kind of
karnevaali	carnival		deep-fried
keräänty-	assembles, gathers		doughnut-like
kunnol**lla**	really (**kunto** 'good		pastry)
	shape')	**vappu**	May Day

Language points

Linking clauses, 1: Partisiippirakenne (PR)

In earlier units you have seen how to link verbs together to form complex constructions such as *Haluaisin ostaa* **uuden sanakirjan** '*I would like to buy* a new dictionary' (Unit 3) and **Mun pitää ostaa uusi sanakirja** '*I have to buy* a new dictionary' (Unit 10). In this section you will learn how to join a clause like **mä näin** 'I saw' with a clause like **se lähti** '(s)he left' to produce the complex construction **Mä näin sen lähtevän** 'I heard her/him leave.'

Constructions of this type are called participial constructions (**partisiippirakente**l**i**l**ta** or PRs). In all PRs, the first clause contains a verb of perceiving, feeling, knowing, thinking, wanting, or speaking. Common examples are **näke-** 'sees', **katso-** 'watches, views', **kuule-** 'hears', **tunte-** 'senses, feels', **huomaX-** 'notices', **kuvittele-** 'imagines, pictures', **toivo-** 'hopes', **pelkäX-** 'fears', **ihmettele-** 'marvels', **ajattele-** 'thinks', **arvele-** 'thinks, assumes', **sano-** 'says', **kerto-** 'tells', **kieltä-** 'denies'.

To link the second clause, you put its subject into the genitive and add the suffix =**vAn** to the stem of the verb. So in the example above we have:

se lähti   se|n lähte|vän

Instead of =**vAn**, you add =**neen** if the time of the second verb is earlier than that of the first:

Minä huomasin hänen lähteneen.
I noticed that (s)he had left.

(*Note*: This =**neen** is a form of the past active participle you learned in Unit 6, so its first **n** assimilates and causes sound changes accordingly: **pääs|seen, huoma***n*|**neen**. In colloquial Finnish such constructions are rare; people use two clauses instead, e.g. **Mä huomasin et se oli lähtenyt.**)
Here are some more examples:

Mä kuulin jo|n||ku|n huuta|van pihalla.
I heard someone shouting in the yard.

Myyjä arvelee minu|n halua|van jutella.
The salesperson thinks I want to chat.

Mikä se kertoi isänsä ol|leen?
What did (s)he say her/his father had been?

Luuletteko minu|n hake|van teekuppia?
Do you think it's a teacup I'm after?

Pelkäsin tämä|n väsyttä|vän häntä.
I was afraid this was tiring him/her.

If the subject of both clauses is the same, the appropriate possessive suffix is added to the form built with =**vAn** or =**neen**, and the pronouns (**minun, sinun, hänen**, etc.) are used or omitted as usual, for example:

Minä tunsin ole|va|ni varma sen saamisesta.
I felt sure of getting it.

Contrast

Mitä Pasi tekee tänä iltana?
What's Pasi doing tonight?

Se soitti vähän ennen kun sä tulit ja sanoi tule|va|nsa käymään.
He rang a little before you came and said that he (Pasi) was coming to visit.

with

Mitä Pekka tekee tänä iltana?
What's Pekka doing tonight?

Pasi soitti vähän ennen kun sä tulit ja sanoi *hänen* tule|va|nsa käymään.
Pasi rang a little before you came and said that *he (Pekka)* was coming to visit.

There are just two hiccups. The first is this: the less the subject is in control, the less likely it is to be put into the genitive. It is more likely to remain in the nominative (or partitive) if it refers to someone or something that is not dynamic, for example something which merely exists. Example: **poik|i|a** 'some boys' in **Siellä on poik|i|a** 'There are some boys there' remains in the partitive in:

Mies sanoi siellä ole|van poikia.
The man said that there were boys there.

Furthermore, the subject is not put into the genitive in PRs built with a clause containing an indefinite verb form. Consider the partitive subject **sukunim|i|ä** 'surnames' in:

Sukunim|i|ä katsotaan *esiinty|neen* Italiassa ja Ranskassa 700-luvulta.
In Italy and France, surnames are viewed as *having arisen* in the eighth century.

The second hiccup concerns intransitive verbs like **tuntu-** and **näyttä-** 'seems', and **kuulu-** 'is said to be', which are also commonly used in this way. In PRs made with these verbs, the subject is the same in both clauses but no possessive suffix is used. Examples:

Aurinko tuntui paista|van vielä kuumemmin.
The sun seemed to be shining even more hotly.

Täti kuuluu ole|van sairaana.
Auntie is said to be ill.

Exercise 2 Translate into Finnish, using PRs:

1 I heard them leave.
2 He saw the train arrive.
3 She said she would come back tomorrow.
4 I hope I will meet him again.
5 He seemed to know who they were.

Exercise 3 You will encounter PRs most often in more formal, especially written, varieties of Finnish. Being able to decode them is more important than being able to form them yourself, so practise by seeing whether you can understand these PRs (if you're stuck, translations are at the back of this book, as usual).

1 Mä näin sen vaihtavan väriä.
2 Maton alla tuntui olevan jotain.
3 Minä kiellän tietäväni mitään.
4 Haluan teidän pyytävän anteeksi.
5 Hän arveli ruoan olevan valmiina.

Dialogue 3 ▣

Juhannus

Midsummer Day

Eeva and Kaarina discuss their plans for spending Midsummer Day

EEVA: Mitä sä meinaat tehdä juhannuksena?
KAARINA: Mä meen mökille niin ku aina.
EEVA: Missä teidän mökki on?
KAARINA: Sipoon saaristossa. Mitäs sä meinaat tehdä?
EEVA: Mä en oo ihan varma. Me ollaan yleensä Mikon kanssa menty Seurasaareen kattoo sitä perinteistä juhannuskokkoa, mut tänä vuonna ajateltiin tehdä jotain muuta!
KAARINA: No kerro mitä.
EEVA: Kun on kerran juhannus[1] niin ajateltiin, että kerran on koettava[2] juhannuksena lavatanssit.
KAARINA: Ai niinku vanhoissa Suomifilmeissä.
EEVA: Just niin, ja sit me ajateltiin yöpyä teltassa jollain leirintäalueella.[3]
KAARINA: Kuulostaa tosi kivalta!

1 **Kun on kerran juhannus** 'seeing that it's Midsummer Day'

2 **koettava** 'has to be experienced'. More on this form in Unit 13.

3 **jollain leirintäalueella** 'at some campground'

Vocabulary

alueQ	area, zone	**kokko**	bonfire
juhannus *kse*	Midsummer Day	**kuulosta-**	sounds
just → **juuri**	just, precisely	**lavatanssi**|**t**	platform dancing
kattoo → **kattoon**		**leirintä**	camping
→ **katsomaan**		**meinaX-**	intends, means
kerra|**n**	(for) once	**Suomifilmi**|**t**	Finn Films
kerro	imperative of	**teltta**	tent
	kerto- 'tells'	**yöpy-**	spends night

Language points

Linking clauses, 2: 'After having X'd' and 'in order to X'

In colloquial Finnish, the usual way to link such clauses is with conjunctions. For example, you say 'after' with simple **kun** 'when' or the more explicit **sen jälkeen kun**:

(Sen jälkeen) kun mä pääsin työstä mä menin kotiin.
After I got out of work, I went home.

and you say 'in order to' with **jotta**, often with the conditional, as in:

Lapsen pitäisi käydä ruotsinkielistä koulua, *jotta saisi* hyvän ruotsin taidon.
The child should attend Swedish-language school, *so that it might acquire* a good knowledge of Swedish.

In more formal Finnish there are verbal constructions which allow both verbs to be squeezed into the same clause. For 'after', you put the verb into the partitive of its past passive participle (Unit 7); if the subject is a noun, it goes into the genitive:

Peka|**n lähde**|**tty**|**ä tö**|**i**|**hin minä soitin Irma**|**lle.**
After Pekka left for work, I rang Irma.

If the subject is a pronoun, it is added as a possessive suffix to the end of the past passive participle form:

Pääs|**ty**|**ä**|**ni töistä mä menin kotiin.**
After I got out of work, I went home.

Pääs|ty|ä|än töistä Pekka meni kotiin.
After he (= Pekka) got out of work, Pekka went home.

As always, **häne|n** or **se|n** is used if the subjects refer to different actors:

Hänen pääs|ty|ä|än töistä hän meni kotiin.
After he (e.g. Pekka) got out of work, he (= someone other than Pekka, e.g. Juuso) went home.

For '(in order) to', a special form of the first infinitive is used; this form resembles the first infinitive in every way except that it ends not in **Q**, but in **KSE** plus the appropriate possessive suffix. This construction is used only if both verbs have the same subject. Examples:

Hän katsoi ikkunasta näh|däkse|en satoiko.
(S)he looked out the window (in order) to see whether it was raining.

Hän meni naimisiin saa|dakse|en rahaa.
(S)he got married in order to acquire money.

Poika on liian nuori men|näkse|en naimisiin.
The boy is too young to get married.

Hän avasi suunsa osoitta|akse|en haluavansa sanoa jotain.
He opened his mouth to show that he wanted to say something.

Notice that the last example includes an example of a PR, as well (**osoittaa haluavansa**).

Exercise 4 Have a look at these rather formal Finnish sentences, making sure you can recognize and decode the verbal constructions. English equivalents are given at the end of this book.

1 Levättyään hetken hän nousi istumaan.
2 Heti hänen sanottuaan sen minä ymmärsin.
3 Mä tein sen jotain tehdäkseni.
4 Minun täytyy lähteä kaupunkiin saadakseni asian toimeen.
5 Me emme ole täällä tutustuaksemme ihmisiin.

Dialogue 4 ▣

Ravintola

Going to restaurants

This dialogue is in two parts. In the first part, Tomi wants to go with Sari to a restaurant, so he discusses options with his friend Pasi. In the second part we hear Tomi and Sari ordering their dishes at the restaurant

Ravintolaan

TOMI:	Mä oon menossa Sarin kanssa tänään ulos. Mä tarttisin vähän ideoita mihin me voitas mennä.
PASI:	Ai, sä oot nyt viimeinkin pyytäny Sarin ulos. Tehän voisitte mennä siihen uuteen Cafe Barockiin Fredalle (Fredrikinkadulle), mä oon kuullu et sen pitäis olla OK paikka.
TOMI:	Ootsä käyny Planet Hollywoodissa, siinä Renny Harlinin paikassa?
PASI:	Joo mut se on enemmän hampurilaispaikka ja disko. Sinne voitte mennä ku ootte syöny. Torni on kans uusittu, jos haluutte kolkytluvun nostalgiaa.
TOMI:	Mä olin kyllä ajatellu vähän jotain rauhallista paikkaa. Kruunuhaassa pitäis olla kans hyvä paikka.
PASI:	Sitte voitte tulla Häppäriin sen jälkeen. Mä, Kati ja Iira ollaan menossa sinne.
TOMI:	No katotaan. Se riippuu vähän Sarista.

Ravintolassa

TARJOILIJA:	Oletteko valmiit tilaamaan?
TOMI:	Joo. Mä ottaisin alkupaloiksi ton katkarapukoktailin ja sit lammasta mokkakastikkeessa.
SARI:	Mulle ensiks mätiä, paahtoleipää ja basilikakastiketta ja sitte tota ankkaa mandariinikastikkeessa.
TARJOILIJA:	Kiitos. Ja mitä saisi olla juotavaksi?[1]
TOMI:	Pullo mineraalivettä ja sitten talon punaviiniä karahvissa.
TARJOILIJA:	Puolikas vai kokonainen?
TOMI:	Kokonainen.

1 **juo|tava|ksi** 'for drinking, to be drunk'.

Vocabulary

ajatel|lu →	
ajatel|lut	
alku|pala	starter
ankka	(domesticated) duck
basilika	basil
disko	disco
ensi|ks	for starters, first of all
haluu|tte →	
halua|tte	
hampurilainen	hamburger
karahvi	carafe
kastikkeQ	sauce
katka|rapu	prawn
katotaan →	let's see
katso|taan	
kokonainen	entire
koktail	cocktail
kolkyt|luku	the Thirties
Kruunuhaka	section of Helsinki east of the station and north of Esplanadi
kuullu →	
kuul|lut	

lampaX	lamb
mandariini	mandarin orange, tangerine
mäti	fish roe
mineraali|vesi	mineral water
mokka	mocha (coffee) flavour
nostalgia	nostalgia
ottasin →	
otta|isi|n	
paahto|leipä	toast
puolikkaX	half-sized
rauhallinen	peaceful
ravintola	restaurant
riippu-	depends
tarjoilija	waiter/waitress
tarttisin →	
tarvits|isi|n	
tilaX-	orders
ton → tuo|n	
tota → tuo|ta	
uusi|ttu	renovated
viimeinkin	at (long) last

Exercise 5 Make up your own short dialogue, in which people ask about dishes on a restaurant menu, then make up their minds and order.

Extra reading 1

A cafeteria menu

Try working out all the dishes on offer at this college cafeteria this week. Do you remember the names of the weekdays?

Ma

Chili tacot
Kanarisotto
Kalaleike
Kasvispihvit

Ti

Uunipaisti
Hernekeitto, laskiaispulla
Jauhelihapihvi
Kasvishernekeitto

Ke

Jauhelihapizza
Maksalaatikko
Herkkusieni-smetanakastike

To

Kreikkalainen salaatti
Aura-ananaslenkki
Unkarilainen uunikala
Kalakeitto
Punajuuri-perunavuoka

Pe

Nasi goreing
Lihamureke
Kuorrutettua kesäkurpitsaa ja
  tomaattia

Kaikenlaiset muutokset ovat
  mahdollisia.

Vocabulary

ananas *kse*	pineapple	**mahdollinen**	possible
Aura	a kind of blue cheese	**maksaǀlaatikko**	liver casserole
		murekkeQ	stuffing
herkku+	gourmet+	**muutos** *kse*	change, alteration
jauheQǀliha	mince		
kana	chicken	**pihvi**	steak
kastikkeQ	sauce	**punaǀjuuri** *e*	beet(root)
kasvis+	vegetarian	**salaatti**	lettuce
kesäǀkurpitsa	summer squash	**tomaatti**	tomato
kreikkalainen	Greek	**uuniǀkala**	baked fish
kuorrutettu	glazed	**uuniǀpaisti**	roast
leikkeQ	slice	**vuoka**	oven dish
lenkki	link (sausage)		

Extra reading 2

Tilaa suurelle perheelle tai edustuskayttöön

An advertisement for a share in a house

Maaseudulla 25 km Porvoosta meren läheisyydessä kolmen perheen talossa osake. Suuri olohuone yli 60 m². Tontti 1.56 ha. Rakennusvuosi 1968. Tontilla ollut ennen kylän koulu, siksi kaunis puutarha ja tilava vanha, suht. hyväkuntoinen ulko-rakennus: talli- ja verstastilaa. Rantaan vajaa puolitoista kilo-metriä. Venepaikkamahdollisuus tienhoitomaksua vastaan (n. 70 mk per vuosi). Öljykeskuslämmitys. Parkettilattia olohuoneessa. Avotakka. Sauna alakerrassa. Iso pihakenttä. Kestopäällystetie melkein perille. Nopea yhteys Helsingin moottoritielle. Hinta vielä toistaiseksi: 550000:- Lisätietoja sähköpostitse allekirjoitta-neelta.

Vocabulary

ala|kerta	lower floor	olo|huoneQ	living room
allekirjoitta|nu|	the undersigned	osakkeQ	share
avo|takka	open hearth	öljy	oil
edustus *kse*	agency	parketti|lattia	parquet floor
hyvä|kunto|inen	in good shape	per	per
käyttö	use (käyttä-'uses')	per|i|lle	as far as (one's) destination (here: all the way to the house)
keskus|lämmitys *kse*	central heating		
kesto	duration (kestä-'lasts')	piha|kenttä	field, yard
lisä|tieto|j|a	additional information	Porvoo	second-oldest town in Finland (after Turku), about 30 miles northeast of Helsinki
läheisyys *te*	proximity, neighbourhood		
maa|seutu	rural area		
mahdollisuus *te*	possibility		
maksu	fee, amount paid (maksa-)	puolitoista	one and a half
		puu|tarha	garden
moottori|tie	motorway	päällysteQ	paving, surfacing

siksi	therefore	**tontti**	lot, plot of land
suht: suhteellisen	relatively	**ulko|rakennus**	outbuilding
sähkö|posti|tse	via e-mail	*kse*	
talli	stable	**vajaa**	scant
tien|hoito	road maintenance	**X|TA vasta|an**	in return for X
tila|a	space, room	**vene|paikka**	place for a boat
tila|va	roomy, spacious	**verstaX**	workshop
toistaise|ksi	for now, temporarily	**yhteys** *te*	connection

13 Mikä laulaen tulee . . .

Easy come . . .

In this unit you will learn:

• how to talk about sightseeing, places to live, and music
• about expressing necessity
• more about linking verbs
• about the eight points of the compass
• some Finnish proverbs

Dialogue 1 ⚉

Ooppera

Opera

RITVA: Oletsä käyny jo Helsingin uudessa oopperatalossa?
LEEA: Joo. Me käytiin Olavin kanssa kuuntelemassa Verdin *Don Carlos* ku Matti Salminen oli laulamassa.
RITVA: Me ollaan nyt vasta menossa ensimmäistä kertaa Simon kanssa. Ajateltiin mennä kuuntelemaan Aulis Sallisen *Viimeisiä kiusauksia*.
LEEA: Se on kuulemma tosi suosittu. Me taas ollaan vähän ajateltu ostaa liput ensi kesän Savonlinnan ooppera-juhlille. Mitäs jos mentäs yhdessä?
RITVA: Mitä niillä on ohjelmistossa?
LEEA: Sallisen *Palatsi*, Wagnerin *Lentävä hollantilainen* ja *Tannhäuser*, Verdin *Macbeth* ja Marinski-teatterin esit-tämänä Tshaikovskin *Mazeppa*.
RITVA: *Palatsi* ja *Mazeppa* vois olla kiinnostavia. Mun täytyy puhua Simon kanssa. Mitä liput maksaa?

LEEA: Noin 200–500 (kakssataa viissataa) markkaa paikoista riip-
puen.

Vocabulary

esittälmälnä	as presented by	**ohjelmisto**	programme
hollantilainen	Dutch(man)	**ooppera**	opera
kiinnostalva	interesting	**palatsi**	palace
kiusaus *kse*	temptation	**riippulen**	depending
kuulemma	they say; I hear;	**suosilttu**	favoured
	allegedly	**teatteri**	theatre
laula-	sings	**vasta**	not before; only
lentälvä	flying		(now)
mentäs →		**viimeinen**	last
menltäisiin			

Exercise 1 Write your own dialogue about your own and others'
interest in music. You'll find the following vocabulary useful:

musiikki	music	**ohjelma**	programme
muusikko	musician	**romppu**	CD-ROM
konsertti	concert	**kasetti**	cassette
bändi	(rock) band	**äänilevy**	record
orkesteri	orchestra		
laulalja	singer	**sopraano**	soprano
säveltäljä	composer	**altto**	alto
sävellys *kse*	composition	**tenori**	tenor
sävel	melody (**sävele-**)	**baritoni**	baritone
kriitikko	critic	**basso**	bass
soitin	instrument	**näyttele-**	acts (on stage)
	(**soittime-**)	**molli**	minor
kuoro	choir	**duuri**	major
laullu	song	**asteikko**	scale
laula-	sings		
suosilttu	popular	**melu**	noise
klassillinen	classical	**jatsi**	jazz
barokki	baroque	**viulu**	violin
moderni	modern	**urult**	organ (**urku-**)
alkulsoitto	overture		

Dialogue 2 ▣

Nähtävyydet

Seeing the sights

In their hotel room, Liz and Nick pore over the tourist brochure and try to decide what to see next in Helsinki

NICK: Mitä museoita siinä esitteessä suositellaan?
LIZ: Kansallismuseo Mannerheimintiellä antaa hyvän yleiskuvan Suomen historiasta, kansasta ja kulttuurista. Ateneumissa on monta eri näyttelyä. Siellä on taidetta 1700-luvulta aina nykytaiteeseen asti.[1]
NICK: Entäs kotimuseoita?
LIZ: Täällä näyttää olevan Marsalkka Mannerheimin kotimuseo, presidentti Urho Kekkosen museo Tamminiemessä ja Suomen kansallistaiteilijan Akseli Gallen-Kallelan Museo Tarvaspäässä Espoossa.
NICK: Mennään huomenna sinne Tarvaspäähän. Tänään voitas mennä sinne Kansallismuseoon. Eiks Eduskuntatalo ja Finlandiatalo oo kans Mannerheimintiellä?
LIZ: Joo. Hyvä idea. Eduskuntatalossa onkin opastettuja kierroksia just lauantaisin ja sunnuntaisin.
NICK: Entä se kallioon rakennettu kirkko.[2]
LIZ: Temppeliaukion kirkko.
NICK: Just se. Se on kyllä kans nähtävä.
LIZ: Katotaan jos ehditään nähdä sekin tänään.

1 **aina nykytaiteeseen asti** 'right up to contemporary art'.

2 **kalliolon rakenneIttu kirkko** 'church (which has been) built into a cliff'.

Vocabulary

Ateneum	(art gallery opposite the National Theatre)	**Espoo**	Finland's second largest city located west of Helsinki
Eduskuntatalo	Parliament (building)	**Finlandiatalo**	Finlandia Hall
ehti-	has enough time (to X)	**kallio**	cliff
		Kansallismuseo	National Museum
esitteQ	brochure	**kansa**	nation

kierros *kse*	tour, turn	opastettu	guided
kulttuurinen	cultural	suosittele-	favours, supports
marsalkka	field-marshall	taiteQ	art
nyky	contemporary	taiteililja	artist
nähltävä	must/should be seen	voitas →	
näyttä-	shows; appears	voiltaisiin	
näyttely	exhibition	yleislkuva	overall picture

Exercise 2 Decode these signs from in front of some museums in order to answer the questions.

Käsityömuseo
Ma-pe 11–17, la 11–15

Kansallismuseo
ti-la 11–15, ti myös 18–21, su 11–16.

Tuomarinkylän museo
su-pe 12–16, to 12–20, la suljettu

Sinebrychoffin taidemuseo
ke 9–20, to-la 9–17, su
11–17, opastukset su 15

Didrichsenin taidemuseo
su ja ke 14–16

1 When is the National Museum open?
2 Which museums aren't open on Saturdays?
3 Are there any guided tours of art museums on Sundays?
4 Can you visit the Handcrafts Museum at weekends? When?

Exercise 3 Translate into Finnish:

1 Let's go to Finlandia Hall tomorrow.
2 Is it open Tuesdays?
3 That's a must-see (nähtävä), I suppose.
4 What museum do you (polite) recommend?
5 I don't know whether I'll have time to see that as well.

Language points

More on linking verbs: expressing simultaneity and manner

Expressing simultaneity

In this construction, one verb refers to an action simultaneous with that of another. Colloquial Finnish has **samalan aikalan kun** 'at the same time as', and **silllä aikala kun** 'while': **Se oli Lontoossa samaan**

aikaan kun minä '(S)he was in London at the same time as I (was).'
More formal Finnish uses the inessive of the second infinitive:

Hänen tul|le|ssa|an takaisin minä olin töissä.
When (s)he came back I was at work.

The second infinitive is identical in form with the first infinitive,
with two exceptions: instead of **A**, it has **e**; and instead of ending
in **Q**, it takes the inessive **-ssA** (as here, to express simultaneity)
or **-n** (to express manner; see below). Compare these forms (all
second infinitives in the first person singular inessive):

	Class I	Class II	Class III	Class IV
	to give	to need	to come	to get
first inf.	**anta|a**	**tarvi|ta**	**tul|la**	**saa|da**
second inf.	**anta|e|ssa|ni**	**tarvi|te|ssa|ni**	**tul|le|ssa|ni**	**saa|de|ssa|ni**
when I	give/gave	need(ed)	come/came	get/got

The inessive form of the second infinitive normally occurs with
either a person suffix (like **-ni** here) or, if the subject is spelled out,
with that noun in the genitive:

Liisa|n nukku|e|ssa minä menin ulos.
While Liisa was sleeping, I went outside.

Expressing manner

This is roughly the equivalent of 'singing' in '(S)he went home
singing.' The form is the second infinitive with the suffix **-n**:

Hän meni kotiin laula|e|n.
Colloquial: *Se lauloi, kun se meni kotiin.*

In colloquial Finnish, this form is frequent only in fixed expressions
such as time expressions built with **lähte-** 'departs' and **alka-**
'begins', e.g. **60-luvun alusta lähtien** 'since the beginning of the
sixties' (notice e>i), **viime syksystä alkaen** 'since last Autumn'.

In more formal Finnish, the second infinitive with this **-n** is also
used to indicate concomitant action on the part of someone else;
this second actor is then put into the genitive. Example:

Tämä otetaan käyttöön vain tarpee|n tullen.
This is used only if the need arises.

A construction with the opposite meaning is mentioned at Unit 6
(abessive of the third infinitive).

Dialogue 3 🔲

Asuminen

A place to live

In the street, Harri runs into Rasse, an acquaintance he's not seen in a while, and does some quick catching-up

Kadulla

HARRI: (*huutaa*) Hei Rasse oota vähän!

RASSE: Moi Harri!

HARRI: Sua ei ookkaan näkyny[1] vähään aikaan.

RASSE: No me ollaan muutettu ja se on vieny tosi paljon aikaa. Kämppä piti ensin remontoida.

HARRI: Mihin te otte muuttaneet?

RASSE: Ostettiin Tapiolasta kaksio.

HARRI: Ai, mistä sieltä?

RASSE: Tietsä ne Otsonkallion kerrostalot, sieltä.

HARRI: Mun täti asuu omakotitalossa Otsolahdessa. Viihdyttekste Tapiolassa?

RASSE: Joo, kämppä on vähän pieni, mut toimiva. Kunhan tässä säästetään muutama vuosi niin sitten me kyllä ostetaan oma rivitaloasunto, jossa on piha, nyt meillä on vain partsi.

HARRI: Mulla ei taida[2] nyt sitte olla sun uutta puhelinnumeroa?

RASSE: Kuule, mun on nyt juostava bussille, mut mä soitan sulle. Jos vaikka[3] tulisitte Emman kanssa käymään ens viikon-loppuna.

HARRI: No soittele, moi.

RASSE: Moi!

1 **Sula ei ookkaan näkyny**: roughly 'Haven't seen much of you', a little more liter-ally: 'Not much of you has been seen'; note the use of partitive in the subject.

2 **Mulla ei taida ... olla** 'I must not have'.

3 **vaikka** used here, as so often, to introduce a suggestion or an alternative.

Vocabulary

asu|minen	living (somewhere)	**juos|tava**	present passive
asunto	flat; apartment		participle of
huuta-	shouts		**juokse-** 'runs'

kaksio	two-room flat	**partsi** →	balcony
kerrostalo⎮t	block of flats;	**parvekkeQ**	
	apartment	**piha**	yard, garden
	building	**remontoi-**	does repair work
kämppä → **asunto**		**rivi⎮talo⎮asunto**	flat/house in a
muutta-	changes, moves		terrace
	house	**soittele-**	gives a ring,
näky⎮ny →			phones
näkynyt		**säästä-**	saves
oma	(one's) own	**Tapiola**	(placename)
oma⎮koti⎮talo	detached house	**tietsä** → **tiedä⎮t⎮sä**	
ookkaan →		**toimi⎮va**	present active
olekkaan			participle of
oota → **odota⎮Q**			**toimi-** 'works,
ootte → **olette**			is functional'
Otsolahi	(placename)	**vieny** → **vienyt**	
Otsonkallio	(placename)	**viihdyttekste** → **viihdyt⎮tte⎮kö te**	

Language points

More on necessity

Back in Unit 10, you learned how to express necessity with modal contructions, as in **Minu⎮n pitä⎮ä lähte⎮ä** 'I must leave.' Necessity may also be expressed with the present passive participle, e.g. **Häne⎮n on men⎮tävä nyt** '(S)he has to go now.' This section shows you how to build and use this form.

In form, the present passive participle is like the past passive participle, but with final **AvA** instead of **U**. Compare the following form-pairs: the first form is the past passive participle, the second is the present passive participle:

stem:	**aja-**	**osaX-**	**mene-**	**vie-**
past passive particle	**aje⎮ttu**	**pala⎮ttu**	**men⎮ty**	**vie⎮ty**
present passive particle	**aje⎮ttava**	**pala⎮ttava**	**men⎮tävä**	**vie⎮tävä**

Here are some examples of the present passive participle in action. As in sentences of the **minun täytyy** type, the actor is put in the genitive. The actor need not be mentioned explicitly, however; the best English equivalent is then quite often a passive sentence.

Sinu\n on ratkais\tava, **lähdetkö vai et.**
You must decide whether you're going or not.

Mu\n on kirjoite\ttava **sille heti.**
I must write to him/her at once.

Se\n on pala\ttava **kotiin pariksi viikoksi.**
(S)he has to return home for a few weeks.

Mei\dän on anne\ttava **ruokaa kahdelletoista lapselle.**
We have to give food to twelve children.

Nii\den on löyde\ttävä **hänet.**
They must find him/her.

Mu\n oli lue\ttava **tenttiin.**
I had to read for an exam.

Mu\n on makse\ttava **vuokra.**
I have to pay the rent.

Vuokra on makse\ttava **kuukauden kymmenenteen päivään**
mennessä.
One must pay the rent by the tenth of the month. (= The rent
must be paid by the tenth of the month.)

As usual, you can mitigate the necessity by using the conditional,
e.g. **Mu\n olisi makse\ttava vuokra** 'I ought to pay the rent.'

Dialogue 4

Ilmansuunnat

The eight points of the compass

Kadulla
TUULA: Kylläpä tänään tuulee kovaa ja kylmästi.
SATU: Pohjoistuuli on aina jäätävä. Säätiedotuksessa ne kyllä lupas
heikkoa idänpuoleista tuulta ja vaihtelevaa pilvisyyttä.
TUULA: No ei se ole ensimmäinen kerta kun säätiedotus on
väärässä. Tänään varmaan rupee satamaankin.
SATU: Syksyt on niin pitkiä. Huvittais tosi paljon lähteä etelän
lämpöön ja auringon paisteeseen.
TUULA: Mun isoisä on aina sanonut että lounaistuuli tuo
tullessaan lämpimän ilman.

SATU: No se on kesällä. Talvella ei varmaan väliä tuuleeko koillisesta, kaakosta tai lounaasta, kylmä on kuitenki. En yhtään ihmettelis, jos vaikka tänään tulis räntäkuuroja.

TUULA: Älä nyt oo niin negatiivinen. Voihan se poutaakin pitää tänään.

SATU: Länsirannikolle ne kyllä tais luvata hyvää säätä.

TUULA: Merellä tuulee kuiteskin kohtalaisesti aina, satoi tai paistoi.

SATU: Elämä olis varmaan vähän ykstoikkosta jos aina aurinko paistais.

TUULA: Enpä tiedä!

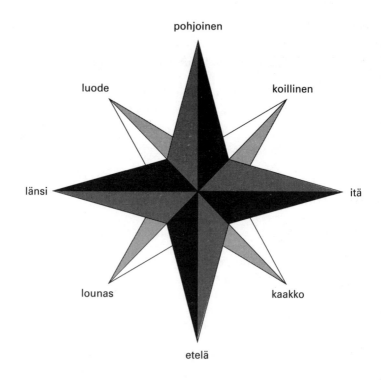

Vocabulary

aurinko	sun	lämpimä|n	sG of **lämmin**
elä|mä	life		'warm'
etelä	south	lämpö	warmth, heat
heikko	weak	länsi *te*	west
huvitta-	it amuses, causes	meri *e*	sP **mer|ta**! 'sea'
	one to have fun	negatiivinen	negative
idän|puoleinen	from the east,	paista-	shines
	easterly	paisteQ	shine, glare
ihmettele-	is surprised,	pilvisyys *te*	cloudiness
	wonders	pohjois+	north(ern)
ilman|suunna|t	the points of the	pouta	fair weather
	compass	rannikko	shore, coast
iso|isä	grandfather	rupeX-	starts, begins
jäätävä	icy	räntä	hail
kaakko	southeast	sata-	rains
kohtalainen	moderate, medium	sää	weather
koillinen	northeast	tais → taisi	
kova|a	hard, fast (adv.)	(stem: **taita**-)	
kuitenki(n)	anyway	tiedotus *kse*	report
kuiteski(n)	anyway	tul|le|ssa|an	when it comes
kuuro	(rain)shower	tuule-	(the wind) blows
lounais|	southwest(ern)	tuuli *e*	wind
lounaX	southwest	vaihtele-	varies
luoteQ	northwest	väärä|ssä	in the wrong;
lupas → lupasi			incorrect
(stem: **lupaX**-)		yhtään	at all
lupaX-	promises	ykstoikkoinen	monotonous

Dialogue 5 📼

Sananlaskuja

Finnish proverbs

Kirsi explains some Finnish proverbs to Paul

PAUL: Musta ois hauska oppia joitakin suomalaisia sananlaskuja.
Tiedät sä yhtään?

KIRSI: No en mä nyt ole kovin hyvä niissä, mutta kyllä mä joitakin

tiedän. Anna kun mietin vähän. *(Hän miettii.)* No
esimerkiks tää:
    Muu maa mustikka
    Oma maa mansikka.

PAUL: Mitä se oikein tarkoittaa?

KIRSI: No jotain semmosta, että oma maa on aina paras maa. On mulla joitain muitakin mielessä. Musta sananlasku 'Se koira älähtää, johon kalikka kalahtaa' on aina osuva. Se tarkottaa sitä, että se joka on syyllinen johonkin, tavallisesti puolustaa itseään äänekkäästi ja yrittää todistaa ettei oo syyllinen.

PAUL: Noi on tosi hyviä. Muistatko vielä muita?

KIRSI: Mitä sä pidät tästä: 'Hullu paljon työtä tekee, viisas selviää vähemmällä.'

PAUL: Mä taidan tietää mitä se tarkoittaa. Luultavasti sitä, että on paras ajatella kunnolla miten joku juttu kannattaa tehdä, ettei joudu tekeen turhaa työtä.

KIRSI: Just niin. On hyvä muistaa myös tätä: 'Joka[1] toiselle kuoppaa kaivaa, se itse siihen lankeaa.'

PAUL: Se onkin hyvä neuvo!

1 **joka** '(s)he who'.

Vocabulary

hullu	fool, crazy, madman	**mietti-**	thinks over, ponders
itse|ä|än	him/herself sP	**mustikka**	whortleberry
joutu-	winds up, ends up	**neuvo**	advice, counsel; council
just = juuri	just		
kaiva-	digs	**oppi-**	learns
kalahta-	clips, claps	**osu|va**	telling (**osu-** 'hits the mark')
kalikka	stick		
kannatta-	is worth while	**puolusta-**	defends
kovin	very, quite	**sanan|lasku**	proverb
kunno|lla	properly	**selviäX-: selviyty-**	manages, comes through OK
kuoppa	pit, hole in the ground		
lankeX-	falls, tumbles	**semmos|ta →**	
luultavasti	probably	**semmois|ta**[1]	
mansikka	strawberry	**= sellais|ta**	
miele|ssä	in mind	**syyllinen**	guilty

tarkotta- →	means, purports	**turha**	useless, vain
tarkoitta-		**viisaX**	wise
tavallisesti	usually	**vähelmmällä**	with less
tekeen →		**yrittä-**	tries
tekemään		**älähtä-**	yelps
todista-	proves	**äänelkkäX**	vociferous

1 Pronunciation note: in colloquial contexts, the **i** final in any diphthong after the first syllable is liable to be dropped, unless the form is a superlative. Thus we have **sano** for **sanoi**, **auttas** for **auttaisi**, and (here) **semmosta** for **semmoista**.

Language points

The present active participle, =vA; participle overview

You have already met the present participle in connection with PRs (Unit 12). In that construction the participle is in the genitive, i.e. its shape is **-vAln**.

But the present participle, like all participles in Finnish, is a full-fledged adjective with a full paradigm of case forms. So a present active participle like **osaalva** 'knowing, who knows' is put into whatever case the rest of the sentence requires, for example the adessive, as in:

> **Hän antoi vihkon suomea osaalvalle ranskalaiselle lehtimiehelle.**
> (S)he gave the notebook to a French journalist who knows/knew Finnish.

On the other hand, the present participle (like all participles) is also a verb, so it can take direct objects (like **suomea** in the example above) and other complements, such as **Ranskalan** 'to France' in:

> **Hän antoi vihkon *Ranskalan lähtelvälle* lehtimiehelle.**
> (S)he gave the notebook to a journalist *who was leaving for France.*

Contrast the following sentence, with the *past* active participle indicating priorness:

> **Hän sai vihkon Ranskalan *lähtelneeltä* lehtimieheltä.**
> (S)he got the notebook from a journalist *who had left* for France.

The English, and for that matter, the colloquial Finnish equivalent of such rather bookish constructions will usually be a clause introduced by a relative pronoun. Thus **Suomesta puhuva nainen** (in less bookish Finnish, **nainen, joka puhuu Suomesta**) is 'a woman who is talking about Finland', and **vaikeita aikoja kokeneita ihmisiä** (= **ihmisiä, jotka on kokeneet vaikeita aikoja**) is 'people who have lived through difficult times'.

> **Ei minulla ole ollut mainittavia ongelmia.**
> I haven't had any problems worth mentioning.

Exercise 4 Unwind these noun phrases by using the relative pronouns **jolka** (or **mikä**).

Example: **vuonna 1955 solmitulla sopimuksella** > **sopimuksella, joka solmittiin vuonna 1955**

1 Saarenmaalla syntynyt lapsi
2 saarta koskeva laki
3 dokumentti (documentary) sata metriä maan alle rakennetusta kaupungista
4 neljännen peräkkäisen mestaruutensa ottanut helsinkiläinen

Additional reading

Sananlaskuja

Finnish proverbs

Here are some more Finnish proverbs for you to have a go at decoding. There's a vocabulary list at the end to help you with the more unusual words and forms; the rest you'll find in the vocabulary at the back of this book. (Also see the Key to Exercises section.)

1 Parempi pyy pivossa kuin kymmenen oksalla.
2 Sanasta miestä, sarvesta härkää.
3 Pata kattilaa soimaa, musta kylki kummallakin.
4 Ei vara venettä kaada.
5 Auta miestä mäessä älä mäen alla.
6 Meni ojasta allikkoon.
7 Se parhaiten nauraa joka viimeksi nauraa.
8 Puhuminen hopeaa, vaikeneminen kultaa.
9 Aamun torkku, illan virkku, se tapa talon hävittää.

10 Mies tulee räkänokastakin, vaan ei tyhjän naurajasta.
11 Kun nokka nousee niin pyrstö tarttuu.
12 Mikä laulaen tulee, se viheltäen menee.

Vocabulary

aamuln torkku	drowsiness in the morning	**pata**	pot
allikko	pool, puddle	**pivo**	(hollow of the) hand
hopea	silver	**pyrstö**	(bird's, fish's) tail
härkä	ox	**pyy**	hazel grouse
hävittä-	ruins, destroys	**räkä**	snot
kaata-	overturns, pours	**sana**	word
kattila	kettle	**sarvi** e	(animal's) horn
kulta	gold	**soimaX-**	reproves, upbraids
kylki e	side		
laulalen	singing	**tarttu-**	gets stuck
naura-	laughs	**tyhjä**	empty
nauralja	one who laughs	**vaikeXE-**	is silent
nokka	bill, beak; nose; prow	**vara**	reserve, spare; foresight
nouse-	rises	**viheltälen**	whistling
oja	ditch	**virkku**	liveliness
oksa	branch, bough		

14 Karhut voi kai olla vaarallisiakin

Bears can be dangerous, I suppose

In this unit you will:

- learn more about Finnish geography, real and fanciful
- learn animal and winter-sports vocabulary
- learn about verbs of motion
- revise the uses of the genitive
- learn new ways of being vague

Dialogue 1 ⚏

Läänit

The administrative districts of Finland

Listen in as Joonas and Orvokki talk about their families' backgrounds

JOONAS: Onks teidän suvussa tehty sukututkimusta?
Orvokki: No ei oikeestaan. Onks sun?
JOONAS: Joo, vähäsen.
Orvokki: Mistä päin sun vanhempas on kotoisin?
JOONAS: Äidin suku tulee pohjoisesta. Mun äiti on syntynyt Kuhmossa, mut paljon sukua on myös Oulussa. Se suku on pysytellyt jokseenkin Oulun läänin sisällä.
Orvokki: Mistä sun isäs suku on kotoisin?
JOONAS: Vaasan läänistä Pietarsaaresta. Mistä sun vanhemmat on kotoisin?

Orvokki: Isän suku on Karjalaisia Viipurista. Mun Isä on syntynyt Lappeenrannassa Kymen läänistä.
Joonas: Onks sun äitis kans sieltä päin?
Orvokki: Ei. Äiti on Turun- ja Porin läänistä, Naantalista.
Joonas: Ootsä sitte uusmaalainen?
Orvokki: Niin monet luulee, ku mä oon asunu jo niin kauan Espoossa, mut mä oon syntynyt Tampereella Hämeessä.
Joonas: Tapasko sun vanhempas Tampereella?
Orvokki: Joo. Ne molemmat opiskeli Tampereen yliopistossa.

Vocabulary

jokseenkin	somewhat	**HämeQ**	region of (south-
kauan	for a long time		west) Finland
lääni	administrative	**Karjalainen**	Karelian
	province	**Kuhmo**	
mone|t	many	**Kymi** e	
oikeestaan →	really	**Lappeenranta**	city in southeast
oikeastaan			Finland
opiskele-	studies	**Naantali**	city south of Turku
pysyttele-	stays, remains	**Oulu**	
päin	abouts	**Pietarsaari**	
sisä|llä	inside	**Pori**	
suku|tutkimus	genealogy	**TampereQ**	
synty-	is born	**uusmaalainen**	someone from the
tapaX-	meets		Uusimaa region
vanhemma|t	parents	**Vaasa**	
		Viipuri	

Suome|n lääni|t
Lapin lääni
Oulun lääni
Vaasan lääni
Kuopion lääni
Pohjoi-Karjalan lääni
Keski-Suomen lääni

Mikkelin lääni
Hämeen lääni
Turun-ja Porin lääni
Uudenmaan lääni
Kymen lääni

(Ahvenanmaa (Åland) on maakunta 'province'.)

Exercise 1 Write out Finnish translations for the following English sentences by raiding the dialogue above. (You may have to change or omit a word here and there.)

1 Where are your mother's people from?
2 That's what a lot of people think.
3 They both studied at the University of Jyväskylä.
4 I've a lot of relatives in Oulu, as well.
5 Is your father also from there?

Dialogue 2 ◘◘

Suomalaisia eläimiä

Finnish fauna

Are there polar bears in Finland? Paula allays some of Greg's apprehension about Finnish wildlife

GREG: Kuule Paula, eihän se pidä paikkaansa, että Suomessa olisi jääkarhuja?
PAULA: No ei tosiaankaan. Se on vaan sellanen myytti Suomesta ulkomailla. Jääkarhuja täällä ei todellakaan kulje kaduilla. Ainut paikka, jossa voi niitä nähdä on eläintarhassa.
GREG: Karhuja täällä nyt kuitenkin on?
PAULA: On, jonkin verran. Mäkin oon nähny yhden kerran karhun marjareissulla. Säikähdin tosi paljon, mut onneks se vaan tuijotti mua vähän aikaa, ja käänty sitten pois.
GREG: Karhut voi kai olla vaarallisiakin?
PAULA: Joo, mut ne käy harvoin ihmisten kimppuun. Ihan viime aikoina on ollu joitakin tapauksia, että sudet on hyökänny karjan kimppuun ja aiheuttaneet suuria vahinkoja.
GREG: Onks Suomessa muitakin petoeläimiä?
PAULA: On meillä ilveksiä ja ahmoja, mut ne on kyllä aika harvinaisia. Yleisimpiä metsäneläimiä Suomessa on hirvet, peurat ja jänikset. Lapissa pidetään paljon poroja elinkeinona, mut ne on samalla tavalla vapaana luonnossa ku hirvetki.
GREG: No hyvä. Nyt mä voinki valistaa ihmisiä kotipuolessa, että Suomi ei olekaan ihan mikään villi Pohjola, vaikka täällä onki paljon mielenkiintoisia eläimiä.

Vocabulary

ahma	wolverine	**peto|eläin**	beast of prey
aiheutta-	causes	**peura**	wild reindeer
ainut	sole, only	**pitä|ä paikka|nsa**	is correct
ei todellakaan	not really	**Pohjola**	the north; ultima
elin|keino	means of survival		Thule
eläin *ime*	animal	**poro**	domesticated
eläin|tarha	zoo		reindeer
harvinainen	rare	**sellanen** →	
harvoin	rarely	**sellainen**	
hirvi *e*	deer	**susi** *te*	wolf
hyökkäX-	attacks	**säikähtä-**	is startled,
ilves *kse*	lynx		alarmed
jänis *kse*	hare	**tapaus** *kse*	case
jää|karhu	polar bear	**tuijotta-**	stares
karhu	bear	**ulkomailla**	abroad
karja	cattle	**vaarallinen**	dangerous
kotipuolessa	back home	**vahinko**	damage; pity
kulje|Q: kulke-	goes	**valista-**	enlighten
käy- kimppu|un	attacks	**X|n verran**	to X extent;
luonto	nature	**jonkin verran**	'to some extent'
marja|reissu	berry-hunting	**villi**	wild
	expedition	**yleinen**	general,
mielenkiintoinen	interesting		widespread
myytti	myth		

Exercise 2 Arrange the following zoological vocabulary according to size of the animal, from the largest down to the smallest:

hiiri   hirvi   susi   mikrobi   kissa   karhu

Exercise 3 Sort according to wild/tame:

poro   ankka   kissa   peura   karja   koira   ilves

Dialogue 3

Talviurheilua

Winter sports

Karsten and Juhani enthuse over the variety of Finnish Winter sports

KARSTEN: Suomen talvi on kyllä ihana, ku on niin paljon lunta, että voi hyvin hiihtää metsässäkin.

JUHANI: Sähän alat kuulostaa ihan suomalaiselta, ku pidät niin kovasti hiihdosta.

KARSTEN: Niin, enpä olis uskonu[1] pari vuotta sitten, että hiihto tulee mulle intohimoksi.

JUHANI: Suomalaisten suosituin talviurheilu on varmaan hiihto. *(He picks up a leaflet.)* Hei, tässä lukee, että sillä on *(he reads)* 'pitkät perinteet. Ennen vanhaan sukset olivat tärkeä liikkumaväline talvella. Nyt juuri kukaan ei käytä niitä siihen tarkoitukseen, vaan lähinnä harrastusmielessä. Hiihtoa pidetään yhtenä parhaimmista liikuntamuodoista, koska se vahvistaa niin monia eri lihaksia.' No niin.

KARSTEN: Suomalaisethan on aina pärjänneet hyvin hiihtokilpailuissa.

JUHANI: Niin on, ja samoin mäkihypyssä. Niitä voi pitää suomalaisten parhaina talviurheilulajeina.

KARSTEN: Onhan sitte vielä jääkiekko. Suomihan voitti maailmanmestaruuden tänä vuonna (1995).

JUHANI: Sähän alat tuntea Suomea paremmin ku mä. Se maailmanmestaruus on kyllä tosi tärkee suomalaisille.

1 enpä olis(i) uskonu(t) 'I really wouldn't have believed'.

Vocabulary

ennen vanhaan	long ago	**kovasti**	very much, a lot
eri	different, diverse	**kuulosta-**	sounds
harrastus|miele|ssä	as a hobby	**lihas** *kse*	muscle
hiihtä-	skis	**liikkuma|**	means of getting
ihana	lovely	**väline**Q	about
into|himo	passion	**liikunta|muoto**	form of exercise
jää|kiekko	ice hockey	**lähin|nä**	primarily

mestaruus *te*	championship,	**talviurheilu**	Winter sport
	mastery	**tarkoitus** *kse*	purpose
mäki|hyppy	skijump	**tä|nä vuon|na**	this year
pärjäX-	gets by OK	**urheilu|laji**	type of sport
suksi *e*	ski	**usko-**	believes
suositu|in	most favoured,	**vahvista-**	strengthens
	favourite	**yhtenä**	sESS of **yksi**

Exercise 4: How things seem (-ltA) *to one* (-stA)
This is a good time to revise the most important verbs which refer to the way things strike our senses. They are **näyttä-** 'looks, seems', **kuulosta-** 'sounds', **maistu-** 'tastes', **haise-** 'smells', and **tuntu-** 'feels, seems'. The way things seem is put in the ablative, and the person who has the impression goes into the elative, e.g. **Minu\|sta vesi tuntuu kylmä\|ltä** 'The water feels cold to me.'

Revise these verbs by building sentences using the following nouns and adjectives in various combinations (if you've forgotten any, look them up in the back of the book):

Nouns	*Adjectives*	*Perceiver*
juusto	hyvä	minä
talo	kallis	sinä
ohjelma	kova	Orvokki
kaupunki	makea	me
kukka	mielenkiintoinen	lääkäri
vuode	paha	lapset
glögi	tuore	nainen
yskä	vanha	hän

Language points

More ways of being vague: submerged subjects

As you have seen in earlier units, Finnish sentences frequently leave the subject or main actor unspecified. There are two main ways in which subjects may be so 'submerged': if the submerged subject is more than one person, the indefinite forms of the verb are used, as in **Espanjassakin vähennetään veroja** 'They're lowering taxes in Spain, as well'. If the submerged subject could be a single person, the third person singular form is used, but without a pronoun – i.e. neither **hän** nor **se**. For example (∅ stands for the omitted pronoun): **Joskus ∅ joutulu odottamaan koko päivän** 'Sometimes one ends up having to wait all day.' Such pronoun omission also works in constructions which mark the actor with the genitive (Unit 10), as in **Talvella ∅ täytyy pukeutua lämpimästi** 'In winter one must dress warmly'; compare **Kesälläkin minun täytyy pukeutua lämpimästi** 'Even in summer I have to dress warmly.'

There is yet another way in which Finnish sentences can be less explicit than their English equivalents: detransitivized verbs. Hundreds of transitive verbs have intransitive analogues which end in =U, =UtU, or =ntU; a sentence built with such a verb requires only a subject. Compare **näke-** 'sees' and **näkly-** 'is visible' in these two sentences:

Mä eln näe kadun loppula.
I can't see the end of the street.

Kadun loppu eli näy.
lit. The end of the street isn't visible.

Here are some more pairs of transitive and intransitive verbs:

English	Transitive	Intransitive	English
contains	**sisältä-**	**sisältly-**	is contained
removes	**poista-**	**poistlu-**	is removed, departs
covers	**peittä-**	**peittly-**	is covered
finishes	**lopetta-**	**lopplu-**	comes to an end
gathers	**keräX-**	**keräälnty-**	is gathered, piles up
adds, appends	**lisäX-**	**lisäälnty-**	is augmented
opens	**avaX-**	**avalutu-**	opens
interrupts	**keskeytltä-**	**keskelyty-**	is interrupted
moistens	**kostultta-**	**kostlu-**	becomes moist (**kostea** 'damp, moist')

Exercise 5 A subject is submerged in each the following sentences. Make up your own explicit versions, starting with the subjects suggested in brackets.

1 Sairaala suljettiin (**hallitus** 'government').
2 Ovi avautui (**tyttö** 'girl').
3 Keskustelu keskeytyy (**isäni** 'my father').
4 Täytyy järjestää huone (**pojat** 'the boys').
5 On pakko lähteä nyt (**me** 'we').
6 Autoa etsitään (**poliisi** 'the police').

Nuances of some very useful verbs: pitä- and verbs of motion

You first met the verb **pitä-** back in Unit 2, where you learned that it means 'likes' when used with the elative (**Etsä pidä kahvi|sta? 'Don't you like coffee?'**). In Unit 10 you saw how **pitä-**, like **täyty-**, expresses necessity in constructions such as **Mun piti mennä kauppaan vaihtamaan** 'I had to go into a shop to get change.' This verb has several other common uses. It can be the equivalent of English 'keeps' (**Pidä ikkuna auki!** 'Keep the window open!'), 'holds' (**Se pitää jotain kädessään** '(S)he's holding something in her/his hand'), and 'considers' (and what you consider something to be is put into the essive: **Hiihtoa pidetään hyvä|nä liikuntamuoto|na** 'Skiing is considered a good form of exercise'). Notice also the following constructions: **pitä|ä hauska|a** *'has* a good time'; **pitä|ä puhee|n** *'gives* a speech'; **pitä|ä huol|ta itsestään** *'takes* care of him/herself', **pitää paikka|nsa** *'holds* true' (lit. 'holds its place').

Verbs of motion

The more specialized verbs of motion are usually fairly similar in scope and use to their English equivalents: you have already met many of the most common of these: **lähte-** 'leaves, departs', **saapu-** 'arrives', **nouse-** 'rises', **laske-** 'descends', **juokse-** 'runs'. Notice also **liikku-** and **siirty-** (intransitive), **liikutta-** and **siirtä-** (transitive), which are all 'moves'. **Liikku-** and **liikutta-** focus more on the motion itself, **siirty-** and **siirtä-** more on the change of location. **Liikutta-** is also 'moves (emotionally)': **Kvartetin viimeinen osa liikutti yleisön kyyneliin** 'The last movement of the quartet moved the audience to tears.' 'Moving house' is **muutta-**.

The more general verbs can cause more difficulty for the learner. Alongside **mene-** 'goes' and **tule-** 'comes', which from an English point of view are fairly straightforward, Finnish has a few other verbs of motion which lack close English equivalents. You have already encountered **käy-**. This verb can mean either 'goes' or 'comes': the essential difference is that a return trip is usually implied. Thus **Se kävi Ruotsi|ssa** '(S)he came/went to Sweden' (note the use of the stative, inessive, case) implies that (s)he is no longer in Sweden, but has returned to wherever (s)he left from. Anther common English equivalent is therefore 'visits': **Tule käymään!** 'Come and pay us a visit!'. **Käy-** has many other common meanings, including:

1 'Goes' in the sense of 'is working', i.e. without locomotion, as in **Mun kello käy edellä** 'My watch is fast (lit. "goes ahead")'; notice also **Olut käy** 'The beer is brewing', **Ulkona käy kova tuuli** 'There's a harsh wind outside'.

2 'Attends', as in **käy koulu|a** 'is attending school'.

3 'Becomes', as in **Kävi selväksi, ettei se auta meitä** 'It became clear that it/(s)he wouldn't help us.' Notice also **käy- ilmi**, as in **Kävi ilmi, että se oli naimisissa** 'It turned out that (s)he was married.' Parallel constructions with the illative are also common, for example: **Mun uneni kävi tote|en** 'My dream came true'.

4 'Walks', but this is more precisely **kävele-**; 'steps', more precisely **astu-**; 'happens' (**tapahtu-**); 'is suitable' (**sopi-**); 'is valid' (**päte-**).

5 With 'motion-to' suffixes, **käy-** means something like 'attacks' or 'gets stuck into', e.g. **Se kävi mua kurkku|un** '(S)he/it went for my throat', **yksityiskoht|i|in käymättä** 'without going into details'; notice also **Karhu ei käynyt lapsen kimppu|un** 'The bear didn't attack the child' (**kimppu** on its own means 'bunch').

Pääse- and **joutu-** deserve special attention because of their focus: whereas **pääse-** focuses on *trying hard to get somewhere, managing to get somewhere (desirable)*, **joutu-** emphasizes a *lack of intention*. So we have **Sen maalaus pääsi kansainväliseen näyttelyyn** 'His/her painting made it into an international exhibition', but **Sen maalaus joutui roskakoriin** 'His/her painting wound up in the bin.' Compare also **Mä pääsin kertomaan koko jutun** 'I managed/had a chance/was allowed to tell the whole story', **Mä jouduin kertomaan koko jutun** 'I ended up/wound up telling the whole story.'

Then there is **kulke-**. This verb is also often translated 'goes', but it usually refers to regular, frequently channelled, motion, especially that of vehicles, as in **Junat kulkee ajallaan** 'The trains run on time'. But notice also **Tästä kulki ennen joki** 'A river used to be/run here', **Kahviloissa huhut kulkivat vauhdikkaasti** 'In the cafés, rumours circulated swiftly.'

Finally, there is **jää-**. This verb is usually translated as 'stays' or 'remains', but you should remember that it takes 'motion-to' cases: '(S)he's staying home' is **Se jää koti|in**.

Exercise 6 Put into Finnish:

1 We went to Sweden last year.
2 Are you staying here or you coming along?

3 The news (**tieto**) travels fast.
4 It turned out that she speaks Finnish.
5 He moved to Harold's place.

Exercise 7 *Viimeiset sanat.* Translate these 'famous last words':

1 Ei ne pure jos sä et pelkää niitä.
2 Kyllä mä nämä vedet tunnen.
3 Ei sieltä junaa tähän aikaan tule.
4 Kyllä siltä sillalta eilen vielä ainakin pääsi.
5 Täällä Lapissa kaikki maisemat näyttää aika samanlaisilta.

Dialogue 4 ▣

Korvatunturi

Some fanciful geography

Anni tries to persuade Paul that there really is a Santa Claus, and that (s)he lives in Finland

ANNI: Hei Paul, ootko jo lähettäny kirjeen joulupukille Korvatunturille?
PAUL: Heh, heh! Mut miten niin Korvatunturille. Joulupukkihan asuu Pohjoisnavalla.
ANNI: No ei varmasti asu, vaan Suomen Lapissa, Korvatunturilla. Kyllä joulupukki on suomalainen, kysy vaikka keneltä tahansa[1] Suomessa.
PAUL: Okei, okei, uskon kyllä sua. Halusin vaan vähän kiusata, kun suomalaiset on niin herkkiä tästä joulupukkiasiasta!
ANNI: Niin, ku joulupukki on niin tärkee osa joulua Suomessa. Kaikki suomalaiset lapset uskoo, että joulupukki asuu Korvatunturilla ja tekee työpajassaan tonttujen kanssa leluja lapsille koko vuoden. Sitten jouluattona pukki jakaa lahjat matkustaen poroillaan ympäri Suomen.
PAUL: Ja tontut on joulupukin korvaamattomia apulaisia?
ANNI: Joo. Ennen joulua ne kiertelevät ikkunoiden takana kurkkimassa, jotta joulupukki tietää kuka on ollu kilttinä ja kuka ei!
PAUL: Tuo on kyllä kiristystä, vaikka se kyllä varmaan toimii hyvin. Lapset yrittävät olla kiltimpiä, jotta saisivat enemmän lahjoja.

ANNI: Onhan se vähän huijausta, mutta kyllä tonttuja on ihan oikeesti olemassa. Kirjoita vaikka joulupukille, jos et usko. Tässä on osoite: Joulupukin kamari, 96930 Napapiiri.

1 **kysy vaikka keneltä tahansa** 'just ask anyone'

Vocabulary

apulainen	assistant	**lelu**	toy
herkkä	sensitive, touchy	**matkusta-**	travels
huijaus *kse*	swindle	**napa|piiri**	arctic circle
jaka-	distributes	**oikeesti** =	
joulu|pukki	Father Christmas	**oikeastaan**	
kamari	chamber	**okei**	OK
ke(ne)ltä	sABL of **kuka**	**on ole|ma|ssa**	exists
kiertele-	travels around, roves	**pohjois|napa**	North Pole
		tahansa	-ever
kiltti	well-behaved, good	**X|n takana**	behind X
		toimi-	works, functions
kiristys *kse*	tension; extortion, blackmail	**tonttu**	elf
		tunturi	mountain with rounded treeless summit
kiusaX-	teases		
korvaamaton	irreplaceable		
Korvatunturi	a tunturi in northern Finland	**työ|paja**	workshop
		usko-	believes
kurkki-	peeps/peeks	**ympäri Suomen**	all over Finland
lahja	gift, present	**yrittä-**	tries
lapsi *e*	child, sP **las|ta**		

Exercise 8 (Refer to the previous dialogue if you're stuck.)

1 Ask a friend whether (s)he has sent a certain letter yet.
2 Tell him/her to ask any Finn.
3 Tell him/her you believe him/her.
4 Say you just wanted to tease him/her.
5 Tell him/her that you know who's been good and who hasn't.

Language points

Revision: uses of the genitive

You have now met most of the constructions which use the genitive. This section provides a quick overview of these uses, which we may group into three basic types:

1 The genitive proper. This group includes possessives like **Heiki|n auto** 'Heikki's car' and postpositional and prepositional constructions like **talo|n takana** 'behind the house' and 'all over Europe' **Kautta Euroopa|n** (Unit 9). Here, too, belongs the adverb of intensity, as in **hirveä|n kaunis** 'frightfully beautiful' (Unit 11).

2 Accusative marker. This use is characteristic only of nouns in the singular, e.g. **Mä näin Heiki|n eilen** 'I saw Heikki yesterday' (Unit 5).

3 Subject in a modal construction, or of a linked verb. There are several subtypes:

   (a) **Heiki|n täyty|y mennä kotiin** 'Heikki must go home' (Unit 10).
   (b) **Heiki|n on mentävä kotiin** 'Heikki must go home' (Unit 13).
   (c) **Heiki|n saapuessa minä lähdin** 'I left as Heikki arrived' (Unit 13).
   (d) **Heiki|n tul|tu|a minä lähdin** 'Once Heikki had come, I left' (Unit 12).
   (e) **Minä lähdin Heiki|n näh|de|n** 'I left in full view of Heikki' (Unit 13).
   (f) **Minä lähdin Heiki|n huomaa|ma|tta** 'I left without Heikki's noticing' (Unit 6).
   (g) **Mä kuulin Heiki|n lähtevän** 'I heard Heikki leave' (Unit 12).

There is also a common construction with **anta-**, expressing permission; for instance:

   (h) **Mä annoin Heiki|n ajaa mun autoa** 'I let Heikki drive my car.'

One last construction, built with the third infinitive, will come up in Unit 15:

   (i) **Heiki|n kirjoitta|ma|ssa kirjee|ssä** 'in a letter which Heikki wrote'.

Additional reading

Olavinlinna

Savonlinnan oopperajuhlat on yksi kesän tärkeimmistä kulttuuritapahtumista Suomessa. Se on kansainvälinen oopperafestivaali. Olavinlinna on juhlien päänäyttämönä. Olavinlinnan sanotaan olevan yksi kauneimmista keskiaikaisista linnoista pohjolassa. Se on vanha esimerkki Pohjoismaisesta yhteistyöstä; Ruotsin kuningas antoi tanskalaiselle ritarille tehtäväksi rakentaa Suomen maaperälle linnan Norjan kuninkaan kunniaksi.

Turunlinna

Turunlinnan voisi luonnehtia yhdeksi Suomen kansallisista symboleista. Retki Turunlinnassa on kuin Suomen historian oppitunti yli neljästä vuosisadasta, 1200-luvulta 1600-luvun loppuun. Linnaa alettiin rakentaa noin 1280. 1500-luku oli linnan historian värikkäin vuosisata. Toisessa maailman sodassa Turunlinna tuhoutui pahoin. Sodan jälkeen aloitettiin restaurointityö, joka saatiin päätökseen 1961.

Kalevala

Kalevala on Suomen kansalliseepos. Se ilmestyi ensimmäisen kerran 1835. Kalevala on käännetty 45 kielelle ja se on hyväksytty, ainoana suomalaisena teoksena, englanninkieliseen 'Maailman klassikot' – sarjaan.

Eduskuntatalo

Eduskuntatalo valmistui 1931 Arkadianmäelle. Rakennuksen suunnitteli professori J.S. Sirén. Rakennuksesta tuli uuden Helsingin symboli.

Suomenlinna

Vuonna 1747 aloitettiin Viaporin/Sveaborgin/Suomenlinnan rakentaminen saarelle Helsingin edustalle. Suomenlinnasta tuli alueen mahtavimpia linnoituksia. Suuri laivasto asettui linnoitukseen. Suomenlinnaa on kutsuttu 'Pohjolan Gibraltariksi'. Suomensodassa linnoituksen oli antauduttava venäläisille joukoille. Nykyään Suomenlinnasta on tullut suosittu vapaa-ajan- viettopaikka. Siellä on myös museoita kuten Armfelt ja Ehrensvärd museo, sukellusvene Vesikko ja pohjoismainen taidegalleria. Osa Suomenlinnaa on vieläkin sotilasaluetta.

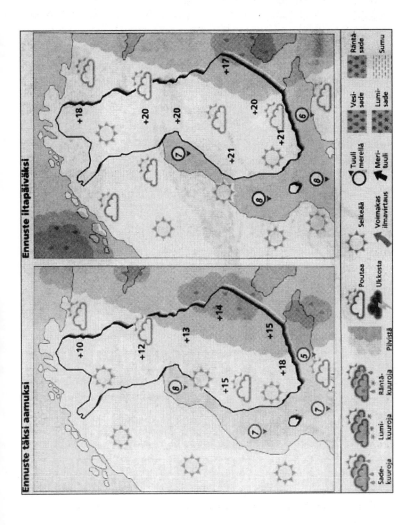

Vocabulary

alettiin	past indefinite of **alka-**	**pohjoismainen**	northern-country (adj.)
asettu-	is set up, takes up a position	**restauroi|nti**	restoration
		retki *e*	trip, excursion
edusta	place in front of X	**ritari**	knight
galleria	gallery	**saari** *e*	island
kansain|välinen	international	**sarja**	series
klassikko	classic	**sotilaX**	soldier
kunnia	honour, glory	**sukellus** *kse*	diving
laiva|sto	fleet	**suunnittele-**	plans
linnoitus *kse*	fortification	**tapahtu|ma**	event, happening
luonnehti-	characterizes	**teh|tävä**	task
maa|perä	soil, ground	**tuhoutu-**	is destroyed, damaged
mahta|va	huge, great, mighty		
Norja	Norway	**valmistu-**	is prep.ared, made ready
oppitunti	class		
päätös *kse*	decision, completion	**värikkäX**	colourful
		yhteis|	joint, mutual

15 Vakavia asioita

Serious matters

In this unit you will:

- read about Finnish authors, Turku, social security, and the European Union
- learn more about how to say 'self' and 'other'
- meet two more uses for the third infinitive
- learn about the remaining four case suffixes
- revise how to say 'everyone', 'no matter what', 'from somewhere', and the like

Dialogue 1 ▣

Euroopa|n Unioni

European Union

In Finland the referendum for EU membership was held on 16 October 1994. Around 60 per cent voted for membership and 40 per cent against. At the same time as Finland, Sweden and Austria also joined the EU, on 1 January 1995. Listen in as Mirka and Seppo argue some of the pros and cons of Finland's joining

MIRKA: Mä tulin just Lontoosta. Oli jotenkin mukavaa kun tunsi[1] kuuluvansa Euroopan Unioniin.

SEPPO: Mä en oikeen ymmärrä mitä iloa siitä tunteesta on.[2]

MIRKA: Sä taisit äänestää EU:ta vastaan kansanäänestyksessä.

SEPPO: Joo.

MIRKA: Uskallanko kysyä, miks?

SEPPO: Musta vaan tuntu siltä, että EU:n toimista ei tiedetty tarpeeks. Toiset sano yhtä ja toiset toista[3] ja se Brysselin byrokratiakin arvellutti.

MIRKA: Mä äänestin puolesta. Musta on kiva matkustaa Euroopassa vapaasti ja vaikka muuttaa Pariisiin jos huvittaa.[4]

SEPPO: Sä et tainnu[5] ottaa äänestystä kovin vakavasti.

MIRKA: Kyllä mä ajattelin myös taloudellisia etuja. Suomi tarttee vapaan pääsyn Euroopan markkinoille.

SEPPO: Musta se politiikka että ollaan neutraaleja, oli hyvä. Nyt se on vähän niinku rikkoutunut.

MIRKA: Nykymaailmassa ei oikeen enää voi pysyä täysin puolueettomana. Eikä meiltä itsenäisyys tässä jäsenyydessä mennyt. Nyt katsotaan länteen idän sijasta.

SEPPO: Mites meidän maataloudelle tulevaisuudessa sitte käy?[6]

MIRKA: No sen aika näyttää.

1 **kun tunsi** 'when I felt'; notice the use of the third person.

2 **mitä iloa siitä tunteesta on** 'what joy there is (to be had) from that feeling'.

3 **Toiset sano yhtä ja toiset toista** 'Some said one (thing) and others another'.

4 **jos (mua) huvittaa** 'if I feel like it'.

5 **tainnu(t)**: the verb **taita-** has two past active participles: **taita|nut** in the meaning 'is skilful', **tain|nut** in the meaning 'is probable (that something happened)'.

6 Cf. **Miten si|lle käy?** 'What will become of him/her/it?'

Vocabulary

arvelutta-	makes X apprehensive	**mites** → **miten**	
		neutraali	neutral
Bryssel	Brussels	**niinku** → **niinkuin**	
byrokratia	bureaucracy	**oikeen** → **oikein**	
et|u	advantage	**Pariisi**	Paris
EU =		**politiikka**	politics
Euroopa|n Unioni		**X|n puolesta**	in favour of X, for X
ilo	joy	**puoluee|ton** *ma*	impartial, disinterested
jotenkin	somehow		
jäsen|yys *te*	membership (**jäsen** 'member')	**pysy-**	stays; doesn't change
kansan| äännestys *kse*	referendum	**rikko|utu- X|n sijasta**	gets broken instead of X

taloudellinen	economic	uskalta-	dares
tarpeelks(i)	enough	vakavalsti	seriously
tarttee → tarvitsele		vastaan	against (post. P)
toimi	functioning	äänestä-	votes
tulevaisuus *te*	future	äänestys kse	vote, voting
tunteQ	feeling		

Exercise 1 Write your own Finnish dialogue, in which someone from Britain explains his or her attitude towards the EU to someone from Finland. You can have them discuss referenda, exports and imports, hopes and fears.

Language points

More submerged subjects: saying how you feel

People are often governed (or at least swayed) by their emotions, and Finnish grammar has a way of reflecting this. Alongside such expressions as **Mä oon iloinen** 'I'm happy', **Mä oon pettynyt** 'I'm disappointed', **Harri on vihainen** 'Harold is angry', Finnish even more commonly uses a construction in which a verb, always in the third person, governs the person with the emotion or feeling. This person is put into the partitive. Thus, for example, Finns are less likely to say **Mä oon väsynyt** 'I am tired' than **Mua väsyttää**, literally 'Tires me', an expression in which there is no agent specified. Other examples include

mua nukuttala	I'm feeling sleepy
mua pyöryttälä	I'm feeling dizzy
mua huvittala	I feel like, I enjoy
mua janottala	I'm feeling thirsty
mua ihmetyttälä	I'm amazed
mua aveluttala	I'm reluctant/concerned

Dialogue 2

Turku (Åbo)

Turku, now Finland's second (or, in population, fourth) city, was originally its first: its heyday began in the sixteenth century, when

what is now southwest Finland was part of the kingdom of Sweden. A university (Turu\n Akatemia, Åbo Akademi) was founded at Turku/Åbo in 1640 (later moved to Helsinki), and it was the capital until 1812. Turku now has two new universities, one Swedish and one Finnish

RIITTA: Mitä sä teit viime viikonloppuna?

JULIA: Kävin Turussa.

RIITTA: Millanen matka oli?

JULIA: Tosi onnistunut. Mä opin paljon Suomen vanhasta pääkaupungista.

RIITTA: Turku taitaa olla perustettu[1] jo 1200-luvulla.

JULIA: Joo. Vuoden 1154 arabialaisessa Idrīsī:n kartassa[2] mainittiin kaks paikkaa Suomesta. Ne oli Turku ja Häme.

RIITTA: Kävitsä Turun Tuomiokirkossa?

JULIA: Tietysti. Se oli upea kirkko. Se vihittiin 1300.

RIITTA: Sitte sä varmaan tutustuit Mikael Agricolaanki.[3]

JULIA: Kyllä. Hänhän[4] oli Turun piispana ja ensimmäisen suomenkielisen aapisen tekijä. Mä kävin myös Turun linnassa.

RIITTA: Tykkäsitkö?

JULIA: Olin haltioissani.[5] Mä olen keskiaikaisten linnojen ihailija.

RIITTA: Mitä muuta sä ehdit nähdä?

JULIA: Kävin Luostarinmäen käsityöläismuseossa katsomassa miten ennen vanhaan elettiin Turussa. Sieltä mä ostin nekkuja ja söin itseni melkein kipeeks.

RIITTA: Tiesitsä että Turusta julistetaan joka vuosi joulurauha kello kaksitoista jouluaattopäivänä.

JULIA: En tienny. Mutta tiedän että Turun Akatemia perustettiin 1640.

RIITTA: Sulla tais olla[6] antoisa viikonloppu.

JULIA: Oli. Mutta vielä jäi paljon näkemättä.[7]

1 **taitaa olla perustettu** 'must have been founded; I guess it was founded'.

2 **arabialaisessa Idrīsī:n kartassa** 'on the Arab map of (ash-Sharīf al-)Idrīsī' (twelfth-century geographer and adviser to Roger II, Norman king of Sicily).

3 **Mikael Agricola** see exercise below.

4 **hän\hän** 'he, (as) you know, . . .'

5 **Olin haltioissani** 'I was on cloud nine'.

6 **Sulla tais olla** 'You must have had'.

7 **(multa) jäi paljon näkemättä** '(I) missed a lot', lit. 'much remained unseen (off me)'.

Vocabulary

aapinen	primer	**käsityöläis|museo**	handicrafts
antoisa	productive, rich		museum
arabialainen	Arab(ic), Arabian	**millanen** →	
elettiin	pt indefinite of	**millainen**	
	elä-	**nekku**	toffee cone
ihaili|ja	admirer	**onnistu-**	succeeds, goes
itse|ni	myself		off well
joulu|aatto|päivä	day before	**perusta-**	founds
	Christmas	**piispa**	bishop
joulu|rauha	Christmas peace	**tais** → **taisi**	pt of **taita-**
julista-	proclaims,	**teki|jä**	maker, author
	declares, makes	**tienny** = **tietä|nyt**	
	public	**tuomio|kirkko**	cathedral
keski|aikainen	medieval	**upea**	magnificent,
kipeeks →			grand
	kipeeksi	**vihki-**	consecrates

Exercise 2 Dig the answers to these out of the dialogue above.

1 When was Turku cathedral consecrated?
2 What was founded in 1640?
3 Who was Mikael Agricola?
4 What kind of museum is at Luostarinmäki?

Language points

Self and other

English 'myself', 'yourself', 'herself', 'ourselves' and the like are rendered in Finnish by the word **itse** with the appropriate possessive suffix. For example:

Mä söin itse\|ni kipeeksi.
I ate myself sick.

Se katselee itse\|ä\|än peilistä.
(S)he looks at him/herself in the mirror.

Tunne itse\|si!
Know thyself!

Mullla on itselllä|ni kolme lasta.
I have three children myself.

But **itse** does not take suffixes when it is used to mean 'even' (= **jopa**) or 'none other than', as in **Itse presidentti on sanonut, että ...** 'None other than the president (him/herself) has said that ...'.

'Other' and 'another' are a bit more complicated. In reciprocal situations such as 'They loved one another' you have a choice: (1) you use **toinen** in the appropriate plural case and with the appropriate possessive suffix, as in **Ne rakasti tois|i|a|an:** or (2) you use **toinen** twice, the first time in the nominative singular and the second time with the appropriate possessive and case suffix, as in **Ne rakasti toinen tois|ta|an.**

Toinen refers to one or the other of two known entities; **muu** is 'other' in the sense of 'something else', or 'different'. Indeclinable **eri** is 'other' in the sense of 'separate', 'distinct', and 'various'. There is some overlap in the use of these three words, but keeping these distinctions in mind should help. Contrast:

toise|ssa huonee|ssa	in the other room
muu|ssa huonee|ssa	in another (= different) room
eri huonee|ssa	in another (= separate) room

Exercise 3 Put into Finnish:

1 They already know one another.
2 He's always talking about himself.
3 I've left my bag in the other room.
4 There were also a few other guests.
5 They came to visit at two different times.
6 I couldn't get anyone to believe me (= myself).

Four more noun suffixes: abessive, instructive, comitative, and prolative

These suffixes are all somewhat rare, but you will need at least to recognize them.

The *abessive*, **-ttA**, you have already met, in connection with the third infinitive (Unit 6). With ordinary nouns, it means 'without'; thus **vaiva|tta** 'without trouble' is just a more formal way of saying **ilman vaiva|a** (Unit 7). It usually occurs with the singular, but notice the expression **mu|i|tta mutk|i|tta** 'without (any further) ado' (**mutka** 'bend, curve'). You'll come across this suffix mostly in fixed phrases; don't try making up your own unless you want to sound silly.

You have also already met the *instructive*: it is the **-n** which is added to the second infinitive (Unit 13). With ordinary nouns, it means something like 'with' or 'by means of', for example:

jala|n	on foot
om|i|n käs|i|n	with one's own hands
koste|i|n silm|i|n	with moist eyes
ehdo|i|n tahdo|i|n	intentionally (**ehto** 'stipulation', **tahto** 'wish')

As these examples indicate, the instructive is used most commonly in the plural. The *comitative*, on the other hand, is *always* used in the plural, even when its meaning is singular. Its form is the suffix **-ne-**; when attached to the last (or only) noun in the phrase, this is followed by the appropriate possessive suffix. For example:

Se lähti ystäv\|i\|ne\|en.
(S)he left with her/his friends.

Se haluaa muuttaa perhe\|i\|ne\|en Suomeen.
(S)he wants to move to Finland with her/his family.

Joulupukki ilmestyi poro\|i\|ne\|en ja lahjo\|i\|ne\|en.
Father Christmas appeared, with his reindeer and his presents.

As these examples suggest, the comitative means something a little more than simple accompaniment (which is expressed by **kanssa** or **kera**, Unit 9). Whereas **perhee\|nsä kanssa** is no more than 'with his/her family', **perhe\|i\|ne\|en** is closer to 'family and all'.

The *prolative*, **-tse**, means 'via' or 'by means of' and is restricted to a few types of expression. Some of the more common uses are: **puhelim\|i\|tse** 'by telephone', **lentoposti\|tse** 'via air mail', **sähkö-posti\|tse** 'by e-mail', **meri\|tse** 'by sea', **ma\|i\|tse** 'by land', **oikeuste\|i\|tse** 'through the courts' (**oikeus** 'justice', **tie** 'road, route').

Exercise 4 Match up the items in columns A and B so that they make some kind of sense.

A	*B*
1 Se kertoi mulle kaiken	vanhempineen.
2 Ne muuttaa Ruotsiin	puhelimitse.
3 Mä näin sen	omin silmin.

Dialogue 3

Vähän Suomen taloudesta

A little about Finland's economy

At the airport, Peter and Heikki discuss unemployment, imports, exports, and souvenirs

Lentokentällä

PETER: Olen kuullut että Suomessa on paljon työttömiä. Pitääkö se paikkansa?

HEIKKI: Valitettavasti se on totta. 80-luvun[1] lopussa Suomen talous kärsi kovasti Neuvostoliiton hajoamisesta ja niinkuin muuallakin maailmassa pankkikriiseistä. Suomen työttömyys on siinä[2] 17 prosenttia.

PETER: Mitkä maat ovat nykyään Suomen suurimpia kauppakumppaneita?

HEIKKI: Saksa ja Ruotsi ovat suurimpia, mutta Suomi tekee paljon kauppaa myös Englannin, Yhdysvaltojen ja Venäjän kanssa.

PETER: Mitkä ovat Suomen vientivaltteja? Olen kuullut Nokian kännyköistä.

HEIKKI: Nokia onkin[3] varmaan yksi Suomen tunnetuimmista yhtiöistä maailmalla. Suomi on suuri metallin, konetekniikan ja paperin viejä. Suomessa on myös iso kemianteollisuus ja tietysti Suomi vie myös puutavaraa.

PETER: Ajattelin ostaa tuliaisia vaimolleni. Se saisi olla[4] jotain suomalaista. Mitä suosittelisit?

HEIKKI: Marimekon tekstiilit ovat tyylikkäitä ja hyvää laatua. Aarikan puiset tavarat, Iittalan lasi ja Arabian posliini ovat myös hyviä tuliaisia. Kannattaa myös katsoa Kalevalakoruja. Fazerin suklaa on myös aina tervetullutta.

PETER: Lähdenpä tästä vähän ostoksille[5] ennen koneen lähtöä.

HEIKKI: Nähdään koneessa!

1 **80-luku** 'the eighties'.

2 **siinä** 'about'.

3 **Nokia onkin** 'It's true, Nokia *is* ...'

4 **se saisi olla** 'it should/ought to be'.

5 **lähden ... ostoksille** 'I'm going shopping'; the **–pA** of **lähdenpä** adds a nuance of immediacy and energy, as usual.

Vocabulary

kannatta-	is worth it	puultavara	things made
kauppalkumppani	trading partner		of wood
kemianlteollisuus *te*	chemical	tavaralt	wares
	industry	tekstiililt	textiles
koru	ornament,	terveltullut	welcome
	jewellery	tunneltulimmlilsta	pELA of
kärsi-	suffers, bears		tunnetuin
laatu	quality		(see unit 8)
metalli	metal	tyylilkkäX	stylish (tyyli
muuallalkin	elsewhere, as		'style')
	well	työtön *mä*	unemployed
Neuvostolliitto	Soviet Union	työttömyys *te*	unemployment
ostos *kse*	purchase,	valtti	trump card
	shopping	vie-	takes away;
pankkilkriisi	banking crisis		exports
posliini	porcelain, china	vieljä	exporter
puinen	wooden	vielnti	export
		yhtliö	company, firm

Dialogue 4 🔊

Suomalaisia kirjailijoita

Finnish authors

In a bookshop, Mrs Marple enquires into Finnish literature

MRS MARPLE: Päivää, haluaisin ostaa suomalaisten kirjailijoiden kirjoittamia kirjoja.[1] Voisitteko suositella joitakin?

MYYJÄ: Aleksis Kiven *Seitsemän veljestä* on hyvin suosittu.

MRS MARPLE: Se minulla jo onkin.[2] Kerään nimittäin suomalaista kirjallisuutta. Minulla on myös Mika Waltarin *Sinuhe-egyptiläinen* ja Emil Sillanpään *Nuorena nukkunut*, se josta[3] hän sai Nobelin kirjallisuus-palkinnon.

MYYJÄ: Tämän vuoden Finlandia-palkinnon saajan Hannu Mäkelän *Mestari* on kuulemma hyvä.

MRS MARPLE: Eikös Hannu Mäkelä ole sen lastenkirjan *Herra Huu* kirjoittaja.

MYYJÄ: Kyllä, mutta hän kirjoittaa myös aikuisille. Voisin
            suositella lämpimästi myös Helvi Hämäläisen
            Kadotettua puutarhaa.
MRS MARPLE: Näin teidän näyteikkunassanne Veijo Meren *Ei tule
            vaivatta vapaus.*
MYYJÄ: Se onkin ollut suosittu viime aikoina.⁴
MRS MARPLE: Olisin myös kiinnostunut nuortenkirjoista ja
            lastenkirjoista.
MYYJÄ: Anna-Leena Härkösen *Häräntappoase* ja *Akvaario-
            rakkautta* ja Rosa Liksomin kirjat ovat ne jotka
            tulevat mieleeni⁵ ensimmäisenä. Lastenkirjoista
            ensimmäisenä tulee mieleeni *Uppo-Nalle* kirjat ja
            Mauri Kunnaksen *Koiramäen lapset* ja tietysti Tove
            Janssonin Muumi-kirjat.
MRS MARPLE: Minun on hetki mietittävä. On niin paljon mistä
            valita. Kiitos avustanne.

1 **suomalaisten kirjailijoiden kirjoittamia kirjoja** 'some books written by Finnish writers'.

2 **Se minulla jo onkin** 'I've already *got* (a copy of) *that*.'

3 **jo|sta** 'for which'.

4 **viime aiko|i|na** 'recently, of late'.

5 **tulevat miele|e|ni** 'they occur to me', lit. 'come into my mind'.

Vocabulary

aikuinen	adult	**mietti-**	ponders, considers
akvaario	aquarium	**nimittäin**	you see
egyptiläinen	Egyptian	**nuoriso**	youth
härän|tappo|aseQ	weapon for killing	**näli|n**	I saw (**näke-**)
	an ox (**härkä**	**näytteQ|ikkuna**	display window
	'ox')	**palkinto**	prize
kadotta-	loses	**puu|tarha**	garden, orchard
keräX-	collects	**rakkavs te**	love
kiinnostu-	takes an interest	**saa|ja**	winner, 'getter'
	in	**suosittele-**	recommends
kirjaili|ja	writer	**vaiva|tta**	without difficulty
kirjallisuus te	literature	**valiTSE-**	chooses
kuulemma	'I hear', they say	**vapaus te**	freedom (**vapaa**
lämpimä|sti	warmly (**lämmin**		'free')
	'warm')	**veljestä**	sP of **veljekse-** 'one
las|ten	pG of **lapsi** *e* child		of a set of
			brothers'

Exercise 5 Explain in Finnish to a Finn about contemporary English-language authors: what books they have written, what prizes they have won, which ones are read by whom, and so on.

Language points

More uses for the 3rd infinitive

In Unit 6, you learned how to form the third infinitive, and its more common uses in colloquial style. Here we look at two more of its uses.

The first use is common enough in both colloquial and more formal Finnish. It consists of the third infinitive plus the suffix-chain:

-is-i-llA-PX

where 'PX' stands for any possessive suffix, and it means something like 'on the verge of doing X'. So, for example, 'I was (just) about to fall' is **Mä olin putoamaisillani**. Roughly equivalent is the first infinitive, with optional **vähällä** (lit. 'with a little'): **Mä olin (vähällä) pudota**.

The second use is much more common in written than in spoken Finnish. It is as if we could, in English, turn 'the house that Jack built' into 'the by-Jack-built house'.

    talo, jonka Jack rakensi   **Jackiｌn rakentaｌma talo**

This construction is fully declinable; for example, in the inessive we have

taloｌssa, jonka Jack rakensi   **Jackiｌn rakentaｌmaｌssa taloｌssa**
'in the house which Jack built', more literally: 'in the by-Jack-built house'

Its conciseness makes this construction very handy, for instance:

Jatkosodassa Suomi koetti saada *talvisodassa menettämänsä alueet* takaisin.
In the War of Continuation, Finland attempted to get back *the areas which it had lost in the Winter War.*

Me totutaan hyvin nopeasti *uuden tekniikan aiheuttamiin muutoksiin* ympäristössämme.
We quickly get used *to changes* in our environment *which have been brought about by new technology.*

Here are a few more examples:

demar\i\en johta\ma\ssa hallitukse\ssa
in a government led by the Social Democrats

kirjeesi, jo\n\ka innoitta\ma\na minä kirjoitin tämän
your letter, *inspired by which* I wrote this

meidän valitse\ma\ssa\mme konee\ssa
in the machine (which) we chose

Exercise 6 Rewrite these phrases in colloquial Finnish.

Model: **Turkan lähettämä paketti > paketti, jonka Turkka lähetti**

1 isän keittämää keittoa
2 lasten kirjoittamat tarinat
3 Goethen mainitsemassa romaanissa

Dialogue 5

Sosiaaliturvasta 1

Social security 1

ANSA: Koska sulla on laskettu aika?[1]
KIRSI: Mä kävin eilen äitiysneuvolassa. Laskettu aika on nyt sitte kesäkuun kymmenes.
ANSA: Milloin sun äitiysloma alkaa?
KIRSI: Toukokuun alkupuolella. Turkka ottaa isyyslomaa sit ku vauva on syntyny.
ANSA: Silloin kun meidän Erkki synty, mä sain äitiysrahaa kahdeksankymmentä (80) prosenttia palkasta, mut nyt ne on tainnu laskee sitä.
KIRSI: Kyllä ne tais sitä laskea, mut mä en nyt muista paljonks se on.
ANSA: Ootsä ajatellu jäädä kotiin äitiysloman loputtua?[2]
KIRSI: No ollaan me sitä ajateltu, kun kerran sitä kotihoidontukea saa siihen asti kun vauva täyttää kolme[3] ja työpaikka säilyy.[4]

Sosiaaliturvasta 2

Social security 2

BRIAN: Miten sä rahoitat sun opiskelut?

TONI: Mä saan valtion opintotukea ja sit mä teen vähän töitä opiskelun ohessa. Mä voisin myös ottaa valtion takaamaa opintolainaa,[5] mut se on sit markkinakorkoista.

BRIAN: Miten sitten opiskelujen jälkeen?

TONI: No tarkoitus olis löytää töitä: Mut jos niit ei heti löydy, niin mä saan sitte työttömyyskorvausta tai sosiaaliavustusta.

BRIAN: Maksaako valtio myös eläkkeet?

TONI: Joo, valtio ja työeläkelaitokset. Eläke on kai noin kuuskyt (60) prosenttia palkasta.

BRIAN: Pitääkö siitä sitten maksaa myös sairaala ja terveyskeskuskulut?

TONI: Kyllä niistä pitää vähän maksaa. Terveyskeskuksissa se on noin viiskymppiä kerta (50mk) tai satasen per vuosi ja sairaalakäynneistä maksetaan myös paljon vähemmän ku mitä ne oikeesti maksaa.[6]

1 **laskettu aika** 'expected date of delivery' (lit. 'reckoned time').

2 **äitiyslomaǀn lopuǀttuǀa** 'once maternity leave has ended'.

3 **siihen asti kun vauva täyttää kolme** 'until the baby reaches three (years old)' (lit. until then when the baby completes three').

4 **työpaikka säilyy** 'they keep (my) place at work' (lit. 'the workplace is kept').

5 **valtioǀn takaaǀmaǀa opintoǀlainaǀa** 'an education/study loan guaranteed by the state'.

6 **maksetaan myös paljon vähemmän ku mitä ne oikeesti maksaa:** note the two senses of **maksa-**: 'one *pays* much less than what they really *cost*'.

Vocabulary

alkuǀpuoleǀlla	in the first half	**korkoǀinen**	having an
asti	as far as, until (post.)		interest rate
avustus *kse*	assistance	**korvaus** *kse*	compensation
eläǀkkeQ	pension (**elä-** 'lives')	**koska**	when
isǀyysǀloma	paternity leave (**isä** 'father')	**kotihoidonǀtuki** *e*	home care support
korko	interest (rate) (**korkea** 'high')	**kuluǀt**	costs, expenses

laske-	counts, reckons; lowers	**taka|X-**	guarantees, backs (**taka|na** 'behind')
neuvo|la	advice centre	**tarkoitus** *kse*	aim, intention, purpose
ohe|ssa	alongside (post. with genitive)	**terveys|keskus** *kse*	health centre (**terveQ** healthy)
opinto|laina	study loan	**työ|eläke|laitos**	work pension
opinto|tuki *e*	support for study, scholarship	*kse*	system
opiskelu|t	studies	**työ|paikka**	place (in work)
palkka	pay, wage, salary	**työ|ttöm|yys** *te*	unemployment
per	per (prep. with nominative)	**täyttä-**	completes, fills
rahoitta-	funds (**raha** 'money')	**valtio**	(the) state (**valta** 'power')
sairaala|käynti	stay in hospital	**vauva**	baby
sosiaali|turva	social security	**äiti|lys** *te*	maternity (**äiti** 'mother')
säily-	is kept, is preserved	**äitiys|loma**	maternity leave

Language points

'Somehow', 'everyone', 'whatever' and 'elsewhere'

The Finnish expressions for these somewhat abstract concepts are formed fairly regularly. We may distinguish seven categories:

1 *The interrogative.* You should know all of these by now. Check that you do with this list: **kuka** 'who?', **mikä** 'what?', **millainen** 'what kind of?', **kumpi** 'which (of two)?', **miten** 'how?, **missä** 'where?', **minne** 'to where?', **mistä** 'from where?', **milloin, koska** 'when?', **miksi** 'why?', **paljonko** 'how much?' Forms of **mikä** and **millainen** also serve to modify nouns, for example **mi|ssä paika|ssa** 'in what place?', **millais|li|a filme|j|ä** 'what kinds of films?'

2 *The indifferent.* Compare English '-ever' as in 'whoever', or 'no matter' as in 'no matter where'. In Finnish, you simply add **vaan** to the interrogative, for example: **kuka vaan** 'no matter who', **missä vaan** 'wherever'. More formal Finnish has **tahansa** or **hyvänsä** instead: **milloin tahansa** 'whenever', **millainen hyvänsä** 'no matter what kind'.

3 *The indefinite.* These are made with 'some-' in English, as in 'someone', 'somewhere'. In Finnish, the root is **jo-**, so we have **jo|ku** 'someone' and **jo|kin** 'something'; **jo|ssa|in** 'somewhere', **jo|sta|in** 'from somewhere', and **jo|nne|kin** 'to somewhere'; and **jo|ten|kin, jo|lla|in tava|lla** 'somehow', **jo|sta|in syy|stä** 'for some reason'.

4 *The negative.* These are used with the negative verb (and with the prohibitive). They are formed by adding -#n to the interrogative if this ends in an **A**, by adding -**kAAn** otherwise. Thus 'no one' is (**ei**) **kuka|an**, and 'to nowhere' is (**ei**) **minne|kään**. 'Never' is (**ei**) **koska|an** or (**ei**) **milloin|kaan**. Again, forms of **mikä|än** modify nouns: **ei mi|ssä|än talo|ssa** 'in no house'.

5 *The universal.* This is the opposite of the negative, and is expressed by a separate set of stems, most of which you should know by now. 'Always' is **aina**, 'all', 'every', 'everyone', and 'everything' are **kaikki**; the words for 'everywhere' are built from **kaikki|a-: kaikki|a|lla, kaikki|a|lle, kaikki|a|lta**.

6 *The demonstrative.* Corresponding to **se** 'this/that/it' we have **silloin** 'then', **sellainen, semmonen** 'such (a)', **siellä** 'there'; corresponding to **tuo** 'that' we have **tuolloin** 'at that time', **tuollainen, tommonen** 'that kind of (a)', **tuolla** 'there (yonder)'. **Semmonen** is widely used in casual speech; cf. English 'kind of'.

7 *The other.* Notice that the words for 'elsewhere' are built to a stem **muu|a-: muu|a|lla, muu|a|lle, muu|a|lta**.

Exercise 7 Translate into English:

1 Sellaista voi tapahtua kenelle tahansa.
2 Onks täällä jossain hyvä hotelli?
3 Älä missään tapauksessa tee sitä!
4 Kuka tahansa teistä olisi tehnyt samoin.
5 Poika ei tiennyt minne muualle katsoa.

16 Älköön sanottako!

Let it not be said!

In this unit you will learn:

- a little about Finnish history, and about *sisu*
- more ways of expressing uncertainty
- more about participles
- some computerese

Dialogue 1 ▣

Sisu

Helka offers Matthew a 'Sisu' pastille, and the conversation turns to the perennial question: how do we define Finnish **sisu**?

HELKA: (*tarjoaa pastillin*) Saako olla sisua?

MATTHEW: Kiitti. Onpas nämä voimakkaita, siksi kai niitä kutsutaan sisuiksi?

HELKA: Joo, näitä pastilleja on valmistettu Suomessa jo pitkään.[1] Nimi viittaa suomalaisten käsitykseen suomalaisesta sisusta, joka on ollut kautta aikojen[2] ja edelleen kuvaa suomalaista perusluonnetta.

MATTHEW: Se on siis eräänlainen myytti, joka kuitenkin on hyvin todellinen suomalaisille.

HELKA: Niin se varmaan on. Sisu on sisu. Sitä ei voi kääntää eri kielille. Se merkitsee jokaiselle henkilökohtaisesti ehkä eri asiaa, mutta silti kaikki ymmärtävät mitä sillä tarkoitetaan. Mä itse kuvaisin sisun joksikin sellaiseksi, että ei anna periksi,[3] vaikka ois kuinka vaikeeta.[4] Suomalaisen sisun on sanottu näkyvän[5] niin urheilussa, kun myös sodassa ja muissa vaikeissa paikoissa.

MATTHEW: No niin. Lähdetään nyt sinne tenttiin ettei myöhästytä.[6] Siellä varmasti tarvitaan suomalaista sisua!

1 **jo pitkälän** 'for a long time now'.

2 **kautta aikoljen** 'through the ages'.

3 **ei anna periksi** 'one doesn't give in'.

4 **vaikka ois kuinka vaikeeta → vaikka olisi kuinka vaikea(t)a** 'no matter how difficult it is'.

5 **Suomalaiseln sisuln on sanottu näkylväln** 'It has been said that Finnish **sisu** is evident'.

6 **ettlei myöhästyltä** 'so that we're not late'.

Vocabulary

erään‖lainen	some kind of	**sisu**	mental/physical
henkilö‖kohtainen	personal		stamina
jokainen	each	**sota**	war
kääntä-	turns, translates	**tarjoX-**	offers
käsitys *kse*	idea, view,	**tentti**	test
	conception	**todellinen**	true
luonteQ	character	**valmista-**	manufactures,
myöhästy-	is late (for X:		prepares
	X-#n)	**viittaX-**	points, beckons;
myytti	myth		refers
pastilli	pastille	**voi‖ma‖kkaX**	strong, powerful
silti	nevertheless		

Exercise 1 Write out Finnish translations for the following English sentences by raiding the dialogue above. (You may have to change or omit a word here and there.)

1 It means something a little different to each person.
2 I suppose that's why they're called 'Sisu'?
3 For Finns, it's quite true.
4 Don't give in!
5 This really *is* strong!

Dialogue 2

Pieni kertaus Suomen historiasta

In history class

The teacher *(opetta\ja)* leads a revision session on some highlights of Finnish history

OPETTAJA: Otetaanpa[1] pieni kertaus Suomen historiasta ennen ensi viikon kokeita. Milloin Suomi itsenäistyi? Pekka!

PEKKA: Kuudes (6.) joulukuuta tuhatyhdeksänsataaseitsemäntoista (1917).

OPETTAJA: Mikä oli Suomen asema ennen itsenäistymistä?

ULLA: Ennen itsenäistymistä Suomi oli Venäjän autonominen suurruhtinaskunta ja Venäjän Tsaari oli Suomen suuriruhtinas.

JUHA: *(viittaa innokkaasti)* 1808–1809 oli Suomen sota, jolloin Ruotsi menetti Suomen Venäjälle.

OPETTAJA: Kenestä tuli[2] Suomen ensimmäinen presidentti tasavallaksi julistamisen jälkeen?[3]

PILVI: Juho Kusti Ståhlberg. Ja eiks sitte 1918 alkanu Sisällissota?

OPETTAJA: Totta. Se kesti vain muutaman kuukauden, mutta sen seurauksena kuoli lähes yhtä paljon ihmisiä kuin[4] Talvisodassa. Kuka muistaa, kuinka kauan Talvisota kesti?

JUKKE: Talvisota alko 30. marraskuuta 1939 ja päätty maaliskuussa 1940.

OPETTAJA: Entäs Jatkosota?

JUKKE: Se alko kesäkuussa 1941 ja rauha tuli syyskuussa 1944.

OPETTAJA: Mitkä olivat 50-luvun tärkeimpiä tapahtumia?

MAIJA: Armi Kuuselasta tuli Miss Universum 1952.

PEKKA: Ja Helsingin olympialaiset oli kans -52.

OPETTAJA: Entäs poliittisesti tärkeitä tapahtumia?

PILVI: Porkkalan luovutus oli tammikuussa 1956 ja Urho Kekkosesta tuli presidentti.

JUHA: Eiks se ystävyys, yhteistyö ja avunanto sopimus Neuvostoliiton kanssa allekirjoitettu joskus 50-luvulla?

OPETTAJA: Ei. YYA-sopimus allekirjoitettiin ensimäisen kerran jo 1948. Mikä on ETYK-sopimus?

ULLA: Se oli se Euroopan turvallisuus- ja yhteistyökonfe-
renssi, joka allekirjoitettiin Helsingissä 1975.

OPETTAJA: Tunti loppuukin kohta. Muistakaa kerrata Suomen
presidentit.

JUKKE: Mauno Koivostosta tuli presidentti 1982 Kekkosen
jälkeen.

OPETTAJA: Hyvä. Muistakaa se sitten kokeissakin. (*Kello soi.*)
Menkäähän nyt välitunnille.

1 Ote|taan|pa 'let's have'.

2 **Kenestä tuli** 'Who became?' (lit. 'out of whom came. . .').

3 **tasavalla|ksi julista|mise|n jälkeen** lit. 'after the declaration (as) becoming
republic'.

4 **yhtä paljon ku(i)n** 'as many as'

Vocabulary

allekirjoitta-	signs	**päätty-**	ends, is finished
autonominen	autonomous	**rauha**	peace
avun|anto	giving of aid	**seuraus** kse	consequence
historian|tunti	history class	**Sisällis|sota**	Civil War
innokkaX	keen, enthusiastic	**soi-**	rings, (re)sounds
Jatko|sota	War of	**sopimus** kse	treaty
	Continuation	**suur|ruhtinaX**	Grand Duke
jolloin	when	**suurruhtinas|**	Grand Duchy
keisari	emperor	**kunta**	
kertaus kse	revision	**Talvi|sota**	Winter War
kertaX-	revises, reviews	**tasa|valta**	republic (**tasa|n**
kohta	soon		'evenly,
kokeQ	examination		equally')
konferenssi	conference	**tsaari**	tsar
kuole-	dies	**turvallisuus** te	security
luovutus kse	surrender, handing	**väli|tunti**	break between
	over		classes
menettä-	loses	**yhteis|työ**	collaboration
olympialaise|t	Olympic (game)s	**ystäv|yys** te	friendship
poliittise|sti	politically		

Exercise 2 Here are the answers. What are the questions? (Peek back at the dialogue if you can't remember.)

1 Se alkoi kesäkuussa 1941.
2 Juho Kusti Ståhlberg.
3 Mauno Koivistosta.
4 1917.12.6
5 Lähes yhtä paljon ihmisiä kuin Talvisodassa

Language points

The potential mood

This mood indicates a degree, however slight, of doubt or hesitation. It occurs extremely rarely in colloquial Finnish, but is easy to form and to recognize.

The suffix is -**Ne**-, added directly to the verb stem. The **N** behaves exactly like the **N** of the past active participle. Compare the forms:

	anta-	huomaX-	nouse-	vie-
past active participle	**anta|nut**	**huoman|nut**	**nous|sut**	**vie|nyt**
s3 potential	**anta|ne|e**	**huoman|ne|e**	**nous|se|e**	**vie|ne|e**
class	I	II	III	IV

The final chunks of class II stems (**X**, **XE**, **TSE**) assimilate to the **N**, but the **N** assimilates to the **s**, **l**, or **r** final in class III stems once their final **e**'s have been cancelled: **tul\|le\|e** 'may/might come', **pur\|re\|e** 'may/might bite'. Parallel to the past active participles **nähnyt**, **tehnyt** we have the potential forms **näh\|ne\|e**, **teh\|ne\|e**. The indefinite potential looks just like the past passive participle, but with =**Aneen** instead of =**U**: **anne\|tt\|aneen**, **huoma\|tt\|aneen**, **nous\|t\|aneen**, **vie\|tt\|äneen**.

The only irregularity is in the verb 'is'. In the personal forms of the potential, this is not **ole**- but **lie**-, so we have **lie\|ne\|e** 'may/might be'. Also, the connegative is **liene\|Q**, as in **Se ei liene⁰ pelkkä sattuma** 'It may not be mere chance.' The perfect potential, too, is formed with **lie\|ne**-: **En tiedä, mihin he lie\|ne\|vät menneet** 'I don't know where they might have gone.' Only the indefinite is built to **ole**-: **ol\|t\|aneen** 'one might be'.

As you have already seen, colloquial Finnish has other ways of expressing such doubts. Besides such little words as **ehkä**, **kai** 'perhaps' there is also widespread use of the verbs **saatta**-, **mahta**-, and

taita-. For example, instead of **Useimmat muista|ne|vat hänen puheensa**, you say **Useimmat taitaa muistaa sen puheen** 'Most will probably remember his speech.' Here are some more examples:

Missä mahta|a olla postilaatikko?
Where might there be a letterbox?

Saatta|a tulla kaunis kesä.
Summer may turn out to be beautiful (this year).

(Third person) directives

These are extremely rare in spoken Finnish. They are similar to imperatives in that they express the wishes of the speaker, but their function is to place the obligation not on the addressee, but on some third party, as in English 'Let them come forward' or 'Let there be light.'

The suffixes are **-kOOn** (third person singular) and **-kOOt** (third person plural). You add them to verb stems in exactly the same way as the second person plural imperative suffix **-kAA**. Compare:

p2 imperative	**anta|kaa**	**huomat|kaa**	**men|kää**	**vie|kää**
s3 directive	**anta|koon**	**huomat|koon**	**men|köön**	**vie|köön**
p3 directive	**anta|koot**	**huomat|koot**	**men|kööt**	**vie|kööt**

Unlike imperative forms (Unit 3), directive forms require their direct object nouns to take the accusative suffix **-n**. Contrast:

p2 imperative	**Anta|kaa minulle lasi!**	Give me a/the glass!
s3 directive	**Anta|koon minulle lasi|n!**	Let him/her give me a/the glass!

The connegative is **-kO**, which is added to the stem in exactly the same way as the **-kO** of the imperative: **Älköön men|kö** 'Let him/ her not go.' There are also indefinite forms: **anne|tta|koon** 'may someone give, may it be given', **äl|köön sano|tta|ko** 'let it not be said'.

The directive is most frequently heard in certain fixed expressions, such as **Onneksi olkoon!** 'Congratulations', and **Olkoon menneeksi!** 'So be it!'

This is a good place to mention the formal first person plural imperative, which is built with the suffix-chain **-kAA-mme** in a manner parallel to the second person plural imperative. You will probably only ever come across it in **rukoil|kaa|mme** 'Let us pray.'

Dialogue 3 ▦

Koli

Alisa invites Cheryl to join her and others on a rambling weekend trip to Koli

ALISA: Hei Cheryl, kiva nähdä sua. Kuule, me ollaan tyttöjen kanssa lähdössä[1] Kolille patikoimaan viikonloppuna. Haluut sä tulla mukaan?

CHERYL: Kuulostaa kivalta. Missä se Koli on?

ALISA: Se on noin 70 kilsan päässä täältä Joensuusta. Me aiotaan vuokrata auto, kun se on helpoin ja halvin tapa mennä sinne kun meitä on lähdössä ainakin Anniina, Paula ja mä.[2] Niin, ja sä, jos haluut tulla mukaan.

CHERYL: Voisin lähteäkin. Nyt on hyvä viikonloppu lähteä, kun ei ole paljon tekemistä ensi viikoksi ja patikoiminen sattuu olemaan yksi lempiharrastuksistani.

ALISA: Sitä paitsi Kolin kansallispuisto – yksi monista Suomen kansallispuistoista – on maisemiltaan[3] aivan upea. Kolin korkein kohta on Ukko-Kolilla, 34 metriä merenpinnasta ja sen huipulta näkee pitkälle Pielis-järvelle.

CHERYL: Talvella siellä on varmaan hyvät laskettelumahdollisuudet, kun se on niin korkealla.

ALISA: Joo on. Näin etelässä ei juuri ole parempia laskettelurinteitä. Mutta mä itse kyllä tykkään enemmän käydä Kolilla näin syksyisin patikoimassa ja katsomassa hienoja maisemia. Metsissä on paljon erilaista kasvillisuutta ja eläimiä ja myös useita uhanalaisia kasvilajeja kasvaa Kolin alueella.

CHERYL: Käytkö sä usein Kolilla?

ALISA: Kyllä mä yleensä käyn pari kertaa vuodessa ja useamminkin,[4] varsinkin jos haluan viedä vieraita tutustumaan Koliin. Vähän aikaa sitten kuulin, että Koli on ollut suosittu pyhiinvaelluspaikka Suomen kansallisromantiikan aikana. Kuulemma lukuisat taiteilijat, esimerkiksi Edelfeldt, Sibelius ja Aho ovat ammentaneet luovuuttaan Kolin maisemissa.

CHERYL: No kyllähän mun historian opiskelijana täytyy[5] lähteä tutustumaan niihin maisemiin!

1 **me ollaan tyttöjen kanssa lähdössä** 'the girls and I are going' (lit. 'we're going with the girls'.

2 **meitä on lähdössä ainakin Anniina, Paula ja mä** 'there'll be at least A, P and me going'.

3 **maisemiltaan** 'by virtue/because of its landscapes'.

4 **ja useamminkin** 'and even more often'.

5 **mu|n historia|n opiskelija|na täyty|y** 'as a history student, I must'.

Vocabulary

Aho	Juhani Aho (1861–1921), short-story writer and novelist	**luovuus** *te*	creativity
		mahdollisuus *te*	possibility, opportunity
		maisema	landscape
		meren|pinta	sea level
ammenta-	scoops, ladles; draws	**metri**	metre
		mukaan	along
Edelfeldt	Albert Edelfeldt (1854–1905), artist	**näin**	like this
		näin etelässä	this far south
		paitsi	except
halv|in	superlative of **halpa**	**si|tä paitsi**	in addition
		patikoi-	hikes, rambles
Joensuu	city in east central Finland	**pyhiin|vaellus** *kse*	pilgrimage
kansallis|puisto	national park	**romantiikka**	Romanticism
kasva-	grows	**sattu-**	happens; hits; hurts
kasvi	plant	
kasvillisuus *te*	vegetation	**Sibelius** *kse*	Jean Sibelius (1865–1957)
kilsa →			
kilometri		**uhan|alainen**	endangered, under threat (**uhka** 'threat')
laskettelu	tobogganing		
lempi *e*	favourite; love		
lukuisa	numerous	**varsinkin**	especially

Exercise 3 Read the following sentences out loud, step by step, in the sequence indicated. The idea is to make the various building blocks come to you naturally.

Kuule
Kuule, me ollaan
Kuule, me ollaan tyttöjen kanssa

Kuule, me ollaan tyttöjen kanssa lähdössä
Kuule, me ollaan tyttöjen kanssa lähdössä Kolille
Kuule, me ollaan tyttöjen kanssa lähdössä Kolille patikoimaan
Kuule, me ollaan tyttöjen kanssa lähdössä Kolille patikoimaan
viikonloppuna.

Now repeat this routine, but replace (a) **tyttöjen kanssa** by (1)
poikien kanssa, (2) **vanhempieni kanssa**, (3) **muutamien ystävien
kanssa**, and (b) **Kolille** by (1) **maalle**, (2) **Kiteelle**, or (3) any other
place you like.

Mä yleensä käyn
Mä yleensä käyn Ruotsissa
Mä yleensä käyn Ruotsissa pari kertaa vuodessa

Replace (a) **Ruotsissa** by (1) **New Yorkissa**, (2) **Ranskassa**, (3)
kirjastossa, and (4) other places of your own choosing, and (b) **pari
kertaa vuodessa** by (1) **kaks kertaa viikossa**, (2) **joka kesällä**, and
(3) **kolme kertaa päivässä**. Picture yourself doing what you're
saying you do: watch out for absurdities (like going to New York
three times a day).

Dialogue 4 ▣

Suomen koulusysteemi

Finnish education

*Mrs Furr and Mrs Skeene, foreigners living in Finland, talk about
the education system there.*

*Kaksi suomessa asuvaa ulkomaalaista rouvaa keskustelee suomen
koulusysteemistä. Mrs Furr on juuri muuttanut Suomeen ja Mrs
Skeene on asunut Suomessa jo useita vuosia*

MRS FURR: Minua huolestuttaa[1] vähän, miten Brian sopeutuu
               uuteen kouluunsa.
MRS SKEENE: Minun mielestä sinun on turha huolestua[2] siitä.
               Suomalainen peruskoulu on mielestäni[3] erittäin
               hyvä. Krista käy nyt peruskoulun 6. (kuudetta)
               luokkaa ja viihtyy oikein hyvin. Ensi vuonna hän
               siirtyykin sitten jo yläasteelle, 7. (seitsemännelle)
               luokalle.

Mrs Furr: Montako vuotta tämä peruskoulu kestää? Se on kai
             pakollista koulua?
Mrs Skeene: Kyllä. Oppivelvollisuus Suomessa päättyy 16
             (kuudentoista) vuoden iässä.⁴ Silloin ollaan perus-
             koulun 9. (yhdeksännellä) eli viimeisellä luokalla.
             Peruskouluun kuuluu siis 9 (yhdeksän) luokkaa,
             jotka jakautuvat ala- ja yläasteeseen. Ala-asteeseen
             kuuluvat luokat 1–6 (yksviivakuus), ja yläasteeseen
             luokat 7–9 (seitsemänviivayhdeksän).
Mrs Furr: Millaisia opiskeluvaihtoehtoja Suomessa on perus-
             koulun jälkeen?
Mrs Skeene: Hyvin monenlaisia. On esimerkiksi lukio, ammatil-
             liset laitokset, ja niiden jälkeen on opistot, ammat-
             tikorkeakoulut ja yliopistot. Lukio kestää yleensä
             2–4 vuotta ja sen päättyessä⁵ saa ylioppilastodis-
             tuksen, jolla voi hakea opiskelemaan yliopistoihin
             ja ammattikorkeakouluihin. Ammatilliset oppi-
             laitokset antavat käytännönläheistä koulutusta eri
             aloille.
Mrs Furr: Mitä Krista aikoo tehdä peruskoulun jälkeen?
Mrs Skeene: Hän ei ole vielä päättänyt sitä. On niin monia hyviä
             vaihtoehtoja. Mutta onhan hänellä vielä kolme
             vuotta aikaa miettiä.

1 minu|la huolestutta|la 'I'm worried'.

2 sinu|n on turha huolestu|la 'there's no point in your worrying'.

3 miele|stä|ni 'in my opinion'.

4 16 [kuudentoista] vuoden iä|ssä 'at the age of sixteen' (ikä 'age').

5 se|n päätty|e|ssä 'when it is finished' (Unit 13).

Vocabulary

ala	area	ikä	age
ala-asteQ	lower grade	iässä	sINE of ikä
ammatillinen	vocational, trade-	jaka|utu-	is divided
erittäin	especially,	keskustele-	chats
	particularly	korkea|koulu	'high school', college
esimerkiksi	for example	koulutus kse	education
huolestu-	worries (over)	käytännön|	hands-on
huolestutta-	it worries X	läheinen	

laitos *kse*	institute	**pakollinen**	compulsory
lukio	(something like a	**perus|koulu**	elementary school
	senior secondary	**päättä-**	finishes; decides
	school or sixth	**sopeutu-**	settles in, fits in
	form college)	**systeemi**	system
luokka	class, form	**todistus** *kse*	certificate
monenlainen	of many sorts	**turha**	vain, empty
mun mielestä	in my opinion	**vaihto|ehto**	alternative
opisto	college	**viihty-**	gets on, thrives
oppi|velvollisuus	compulsory	**yleensä**	in general
te	education (lit.	**ylä|asteQ**	upper grade
	learning duty)	**yli|oppilaX**	university
oppi|laitos *kse*	educational		student
	institution		

Exercise 4 Raid the dialogue above for ideas about how to say the following in Finnish:

1 What do you intend to do after university?
2 In my opinion, Scottish elementary schools are especially good.
3 It's compulsory, I suppose?
4 I'm a little worried (about) how the cat is going to get used to its new home.

Language points

Participles as adjectives

In the previous unit, you learned how the third infinitive can be used instead of an entire clause. All four participles can be used in this way, as well. The constructions are typical of more formal varieties of Finnish, but you will need to be able to recognize and decode them if you want to be able to read most written Finnish.

Study the similarities and differences between the clause (C) and participle (P) constructions in the following examples:

Present active participle
P **kaunasta johtu\|va** kaksintaistelu
C **kaksintaistelu,** *joka johtuu kaunasta*
   a duel *which derives from a grudge*
P **uusissa** *markkinoilla olevissa* **tietokoneissa**

C **uusissa tietokoneissa,** *jotka ovat markkinoilla*
in the new computers *which are on the market*

Past active participle
P **lahja heidän** *80 vuotta täyttäneelle* **naapurilleen**
C **lahja heidän naapurilleen,** *joka on täyttänyt 80 vuotta*
a gift to their neighbour, *who has reached his/her eightieth birthday*

Present passive participle
P *sairaalassa hoidettavat* **tapaukset**
C **tapaukset,** *joita täytyy hoitaa sairaalassa*
the cases *which have to be treated in hospital*

Past passive participle
P **vain pieni osa** *vuonna 1981 Afrikkaan annetusta avusta*
C **vain pieni osa siitä avusta,** *joka vuonna 1981 annettiin Afrikkaan*
only a small part *of the aid which was given to Africa in the year 1981*

Dialogue 5 ▣

Mikroilemassa

Coping with computers

Ville asks Riikka, the computer expert, for advice and help with setting up his new machine

VILLE: Riikka hei, et haluis tulla vilkaseen mun uutta tietokonetta, kun mä tarttisin vähän opastusta sen käytössä ja sähän oot niissä asioissa niin hyvä.[1]
RIIKKA: Okei, mikäs siinä.[2] Onks sulla jokin erityisongelma?
VILLE: No ei oikeestaan. Mä en vaan tiedä mitä kaikkia mahdollisuuksia siinä on. Mä osaan kyllä käyttää kirjotus- ja piirustusohjelmia, mutta siinä on sen lisäks kaikkia laskenta- ym. ohjelmia.
RIIKKA: Onks sulla printteri kans?
VILLE: On. Mä ostin sellasen mustesuihkukirjottimen,[3] kun se oli edullinen ja siinä on lähes yhtä hyvä jälki kun laserprintterissä.

RIIKKA: Joo, ne on ihan hyviä. Onks sun tietokoneessa värinäyttö vai tavallinen mustavalkonäyttö?

VILLE: Ihan mustavalkonäyttö vaan. Mun mielestä on turha maksaa siitä värinäytöstä, kun mä pääasiassa käytän sitä vaan kirjottamiseen.[4] Tärkeempi mun mielestä on hiiri, kun mä oon tottunu käyttään sitä. Mun mielestä sen avulla on helpompi toimia kun pelkällä näppäimistöllä[5] ja funktionäppäimillä.

RIIKKA: Se on tietysti siitäki kii,[6] mihin on tottunu. Miten iso muisti sun koneessa on?

VILLE: En mä nyt muista, mut kyllä se on ihan riittävä mun käyttöön. Käviskö sulle,[7] että mennään nyt kattoon sitä konetta, niin voit sit itse tarkastaa sen toiminnot.

RIIKKA: Mikäs siinä, jos tarjoot kupin kahvia.

VILLE: Selvä.

1 nii|i|ssä asio|i|ssa niin hyvä 'so good at these things', with the inessive; verbs go into the third infinitive illative in such constructions, e.g. hyvä laula|ma|an.

2 mi|käs sii|nä 'why not? (= OK)'.

3 Mä ostin sellase|n muste|suihku|kirjottime|n 'I've bought this ink-jet printer', with sellanen (= semmonen) as a buffer to help introduce a term Ville is not particularly at home with.

4 käytän sitä vaan kirjo(i)tta|mise|en 'I'm going to be using it only for writing'.

5 pelkä|llä näppäimistö|llä 'with just the keyboard'.

6 Se on siitäki kii(nni) 'It depends on ...' (= se riippuu siitä, ...).

7 Käviskö sulle 'Would it be OK with you?'

Vocabulary

edullinen	advantageous (etu 'advantage'); cheap	käyttö	use (käyttä- 'uses')
erityisongelma	particular problem	laskenta	calculation (laske- 'counts')
funktio	function		
jälki e	trace, (foot)print; mark, (im)print	lisäks(i)	in addition
		muisti	memory (capacity to remember)
kattoon → katso|ma|an			
		musteQ	ink (musta 'black')
kirjoitin ime	printer	näppäimistö	(typewriter) keyboard
kirjoitus kse	writing; document		
käyttään → käyttä|mä|än		näytt|ö	(computer) display

opastus *kse*	guidance (**opasta-** 'guides')	**tieto**	data; fact
		tieto|koneQ	computer
piirustus *kse*	drawing, design	**toiminto**	function(ing)
printteri	printer	**tottu-**	gets used to
pääl|asiassa	chiefly		**(X|#n)**
riittä|vä	sufficient	**vilkaise-**	glances at
suihku	shower, jet	**vilkaseen** →	
tarkasta-	checks	**vilkaise|ma|an**	
tarttisin →		**ym.** = **ynnä**	etc.
tarvitsisin		**muu|ta**	

Additional vocabulary

Here's some extra vocabulary that is useful in discussing anything to do with computers.

romppu	CD(-ROM)	**kova|levy**	hard disk
kello|nopeus *te*	clock speed	**koti|sivu**	homepage
oletus|arvo	default value	**kilo|tavu**	megabyte
eheyttä-	defrags	**emo**	motherboard
hakemisto|puu	directory tree	**hiiri|ajuri**	mouse driver
hakemisto	directory	**siirtä-**	moves/transfers
imuroi-	downloads	**tulosta-**, **printtaX-**	prints
tiedo|sto	file	**ruutu**, **näyttö**	screen, display
korppu	small (3.5 inch) floppy	**palvelin** *ime*	server
		arkin|syöttö	sheetfeeder
lerppu	large (5.25 inch) floppy	**purka-**	unzips, decompresses
levykkeQ|asema	floppy drive	**päivittä-**	upgrades
alusta-	formats	**tiivistä-**	zips, compresses

Exercise 5 When it comes to vocabulary, you're on your own from here on. But you already have learned enough so that you can extrapolate. Start now by making intelligent guesses at the forms and meanings of the empty cells on the next page:

	A	B
1		**mahdollisuus** *te* possibility
2		**turvallisuus** *te* security
3	**todellinen** true	
4		**velvollisuus** *te* duty, obligation
5	**ystävä** friend	**ystävyys** *te* friendship
6		**luovuus** *te* creativity

Key to exercises

Lesson 1

Exercise 2 1 I am English. 2 I am an engineer. 3 I am a Scottish musician. 4 You are a foreigner (= not Finnish). 5 You are an Italian diplomat.

Exercise 3 1 Oletteko te lääkäri? 2 Hän/se on unkarilainen ohjaaja. 3 Mä olen englantilainen liikemies. 4 Hän/se on ranskalainen matemaatikko. 5 Mä olen kanadalainen opiskelija.

Exercise 4 1 tanskalainen 2 Kreikka 3 norjalainen 4 hollantilainen 5 Albania 6 ukrainalainen 7 turkkilainen 8 portugalilainen

Exercise 5 1 Oletteko te suomalainen? 2 Oletteko te lukkoseppä? 3 Oletteko te venäläinen? 4 Oletteko te poliisi? 5 Oletteko te ranskalainen?

Exercise 6 1 Japanilainenko se on? 2 Insinöörikö sä olet (*or*: te olette)? 3 Palomieskö se on? 4 Saksalainenko sä olet (*or*: te olette)? 5 Poliitikkoko se on?

Exercise 7 1 the fish's tail 2 the door of the house 3 the taste of the fish 4 the end of summer 5 the owl's wing 6 the size of the disk

Exercise 8 1 ranskalaisen viinin maku 2 rahan väri 3 pienen talon ovi 4 talon pieni ovi 5 Ruotsin pääkaupunki 6 lääkärin italialainen ystävä 7 Lontoon historia 8 puvun uusi hinta 9 uuden puvun hinta 10 muusikon parta

Lesson 2

Exercise 1 1 M(in)ä pidän kahvista. 2 Pidätkö s(in)ä (or, more colloquial: pidätsä) teestä? 3 Se (or formal: hän) pitää keväästä. 4 M(in)ä pidän viinasta, se (hän) pitää viinistä. 5 Me pidämme Suomesta.

Exercise 2 1 m(in)ä sanon 2 me näemme 3 Pidättekö (te) Pariisista? 4. He puhuvat. 5 Se (more formal: hän) puhuu Suomesta. 6 Näetkö s(in)ä? (or, even less formal: näetsä?)

Exercise 3 1 Mä pidän vedestä, mutta mä juon mieluummin maitoa. 2 Mä pidän kalasta, mutta mä syön mieluummin juustoa. 3 Mä katselen televisiota, mutta mä kuuntelen mieluummin radiota. 4 Mä puhun englantia, mutta mä puhun mieluummin suomea. 5 Mä pidän klarinetista, mutta mä kuuntelen mieluummin pianoa.

Exercise 4 1 saunan jälkeen 2 sodan jälkeen 3 aamiaisen jälkeen 4 kokeen jälkeen 5 tauon jälkeen

Exercise 5 1 ennen saunaa 2 ennen sotaa 3 ennen aamiaista 4 ennen koetta 5 ennen taukoa

Exercise 6 1 unkaria 2 italiaa 3 ruotsia 4 ranskaa 5 hollantia

Exercise 7 Some possible answers include: Jari katsoo televisiota. Anna etsii kynää. Jussi pesee autoa, lattiaa. Satu maalaa taloa. Se lukee lehteä, kirjaa. Se kirjoittaa postikorttia. Se kuuntelee kasettia, levyä. Lapsi syö omenaa.

Exercise 9 1 Presidentillä on iso auto. 2 Onks sun olut tummaa? 3 Talon ovi on vihreä. 4 Baarimikolla on ruotsalainen vaimo. 5 Onko teidän asunto pieni?

Exercise 10 1 Hänellä on paljon rahaa. 2 Pekalla on monta ystävää. 3 Meillä on sukua Lapissa. 4 Onko sinulla koira?

Exercise 11 Some possible answers: Minulla on tietokone, mutta mulla ei ole radiota. Minulla ei ole autoa, minulla on pyörä. Minulla ei ole kynää, mutta minulla on paperia.

Lesson 3

Exercise 3 1 seuraa/seuratkaa minua 2 tuo(kaa) mehua 3 avaa/ avatkaa ovi 4 sulje/sulkekaa ikkuna 5 pane/pankaa kissa ulos 6 hae/ hakekaa lääkäri 7 vie(kää) televisio pois 8 syö(kää) kakkua 9 auta/ auttakaa poliisia 10 unohda/unohtakaa se

Exercise 6 1 Se saapuu Turusta. 2 Ne asuu (or, formal: He asuvat) Helsingissä. 3 Ne odottaa ulkona. 4 Mitä se sanoo? 5 Missä te asutte? 6 Missä ne nukkuu? 7 Miksi sä odotat? 8 Milloin me lähdemme? 9 Kuka tulee? 10 Ne tietää, missä me asumme (colloquial: asutaan. See Unit 5).

Exercise 7 1 Valitettavasti mä en tiedä sen osoitetta. 2 Olen pahoillani, mutta mä en tiedä sen puhelinnumeroa. 3 Mä en tunne sen isää. 4 Mä en tunne sen poikaa. 5 Mä en tunne sen vaimoa.

Exercise 8 1 Sanokaa jotain suomeksi! 2 Kertokaa jotain Helsingistä! 3 Lukekaa se mulle! 4 Istukaa! 5 Kirjoittakaa mulle postikortti! 6 Odottakaa ulkona!

Exercise 9 1 sano 2 kerro 3 lue 4 istu 5 kirjoita 6 odota.

Exercise 10 1 Kuuntele vaan! 2 Sammuta vaan! 3 Avaa vaan! 4 Imuroi vaan! 5 Ota vaan!

Exercise 11 1 Kuunnelkaa vaan! 2 Sammuttakaa vaan! 3 Avatkaa vaan! 4 Imuroikaa vaan! 5 Ottakaa vaan!

Exercise 12 1 kieltä- 2 niele- 3 tuo- 4 reagoi- 5 sano-

Exercise 14 1 Se/hän taitaa olla ruotsalainen. 2 Niillä/heillä taitaa olla iso talo. 3 Te taidatte tarvita kahvia.

Lesson 4

Exercise 1 1 Helsingissä 2 pullossa 3 pöydällä 4 asemalla 5 yhdessä päivässä 6 Suomessa 7 Englannissa 8 kesällä 9 ensi kuussa 10 oikealla

Exercise 2 1 asemalta 2 asemalla 3 laiturilla 4 junalla 5 kello kuudelta 6 Juusosta 7 Juusolta 8 pöydältä 9 kupista 10 oikealla

Exercise 3 1 asemalle 2 pöydälle 3 Eilalle 4 hyllylle 5 kuppiin 6 Tanskaan 7 kaupunkiin

Exercise 4 1 Jätä laukku eteiseen. 2 Mä pistän lasin takaisin kaappiin. 3 Aila on vielä junassa. 4 Mä kirjoitan kirjeen Juusolle. 5 Lähetä postikortti Heikille Lontooseen. 6 Aikataulu on hyllyn takana. 7 Auto on aseman edessä. 8 Vie minut Pariisiin! 9 Milloin me ollaan perillä? 10 Onks mehua lasissa?

Exercise 7 1 ulos ovesta ja vasemmalle. 2 Missä mahtaa olla pankki? 3 Se tekee kaksikymmentä markkaa. 4 Mitä maksaa postimerkki Englantiin?

Lesson 5

Exercise 1 1 asutaan 2 menemme 3 halutaan 4 ei pidetä 5 emme lue 6 puhumme 7 ei tarvita

Exercise 2 1 jalat 2 huone 3 kaupungit 4 kadut 5 hammas

Exercise 3 1 kirjoissa 2 talossa 3 saarelta 4 laseista 5 pankeille 6 hampaaseen 7 taloihin 8 töihin 9 vesiin 10 jalkaan

Exercise 4 1 uuslila taloljla 2 halpoljla takkeljla 3 vapalilta kansoljla 4 hyvlilä ystävlilä 5 nuorlila opiskelijolilta 6 vanholjla opettajlila

Exercise 5 1 lampun 2 voileipiä 3 ovi 4 autoa

Lesson 6

Exercise 1 1 Mitä s(in)ä haluat, näitä vai noita? 2 Mitä s(in)ä haluat, jäätelöä vai kakkua? 3 Haluatsä (Haluatko sinä) viiniä, olutta, vai mehua? 4 Mä syön nä(m)ä voileivät. 5 T(u)ossa on suklaatuutti.

Exercise 2 1 sä ostat 2 he sanoivat 3 te osasitte 4 me haluamme 5 mä voin: voiln and voliln 6 hän muuttaa 7 ne saapui 8 mä tarvitsin 9 se joi 10 me huusimme

Exercise 3 1 Missä sä olit? 2 Mitä se sanoi? 3 Kissa söi hiiren. 4 Mä autoin vähän. 5 Näitsä sen? 6 Ne otti (more formal: he ottivat) sen pois. 7 Mihin sä pistit sen? 8 Kuka mainitsi siitä? 9 Kenelle sä annoit sen? 10 Mistä sä löysit sen?

Exercise 4 1 Se meni. 2 Ne ei tulleet. 3 Mä istuin tässä. 4 He sanoivat. 5 Etkö nähnyt sitä? 6 Mä luin sen. 7 Me ostimme uuden auton. 8 Me emme tavanneet. 9 Hän ei saanut kirjettä Tanjalta. 10 Ne lähetti(vät) rahan (= the money)/rahaa (= some money).

Exercise 5 1 Tulkaa kotiin syömään! 2 Juokse tuonne katsomaan! 3 Mene uimaan! 4 Lähtekää kävelemään!

Exercise 6 1 mentiin 2 katsotaan 3 syödään 4 haluttiin

Exercise 7 1 tärkeä 2 oikeastaan 3 hulluksi 4 puhumaan 5 pitäisi

Lesson 7

Exercise 1 1 loputon 2 kengätön 3 työtön 4 poluton 5 hampaaton 6 mauton 7 muodoton 8 lumeton 9 auringoton 10 virheetön

Exercise 2 1 non-existent 2 unwritten 3 unwashed 4 unbaked 5 uneaten 6 uninhabited

Exercise 3 1 rakennettu 2 käyttämätön 3 maalaamaton 4 syöty 5 keitetty 6 kuorimaton

Exercise 4 1 **Mä oon tullut** 'I have come'. 2 **Se on hakenut** 'She has fetched/applied for'. 3 **Ne on saapuneet** 'They have arrived'. 4 **Ootsä ollut Hesassa?** 'Have you been in Helsinki?' 5 **Mä oon avannut ikkunan** 'I've opened the window'. 6 **Me ollaan avattu ikkuna** 'We've opened the window'. 7 **Me ollan tultu** 'We've come'. 8 **Hän on tarvinnut apua** 'He has needed some help'. 9 **Mistä se on saanut rahan** 'Where has (s)he got the money from?' 10 **Se on paennut** '(S)he/it has escaped'.

Exercise 5 1 Se ei ole[l] lähtenyt. 2 Mä en ole huomannut sitä. 3 Ne on sanoneet jotain. 4 Mä olen nähnyt sen jo. 5 Me ei olla[v] vielä puhuttu siitä. 6 Mä olen tavannut hänet.

Exercise 7 Malted potato casserole

2 kg potatoes	2–3 tbs melted butter
1 dl wheat flour	2 tsp salt
4–5 dl milk	nutmeg

Boil the potatoes until they are done, and peel them immediately after letting them give off their steam. Mash the potatoes and sprinkle the flour into them (lit. into the mass). Let the mixture malt/ferment for a few hours or even until the next day. Stir a few times. Add the milk, butter, and flavourings. Pour the mixture into a buttered oven dish and bake (it) at 150 degrees for about two hours.

Lesson 8

Exercise 1 1 nopeampi 2 selvempi 3 mukavampi 4 kiltimpi 5 voimakkaampi 6 pienempi 7 paksumpi 8 ohuempi 9 punaisempi 10 terveempi

Exercise 2 1 Sä olet/oot nuorempi ku(i)n mä (*or*: mä olen/oon nuorempi kun sä). 2 Pihvi on kalliimpi ku(i)n keitto. 3 Espanja on isompi ku(i)n Portugali. 4 Lääkäri on vanhempi ku(i)n lapsi. 5 Paperi on kevyempi ku(i)n kulta.

Exercise 3 1 Mä etsin kuivempaa viiniä. 2 Mä etsin halvempaa vihkoa. 3 Mä etsin pienempää laukkua. 4 Mä etsin yksinkertaisempaa vastausta. 5 Mä etsin makeampaa mehua.

Exercise 4 1 Mä oon löytänyt kuivemman viinin. 2 Mä oon löytänyt halvemman vihkon. 3 Mä oon löytänyt pienemmän laukun. 4 Mä oon löytänyt yksinkertaisemman vastauksen. 5 Mä oon löytänyt makeamman mehun.

Exercise 7 1 ujoimmalta 2 tummin 3 kylmin 4 kovimmasta 5 isoimpaan 6 suurimmat 7 nuorimmissa 8 tervein 9 iloisin 10 pisimmälle

Exercise 8 1 Se on luokan nuorin. 2 Tanska on Euroopan vanhin kuningaskunta. 3 Tämä laukku on raskaampi kun m(in)un, mut(ta) s(in)un on raskain. 4 Nopein voittaa, mut(ta) hitain on paras.

Lesson 9

Exercise 1 1 poikien isä 2 tyttöjen nimet 3 suurempien radioiden hinnat 4 huoneiden numerot 5 monien muiden maiden lait

Exercise 2 Some sample answers: 1 Mä herään tavallisesti noin puoli kahdeksan. 2 Mä lähden kello seitsemän. 3 Meillä syödään illallista yleensä kello kuudelta. 4 Arkipäivinä mä meen nukkumaan noin puoli yhdeltätoista.

Exercise 3 1 seitsemän kertaa 2 päivässä 3 kaksi kertaa 4 vuodessa

Exercise 4 1 Se seisoi poikien edessä. 2 Ne pani kirjeen takaisin lampun alle. 3 Mä haluaisin mennä Tukholmaan Turun kautta. 4 Kirkko on koulun vieressä. 5 Ne vei meidät (*or*: Meidät vietiin) rakennuksen taakse.

Lesson 10

Exercise 2 1 Jospa minulla olisi (mulla ois) aikaa! 2 Jospa mä tietäisin, mitä sä tarkoitat! 3 Jospa sä jäisit vähäks aikaa! 4 Jospa me ei tehtäs sitä! 5 Kunpa me ei oltas ois menty sinne eilen!

Exercise 3 1 M(in)un täytyy/pitää mennä kotiin. 2 Irma voisi tietää siitä. 3 Ne ei viitsi tulla (meidän) mukaan. 4 Minne sä meinaat/ajattelet mennä tänä iltana? 5 Se joutui kirjoittamaan koko kirjeen. 6 M(in)un on tärkeä(t)ä/tärkeetä voimistella vähintään kolme kertaa viikossa. 7 Meidän pitäis(i) kirjoittaa sille. 8 S(in)un ei pidä vastata. 9 S(in)ä et saa vastata.

Exercise 4 1 Sulla on varmaan joku hyvä syy lukea sitä, vai? 2 Se vaaditaan kaikilta opiskelijoilta. 3 Ruotsi on Suomen toinen virallinen kieli. 4 Eiks suurin osa suomalaisista osaa ruotsiakin? 5 Ranskassa kaikkien virkamiesten pitää osata ranskaa.

Exercise 5 1 sen huoneeseen 2 sen puhetta 3 sen vaimo 4 mun kuppiin 5 teidän vuoro 6 sen luona (NB: remember that it is also less formal to say **mä juoksin** than **(minä) juoksin**, **mun** than **minun**, **mä oon ollu** than **olen ollut**)

Exercise 6 1 Se seisoi meidän takanalmme. 2 Avaimet löydettiin teidän huoneelstalnne. 3 Se ei halunnut esitellä ystävälälnsä. 4 Miksi pudistat päältälsi? 5 Se joi puolet oluelstalan.

Exercise 7 1 Mieluummin mä otan kahvia partsilla (parvekkeella). 2 Mitä kello on nyt? Puol neljä. 3 Me sovittiin tyttöjen kanssa et tavataan Espalla (Esplanaadilla) kahdeksalta. 4 Kat(s)otaan siellä mitä tehdään. 5 Mun täytyy hoitaa ensin pari juttuu (juttua).

Lesson 11

Exercise 2 Tämä on se huone, jolsta/milstä me puhuttiin. Noi kirjat, jotka/mitkä on ylimmäisellä hyllyllä, on mun. Sanakirja, jolnlka/milnlkä mä unohdin kotiin, on parempi. Uusi opettaja, jolta te ette tunne, tulee huomenna.

Exercise 3 1 yhä yksinkertaisemmin 2 halvimmin 3 mitä pikimmin 4 syvemmin 5 Se tuli aikaisemmin.

Exercise 4 1 kolme viidennestä 2 neljä kuudennesta 3 seitsemän kahdeksannesta 4 kaksi kolmannesta 5 kaksikymmentäkaksi seitsemännestä

Exercise 5 1 someone else 2 something else 3 some people 4 all kinds of (stuff) 5 many people think

Lesson 12

Exercise 2 1 Mä kuulin niitten/niiden lähtevän. 2 Hän näki junan saapuvan. 3 Se sanoi tulevansa takaisin huomenna. 4 Toivon tapaavani hänet jälleen. 5 Se tuntui tietävän keitä ne oli.

Exercise 3 1 I saw it change colour. 2 There seemed to be something under the carpet. 3 I deny knowing anything. 4 I want you to apologise. 5 (S)he thought the food was ready.

Exercise 4 1 After (s)he had rested (s)he stood up. 2 As soon as (s)he said it I understood. 3 I did it in order to have something to do. 4 I have to go into town in order to see to something. 5 We aren't here to meet people.

Lesson 13

Exercise 2 1 Tuesday to Saturday, 11–15 (Tuesdays also in the evenings, 18–21), and Sundays, 11–16. 2 Tuomarinkylä, Didrichsen. 3 Yes: at the Sinebrychoff museum, at 3 in the afternoon. 4 Yes. Saturdays, 11–15

Exercise 3 1 Mennään sinne Finlandiataloon huomenna. 2 Onks se auki tiistaisin? 3 Se taitaa olla nähtävä. 4 Mitä museota te suosittelette? 5 Mä en tiedä, ehdinkö nähdä senkin.

Exercise 4 1 lapsi, joka on syntynyt Saarenmaalla 2 laki, joka koskee saarta 3 dokumentti kaupungista, joka rakennettiin sata metriä maan alle 4 helsinkiläinen, joka on ottanut neljännen peräkkäisen mestaruutensa

Proverbs: Here are some English (very rough) equivalents of some of the proverbs:

1 Better a bird in the hand than two in the bush. 3 The pot calling the kettle black. 6 Out of the fying pan into the fire. 7 He who laughs last laughs loudest/best. 8 Silence is golden. 9 Early to bed and early to rise makes a man healthy, wealthy, and wise. 12 Easy come, easy go.

Lesson 14

Exercise 1 1 Mistä sun äitis suku on kotoisin? 2 Niin monet luulee. 3 Ne molemmat opiskeli Jyväskylän yliopistossa. 4 Mulla on paljon sukua myös Oulussa. 5 Onks sun isäs kans sieltä päin?

Exercise 2 karhu hirvi susi kissa hiiri mikrobi

Exercise 3 *Wild*: peura, ilves; *tame*: poro, ankka ('wild duck' is **sorsa**), kissa, karja, koira

Exercise 5 1 Hallitus sulki sairaalan. 2 Tyttö avasi oven. 3 Isäni keskeyttää keskustelun. 4 Poikien täytyy järjestää huone. 5 Meidän on pakko lähteä nyt. 6 Poliisi etsii autoa.

Exercise 6 1 Viime vuonna me käytiin Ruotsissa. 2 Jäät sä tänne, vai tuut sä mukaan? 3 Tieto kulkee nopeasti. 4 Kävi ilmi, että se puhuu suomea. 5 Se muutti Harrin luo.

Exercise 7 1 They won't bite (you) if you're not afraid of them. 2 Of course I know these waters! 3 No train's going to come from that direction at this hour. 4 You could still get across that bridge last night, anyway. 5 All the landscape looks pretty much the same up here in Lappi.

Lesson 15

Exercise 2 1 1300. 2 Turku Academy. 3 Bishop of Turku and author of the first Finnish primer. 4 A handicrafts museum, with exhibits illustrating old Turku ways of life.

Exercise 3 1 Ne tuntee jo toisensa. (more formal: He tuntevat jo toisensa.) 2 Se puhuu aina itsestään. 3 Mä jätin mun laukun toiseen huoneeseen. (= on purpose). Mun laukku jäi toiseen huoneeseen (= inadvertently). 4 Siellä oli myös pari muuta vierasta. 5 Ne tuli käymään kahtena eri aikana (or: kanteen kertaan). 6 Mä en saanut ketään uskomaan itseäni.

Exercise 4 1 Se kertoi mulle kaiken puhelimitse. 2 Ne muuttaa Ruotsiin vanhempineen. 3 Mä näin sen omin silmin.

Exercise 6 1 keittoa, jota isä keitti 2 tarinat, jotka lapset kirjoitti(vat) 3 romaanissa, jota Goethe mainitsi

Exercise 7 1 That sort of thing can happen to anyone. 2 Is there a good hotel somewhere (around) here? 3 Don't do it under any circumstances! 4 Any one of you (= it doesn't matter which) would have done the same. 5 The boy didn't know where else to look.

Lesson 16

Exercise 1 1 Se merkitsee jokaiselle vähän eri asiaa. 2 Siksi kai nütä kutsutaan sisuiksi. 3 Se on hyvin todellinen suomalaisille. 4 Älä anna periksi! 5 Onpas tämä voimakasta!

Exercise 2 1 Milloin alkoi jatkosota? 2 Kuka oli Suomen ensimmäinen presidentti? 3 Kenestä tuli presidentti Kekkosen jälkeen? 4 Milloin Suomi itsenäistyi? 5 Kuinka paljon ihmisiä kuoli Suomen sisällissodassa?

Exercise 4 1 Mitä sä aiot tehdä yliopiston jälkeen? 2 Minusta skotlantilainen peruskoulu on erittäin hyvä. 3 Se on kai pakollista? 4 Mi(nu)a huolestuttaa vähän, miten kissa sopeutuu uuteen kotiinsa.

Exercise 5 A1 **mahdollinen** 'possible'; A2 **turvallinen** 'secure'; B3 **todellisuus** *te* 'reality'; A4 **velvollinen** 'obliged'; B6 **luova** 'creative'

Appendix: Finnish names

You'll meet over thirty Finnish given names in this book, and will probably have noticed that only a few are familiar-looking. To give you an overview, here's a list of some of the more common ones. Notice that most (but not all!) names ending in **a** refer to females, and most (but not all!) ending in **o** refer to males.

Women

Aija	Ilona	Lilja	Reija	Sonia
Aila	Irja	Maija	Riitta	Sorja
Aliisa	Irma	Marja	Ritva	Susanna
Anja	Juulia	Martta	Saija	Tarja
Arja	Kaarina	Milja	Saima	Tuija
Eeva	Karoliina	Minna	Sanna	Tuula
Eija	Laila	Mirja	Seija	Unelma
Elina	Laina	Netta	Selja	Ursula
Erja	Launa	Niina	Senja	Veera
Hanna	Lea	Onerva	Silja	Veija
Helena	Leea	Paula	Sirkka	Viia
Hilja	Leena	Raija	Solja	Vilja
Hilkka	Liisa			

Aale	Hele	Irene	Roine	Salome
Aune	Helle			
Enne	Hille	Laine	Salme	Synnöve

Aili	Armi	Helmi	Meri	Taimi
Ainikka	Auni	Kirsti	Outi	Terhi
Allikki	Heidi	Kyllikki	Päivikki	Tuulikki
Anneli	Heli	Meeri	Salli	Virpi
Annikki	Hellikki			

Aino	Pirkko	Tellervo	Vuokko

| Aamu | | Keiju | Maiju | Eedit |
| Anu | | | | |

Men:

Elja	Jorma	Konsta	Miikka	Pekka
Ilkka	Juha	Kustaa	Mika	Turkka
Joosua				

Aare	Aarne	Aarre	Aate	Aatte
Ale	Joose	Kalle	Tuure	Valle
Helge				

Aarni	Eemeli	Jooseppi	Lauri	Pentti
Ahti	Eenokki	Juhani	Leevi	Sakari
Antti	Erkki	Jussi	Martti	Seeli
Artturi	Heikki	Kai	Matti	Taavetti
Eeerikki	Ilmari	Kalevi	Olavi	Tapani
Eeli	Joni	Lassi	Olli	

Aapo	Eero	Keijo	Risto	Timo
Aarto	Eino	Launo	Sampo	Toivo
Aatto	Esko	Leo	Simo	Urho
Aimo	Into	Mauno	Sorjo	Urpo
Alho	Jaakko	Niilo	Tapio	Usko
Alpo	Jalo	Paavo	Tauno	Veijo
Antero	Jarkko	Raimo	Teijo	Veikko
Arvo	Kaarlo	Reijo	Terho	Viljo
Asko	Kauko			

| Eetu | Hannu | Samu | Teemu | |

| Äijö | Väinö | Yrjö | | |

| Aleksis | Aulis | Hannes | Mooses | Uljas |
| Armas | Eelis | Joonas | Tuomas | |

| Eevert | Roobert | | | |

Finnish surnames are many: there are about 76,000 of them. Natural and topographic features are quite common, either alone as in **Laakso** ('valley'), **Saari** ('island'), **Koski** ('rapids'), or in derived forms (**Saarinen, Koskela, Koivisto, Sinisalo**). Roughly half end in **=nen** or **=lA** (like **Mäkinen** and **Mäkelä**, both from **mäki** *e* 'hill').

Nicknames also abound: for example, someone named **Matti** may also be called **Masa, Masi** or **Matsu** by friends.

Finnish–English glossary

For nouns written here as ending in X or Q, see pages 30–31; for verbs written here as ending in X, XE, or TSE, see page 52.

aalto	wave	**ammatillinen**	professional-, trade-
aamu	morning		
aapinen	primer	**ammatti**	profession, trade
aatto	eve; night before X		
		ankka	(domesticated) duck
aiheuttaa-	causes		
aika[1]	time (sG aja|n)	**anta-**	gives
aika[2]	(adv.) fairly, somewhat	**antautu-**	surrenders
		anteeksi	excuse me
aikaisemmin	earlier	**apu**	aid, assistance
aiko-	intends	**asia**	matter, affair
aikuinen	adult	**asema**	station, position
aina	always	**asteQ**	degree, stage
ainakin	at least	**asti**	as far as, until (post.)
aineQ	(subject) matter		
ainoa	only, sole	**asu-**	resides, inhabits, lives
ainut	only, sole		
aivan	quite; precisely	**asunto**	flat; apartment
aja-	drives	**aukaise-**	opens
ajattele-	thinks	**aurinko**	sun
al|lA	under PP	**autta-**	helps, assists
al|le	(to) under PP	**avaX-**	opens
al|tA	from under PP	**baari**	bar
ala|	lower	**e-**	*negative verb*
alEXE-	drops, falls, descends	**ede|ssä**	in front of X PP
alka-	begins	**eduskunta**	parliament
alku	beginning	**edusta-**	represents
aloitta-	begins (tr.)	**eepos** *kse*	epic
alueQ	region, area	**ehkä**	maybe, perhaps
amerikkalainen	American		

ehti-	has time, does X in time, has enough time to X	**hake-**	fetches, applies for
eli	or (=)	**halki**	across PP
elokuu	August	**hallinto**	administration
eläin *ime*	animal	**halpa**	cheap
elämä	life	**haluX-**	wants
enempä-	more	**hampurilainen**	hamburger
englanti	English (language)	**harmaa**	grey
		harrastus *kse*	hobby, interest
Englanti	England	**harva**	rare
enimpä-	most	**harvinainen**	rare
ennen	before; prep. w/P	**harvoin**	rarely
		hauska	nice, pleasant
ensi	next	**hedelmä**	fruit
ensimmäinen	first	**heikko**	weak
ensin	first	**heinäkuu**	July
entä(s)	what about?	**heittä-**	throws
eri	various, different	**helmikuu**	February
		helppo	easy
erikoinen	separate, special	**henki** *e*	spirit, life, person
erilainen	different, dissimilar	**henkilö**	person
		herkkä	sensitive, touchy
erittäin	especially	**herkullinen**	gourmet-
erityinen	particular, individual	**herneQ**	pea
		heti	at once, right away
eräX	a certain	**hetki**	moment
esimerkki	example	**hetkinen**	moment
esineQ	object	**hieno**	fine
esittele-	introduces	**hiihto**	skiing
esitteQ	brochure	**hiihtä-**	skis
esittä-	presents	**hiiri** *e*	mouse
etelen	into the space in front of PP	**hikoile-**	sweats
		hillo	jam
etelä	south	**hirveä**	frightful
että	that (cj.)	**hirvi** *e*	deer, stag
flunssa	'flu, headcold	**hoita-**	takes care of, tends (to)
hajoX-	breaks up, dismantles, dissolves	**hopea**	silver
		huhtikuu	April
		huippu	peak, summit

hullu	fool(ish), mad		distributes
huomaX-	notices	**jakautu-**	is distributed, is
huomenna	tomorrow		divided
huoneQ	room	**jalka**	foot, leg
huuta-	shouts	**jatka-**	continues (tr.)
huvitta-	amuses	**jauha-**	grinds
hylly	shelf	**jauheQ|liha**	mince
hyppäX-	jumps, hops	**jauho|t**	flour
hyvin	well	**jo**	already; (in
hyvä	good		questions) yet
hyväksy-	approves	**joka**	each, every
hyvästi	farewell!	**joo**	yeah
hyökkäX-	attacks	**jos**	if
--hän	you know, after	**joskus**	sometime(s)
	all	**joukko**	mass; troop
härkä	ox	**joulu**	Christmas
hävittä-	destroys	**joulukuu**	December
ihan	quite	**joutu-**	ends up in X,
ihana	lovely		winds up
ihmeQ	wonder, miracle		Xing; hurries
ihmettele-	wonders, is	**juhla**	celebration
	amazed	**julista-**	declares,
ihminen	human being		proclaims
ikkuna	window	**jumala**	god, God
ikä	age	**juo-**	drinks
ilma	air	**juokse-**	runs
ilman	without X prep.	**juotava**	drinkable; for
	w/P		drinking
ilmesty-	appears, is	**just**	just
	published	**juttu**	story; matter,
ilta	evening		affair
iso	big	**juuri**	just
istu-	sits	**jäljellä**	left over
isä	father	**jälke|en**	after X PP
itse	self; (him-, her-,	**järjestelmä**	system
	it-)self	**järvi** *e*	lake
itsenäisyys *te*	independence	**jättä-**	leaves behind
itä	east	**jää**	ice
ja	and	**jää-**	remains, stays
jaa	yeah		behind
jaka-	divides,	**kaata-**	pours
	apportions,	**kadotta-**	loses

kahdeksan	eight	**kerros** *kse*	storey
kahvi	coffee	**kerta**	time, occasion
kai	maybe, perhaps	**kertaX-**	repeats, revises
kaikenlainen	all kinds of	**kerto-**	tells, recounts
kaikki *e*	all, every(one)	**keräX-**	gathers
kakku	cake	**keskelllä**	in the middle of
kaksi	(**kahte-**) two		PP
kala	fish	**keskellle**	to the middle
kalja	(weak) beer		of PP
kallio	cliff	**keskelltä**	from the middle
kalliX	expensive, dear		of
kannatta-	is worth while	**kesken**	amid
kans	also, too	**keski** *e*	middle
kansa	nation, people	**keskiaikainen**	medieval
kansallinen	national	**keskiviikko**	Wednesday
kanssa	with PP	**keskus** *kse*	centre
kanta-	carries, bears	**keskusta**	centre
karhu	bear	**keskustele-**	converses, chats
kartta	map	**kestä-**	lasts, endures;
kaskitoista	twelve		can (with-)
kastikkeQ	gravy, sauce		stand
kasva-	grows **äintrö**	**kesä**	Summer
kasvi	plant	**kesäkuu**	June
katkalrapu	prawn	**kevät**	spring (kevää-)
katoX-	goes missing,	**kiekko**	disk, puck
	disappears	**kieli** *e*	language;
katso-	watches, looks		tongue
	at, beholds	**kielioppi**	grammar
katu	street	**kiinnosta-**	interests
kauan	for a long time	**kiinnostu-**	is interested in
kauas	(to) far away	**kiitos**	thank you!
kaukaa	from far away	**kiitti**	thanks!
kaukana	far away	**kilpailu**	contest,
kauniX	beautiful		competition
kauppa	shop	**kilsa** ·	kilometre (sl.)
kaupunki	city	**kiltti**	well-behaved,
kautlta	via		'good'
keino	means	**kimppu**	bunch
kello	clock; at X	**kioski**	kiosk
	o'clock; bell	**kipeä**	sore; ill
kera	with X PP	**kirja**	book
kerraln	once	**kirjailija**	writer

kirjallisuus *te*	literature	**kunnes**	until
kirjeQ	(postal) letter	**kunta**	commune
kirjoitta-	writes	**kunto**	good shape; ability
kirkkaX	bright, clear		
kirkko	church	**kuole-**	dies
kiva	fine, great, lovely	**kuppi**	cup
		kutsu	invitation
kivi *e*	stone	**kutsu-**	calls; invites
koetta-	tries	**kuu**	moon; month
kohta[1]	spot, place, point	**kuukausi**	month
		kuule-	hears
kohta[2]	soon	**kuulemma**	I hear/they say that
koira	dog		
koko	whole, entire; size	**kuulosta-**	sounds
		kuulu-	is audible, can be heard; belongs
kolme	three		
koneQ	machine; aeroplane		
		Mitä kuuluu?	How are you?
korkea	high	**kuuma**	hot, warm
kortti	card	**kuuntele-**	listens
korva	ear	**kuusi** *te*	six
koska	because; when	**kuva**	picture
koskaan	never (with *neg. verb*)	**kuva|X-**	describes, depicts
kotiin	(to, headed) home(ward)	**kyllä**	surely, really
		kylmeXE-	it gets cold
kotoisin	originally from (**X-stA**)	**kylmä**	cold
		kylä	village
kotona	at home	**kymmenen**	ten
koulu	school	**kynttilä**	candle
kova	hard	**kysy-**	asks (question; cf. **pyytä-**)
kovin	very		
kuin	as; than	**kysymys** *kse*	question
kuinka	how	**kyynärpää**	elbow
kuitenkin	anyway	**kämppä**	hut; flat
kuka	who?	**kännykkä**	cellular telephone
kukka	flower		
kulta	gold	**käv|i(si)**	pt. (cd.) of **käy-**
kumpi	which? (of two)	**käy-**	goes (and comes back); turns out (see unit 14)
kun[1]	when; if; seeing that ...		
kun[2] = **kuin**			

käyttä-	uses	luol(kse)	to X's place PP
käänty-	turns (intr.)	luolnA	at X's place PP
kääntä-	turns (tr.),	luoltA	from X's place
	translates		PP
laatikko	box	luokka	class
lahja	gift, present	luonteQ	character
laitta-	prepares, makes	lupaX-	promises
laiva	ship	luule-	thinks (that ...)
laji	type, sort, kind	luultavasti	probably
lakka	arctic cloud-	lähelllA	near PP
	berry	lähelle	(to) near PP
lapsi e	child (sP laslta)	läheltA	from near PP
lasi	glass	lähes	nearly
laske-	descends, comes	lähettä-	sends
	down; counts	lähte-	leaves (intr.),
lauantai	Saturday		departs, goes
laula-	sings	lähtö	departure
laulu	song	lämmin	warm
lauseQ	sentence		(lämpimä-)
lautanen	plate, dish	länsi te	west
lehti e	leaf; newspaper	läpi	through PP
leipo-	bakes	lääkäri	doctor, GP
leipä	bread	lääni	(county)
lempi e	favourite; love	löyty-	is found
lentokenttä	airport	löytä-	finds
lepäX-	rests (intr.)	maa	land; country-
liha	meat		(side); ground
liian	too (much)	maailma	world
liitty-	joins, is added	maaliskuu	March
linna	fortress, castle	maanantai	Monday
lippu	ticket; flag	maatalous te	agriculture
lisäl	additional	mainiTSE-	mentions
lokakuu	October	maisema	landscape
loma	break	maista-	tastes (tr.)
Lontoo	London	maito	milk
loppu	end	makea	sweet; pleasant-
loppu-	ends (intr.)		tasting
loputta-	ends (tr.)	maksa-	pays; costs
luke-	reads	malli	model, pattern
luku	chapter;	mansikka	strawberry
	number	marja	berry
lumi	snow	markka	(Finnish) Mark

markkina(lt)	market(s)	**museo**	museum
marraskuu	November	**musta**	black
matka	journey, trip	**musteQ**	ink
matkusta-	travels	**mustikka**	bilberry
meinaX-	means (to), intends	**mutta**	but
		muu	other
melkein	fairly, quite	**muualla**	elsewhere
mene-	goes	**muuan**	a few
meno	going		**(muutama-)**
on menossa	is going	**muutta-**	changes (tr.); moves house
meri	sea, ocean		
merkiTSE-	means, signifies	**myy-**	sells
merkki	mark, symbol, sign	**myyljä**	salesperson
		myöhästy-	is late
metsä	forest	**myös**	also, as well
milssä	where?	**myöten**	along; as far as PP w/P
mielenkiintoinen	interesting		
mieli *e*	mind	**mäki** *e*	hill
mies	man; husband **(miehe-)**	**mökki**	cabin, hut
		naura-	laughs
mietti-	thinks over, considers, ponders	**neiti**	young lady; Miss
		neljä	four
mikä	what?	**niinkuin**	like, as
millainen	what kind of?	**nimi** *e*	name
milloin	when?	**nimittäin**	you see; I say that because
minuln	mine, my		
miten	how	**noin**	like that; about, roughly
mm: muun muassa	inter alia		
		nouse-	rises
moi	Hi!; Bye!	**nukku-**	sleeps
molemmalt	both	**numero**	number
moni *e*	many	**nuori** *e*	young
muista-	remembers	**nykyl**	present-day, contemporary
mukalna	along with X PP		
		nykyään	nowadays
mukalan	along with X; according to X PP	**nyt**	now
		näin	like this, in this way
mukava	pleasant, comfortable	**näke-**	sees (inf. **nähldä**)
mummo	Grandma	**näke-**	sees

näkemiin	Goodbye!	**pankki**	bank
näyttä-	shows; looks, appears	**paperi**	paper
		paras	best
odotta-	waits for, expects	**parempi**	better
		pari	pair, a few
ohli	past PP	**passi**	passport
oikea	correct	**peli**	game
oikein	really, very	**pelkäX-**	fears
ojenta-	offers, extends, passes	**perheQ**	family
		perinteinen	traditional
ole-	is	**perinteQ**	tradition
olo	the way it is; condition	**perjantai**	Friday
		peruna	potato
olut	beer (**olue-**)	**perusl**	basic
oma	one's own	**perusta-**	founds, bases
onnistu-	succeeds, comes out OK	**peura**	wild reindeer
		pieni	small, little
opettele-	learns	**piirakka**	pasty
opiskele-	studies	**pikku**	little
opiskelija	student	**pilvi** *e*	cloud
oppi-	learns, studies	**pitkin**	along PP w/P
osa	part	**pitkä**	long
osaX-	knows how (to X)	**pitä-**	holds; likes (-**stA**)
osoitteQ	address	**pohja**	bottom; north
osta-	buys	**pohjoinen**	north(ern)
otsa	forehead	**poika**	boy (sG **pojaln**)
otta-	takes	**poikki**	through, across PP
ovi *e*	door		
paha	bad	**poltta-**	burns; smokes (tobacco)
paikka	place		
paista-	shines	**polvi** *e*	knee
paitsi	beside, except PP	**poro**	domesticated reindeer
paketti	package	**posti**	mail; post
pala	piece	**postimerkki**	stamp
paljoln	lots, many	**prosentti**	per cent
paljonko	how much?	**puhtaX**	clean
palkinto	prize, award	**puhelin** *ime*	telephone
palkka	salary, wage, pay	**puhu-**	speaks
		pukki	ram
pallo	ball	**pulla**	bun

pullo	bottle	**ranta**	shore, coast
punal	red	**rauha**	peace, quiet
punainen	red	**rauta**	iron
puolel**sta**	on behalf of PP	**rautatie**	railroad
puoli *e*	(be)half; side	**ravintola**	restaurant
puolueQ	(political) party	**riippu-**	hangs;
puolusta-	defends		depends
pure-	bites	**riittä-**	is enough;
pussi	bag		suffices
puu	tree, wood	**rikkoutu-**	is broken
puutarha	garden	**rinta**	breast, chest
pysty-	is able	**rinteQ**	slope
pysy-	stays, remains,	**rouva**	married woman,
	doesn't move/		Mrs
	change	**rukiX**	rye
pyytä-	asks (for; cf.	**runo**	poem
	kysy-)	**ruoka**	food
päin	abouts; towards	**ruotsalainen**	Swedish
päivä	day	**ruotsi**	Swedish
pärjäX-	gets by		(language);
pää	head; end		Sweden
pääkaupunki	capital	**rupeX-**	starts, gets stuck
pääll**lä**	on		in
pääse-	manages to go/	**saa-**	gets, receives; is
	come; gets		allowed to
	(through/by/	**saame**	Saami,
	in, etc.)		Lapp(ish)
pääsy	entry		(language)
päätty-	ends (intr.)	**saapu-**	arrives
päättä-	ends (tr.),	**saaristo**	archipelago
	decides	**sairaala**	hospital
pöytä	table	**sairaX**	ill, sick;
raha	money		patient
rahoitta-	funds, provides	**saksa**	German
	with money		(language)
rakennus *kse*	building	**Saksa**	Germany
rakenta-	builds	**sama**	same
rakenteQ	structure	**samanlainen**	similar
rannikko	shore, coast	**sana**	word
ranska	French	**sano-**	says
	(language)	**sata**	hundred
Ranska	France	**sata-**	rains

satanen	100(-mark) note; the number 100	**sunnuntai**	Sunday
		suomalainen	Finnish (adj)
		suomi *e*	Finnish (language)
sateQ	rain		
sattu-	happens	**Suomi** *e*	Finland
sauna	sauna (see unit 9)	**suoritta-**	performs, executes, carries out
seitsemän	seven		
sekaisin	mixed up, jumbled	**suosittele-**	recommends
		suosittu	favoured, popular
sekä:			
sekä X että Y	both X and Y	**suu**	mouth
		suuri *e*	great, large
selkä	back	**syksy**	Autumn
selvä	clear; OK	**symboli**	symbol
seteli	banknote	**synty**	birth
seuraX-	follows	**synty-**	is born
sija|an	instead of X PP	**sytyttä-**	lights, ignites
silloin	then (at that time)	**syy**	cause, reason; blame, guilt
sisko	sister	**syyskuu**	September
sisä|llA	inside PP	**syö-**	eats
sisä|ssA	inside PP	**säily-**	is preserved
sisä|än	(to) inside PP	**sää**	weather
sitten	then (subsequently); so	**sääri** *e*	leg
		säästä-	pollutes
soi-	rings, sounds	**taa|kseQ**	to behind X PP
soitta-	makes X ring/ sound; plays	**taas**	again
		tai	or
soittele-	calls, phones	**taita-**	is capable; is likely; 'must'
sopeutu-	settles in, fits in		
sopi-	agrees (tr.)	**taiteQ**	art
sopimus *kse*	agreement, treaty	**taiteilija**	artist
		taka|A	from behind X PP
sosiaaliturva	social security		
sota	war	**taka|nA**	behind X PP
sovitta-	fits (tr.), accommodates (tr.)	**takaisin**	back (adv)
		takia	on account of X PP
sukellus *kse*	diving		
suklaa	chocolate	**talo**	house; building
suku	kin, relatives	**talvi** *e*	Winter
sulkeutu-	closes (intr.)	**tammikuu**	January

tapa	way, custom	**torstai**	Thursday
tapahtu-	happens	**torttu**	cake
tapaX-	meets	**tosi** *te*	true; truly,
tarha	enclosure, yard		really
tarina	story	**toukokuu**	May
tarjoX-	offers	**tuhat** *nte*	thousand
tarkasta-	checks	**tuke-**	supports
tarkista-	checks (and	**tuki** *e*	support
	rectifies)	**tule-**	comes
tarkoitta-	means, intends	**tuliaiseIt**	gifts given by,
tarkoitus *kse*	purpose		or party
tarpeeksi	sufficiently,		thrown for,
	enough		one arriving
tartte-→		**tunnelma**	feeling, mood
tarviTSE-		**tunte-**	knows; feels
tarviTSE-	needs; is	**tunteQ**	feeling
	necessary	**tunti**	hour; lesson
tavallinen	usual,	**tuntu-**	feels (intr.),
	customary		seems
tavara	stuff	**tuo-**	brings;
tavaraIt	wares		imports
teke-	does, makes	**tutustu-**	gets to know
	(inf. **tehIdä**)	**tuuli** *e*	wind
teos *kse*	work (of art)	**tyhjä**	empty
terveQ	healthy	**tykkäX-**	likes
terveys *te*	health	**tyttö**	girl
tie	road	**työ**	work
tietysti	of course	**työttömyys** *te*	unemployment
tietä-	knows	**tähden**	for the sake of
tiistai	Tuesday		X PP
tila	room, space	**tänään**	today
todeIlla	truly	**tärkeä**	important
toimi *e*	function(ing)	**täti**	aunt(ie)
tule- toimeIen	manages	**täysin**	completely
toimi-	works,	**täyttä-**	fills, completes
	functions	**täyty-**	is necessary
toinen	other (of two);	**ulkomaalainen**	foreigner
	the other	**upea**	splendid
Itoista	+teen, e.g.	**urheilu**	sport
	viisitoista	**usea**	frequent
	'fifteen'	**uskalta-**	dares, is so bold
tori	market		(as to . . .)

usko-	believes	**vastoin**	contrary to X
uudelleen	again		prep. w/P
uusi *te*	new	**vauva**	baby
vaali	election	**veli**	brother (sG
vaan[1]	(but) rather; go		velje|n)
	ahead!	**veneQ**	boat
vaan[2] = **vain**		**venäjä**	Russian
vaati-	demands,		(language);
	requires		Russia
vai	or (in	**vesi** *te*	water
	questions)	**vie-**	takes (away);
vaihta-	changes		exports
vaihtoehto	alternative	**vielä**	still, yet
vaikea	difficult	**vieraX**	stranger; guest
vaikka	although; even;	**viere|llä**	next to X PP
	for example	**viere|ssä**	next to X PP
vaimo	wife	**vietto**	spending,
vain	only		celebrating
vaiva	difficulty	**viettä-**	spends,
vakavasti	seriously		celebrates
valitettavasti	unfortunately	**vihannes** *kse*	vegetable
valitta-	complains	**viihty-**	gets on, thrives
valkoinen	white	**viikko**	week
valmiX	ready; finished	**viiko|n+loppu**	weekend
valta	power	**viimeinen**	last (= final)
valtio	(the) state	**viimeksi**	for the last time
vanha	old	**viimeQ**	last (= most
vanhemma|t	parents		recent)
vapaa	free	**viina**	spirits
varaX-	books, reserves	**viini**	wine
varma	sure, certain	**viipy-**	stays, tarries
varmaan	certainly	**viisaX**	wise
varten	for X PP	**viisi** *te*	five
vasemmalle	to the left	**viittaX-**	refers; beckons
vasta	not until	**viitsi-**	feels like (X-
vasta|an	against X;		ing: **X|TAQ**)
	opposite	**viiva**	line, dash
	X PP	**voi**	butter
vastapäätä	opposite PP	**voi-**	is able; can
vastaX-	answers,	**voitta-**	wins
	replies	**vuo|ksi**	for X PP
vasten	against X PP	**vuokraX-**	hires, rents

vuosi *te*	year	**yksitoista**	eleven
vähitellen	gradually, little by little	**yl|lä** = **pää|llä**	
		yleensä	in general
vähä|n	a little	**yli**	over X PP
väli	interval	**yliopisto**	university
väli|llä	between X and Y PP	**yläpuole|lla**	above X PP
		ymmärtä-	understands
väri	colour	**ympäri**	around X PP
yhdeksän	nine	**yrittä-**	attempts, tries
yhdessä	together	**yskä**	cough
Yhdysvalla|t	the United States	**yskä-**	coughs
		ystävä	friend
yhteensä	all together	**yö**	night
yhtä	(just) as	**äiti**	mother
yhtään	at all	**äänekkäX**	loud
yhä	ever, still; *with comparative* Xer and Xer	**äänestä-**	votes
		ääni *e*	voice; sound
		ääre|ssA	at X PP
yksi	one (**yhte-**)	**öljy**	oil

English–Finnish glossary

See note on page 279.

English	Finnish
a little	**vähä|n**
about, roughly	**noin**
according to	**mukaan**
address	**osoitteQ**
administration	**hallinto**
adult	**aikuinen**
aeroplane	**lentokoneQ**
again	**taas, uudelleen**
age	**ikä**
agreement, treaty	**sopimus** *kse*
agrees (tr.)	**sopi-**
aid, assistance	**apu**
air	**ilma**
airport	**lentokenttä**
all kinds of	**kaikenlainen**
all, every(one)	**kaikki** *e*
along with	**mukana**
already	**jo**
also	**myös, kans**
alternative	**vaihtoehto**
although	**vaikka**
altogether	**yhteensä**
always	**aina**
American	**amerikkalainen**
amuses	**huvitta-**
and	**ja**
animal	**eläin** *ime*
answers	**vastaX-**
anyway	**kuitenkin**
approves	**hyväksy-**
around	**ympäri**
arrives	**saapu-**
art	**taiteQ**
as far as, until	**asti**
as; than	**kuin**
asks (question)	**kysy-**
asks (for)	**pyytä-**
at home	**kotona**
at all	**yhtään**
at least	**ainakin**
at once, right away	**heti**
at X's place	**luo|nA PP**
aunt(ie)	**täti**
Autumn	**syksy**
baby	**vauva**
back (adv)	**takaisin**
back	**selkä**
bad	**paha**
bag	**pussi**
ball	**pallo**
bank	**pankki**
banknote	**seteli**
bar	**baari**
beautiful	**kauniX**
because; when	**koska**
beer	**olut (oluTe-)**
before	**ennen**
beginning	**alku**
begins	**alka-**
behind	**taka|nA**

believes	**usko-**	changes (tr)	**muutta-**
bell	**kello**	chats	**keskustele-**
belongs	**kuulu-**	cheap	**halpa**
besides	**paitsi**	checks	**tarkasta-**
best	**paras**	child	**lapsi** *e*
better	**parempi**	chocolate	**suklaa**
between	**väli|llä**	church	**kirkko**
big	**iso**	city	**kaupunki**
bites	**pure-**	class	**luokka**
black	**musta**	clean	**puhtaX**
boat	**veneQ**	clear; OK	**selvä**
book	**kirja**	clock	**kello**
books, reserves	**varaX-**	closes (intr)	**sulkeutu-**
both	**molemma|t**	cloud	**pilvi** *e*
bottle	**pullo**	coffee	**kahvi**
bottom; north	**pohja**	cold	**kylmä**
box	**laatikko**	colour	**väri**
boy	**poika (sG pojа|n)**	comes	**tule-**
		complains	**valitta-**
bread	**leipä**	completely	**täysin**
breast, chest	**rinta**	continues (tr)	**jatka-**
brings; imports	**tuo-**	correct	**oikea**
brother	**veli (sG velje|n)**	country(side)	**maa**
building	**rakennus** *kse*	cup	**kuppi**
builds	**rakenta-**	day	**päivä**
bunch	**kimppu**	decides	**päättä-**
burns	**poltta-**	demands	**vaati-**
but	**mutta**	depends	**riippu-**
butter	**voi**	descends	**laske-**
buys	**osta-**	describes	**kuva|X-**
cake	**kakku**	dies	**kuole-**
calls, phones	**soitta-**	different	**erilainen**
calls; invites	**kutsu-**	difficult	**vaikea**
can	**voi-**	difficulty	**vaiva**
capital	**pääkaupunki**	doctor, GP	**lääkäri**
card	**kortti**	does, makes	**teke- (inf. teh|dä)**
carries, bears	**kanta-**		
causes	**aiheuttaa-**	dog	**koira**
celebration	**juhla**	door	**ovi** *e*
centre	**keskusta**	drinkable	**juotava**
certainly	**varmaan**	drinks	**juo-**
changes, converts	**vaihta-**	drives	**aja-**

duck	**ankka**	fish	**kala**
each, every	**joka**	flat; apartment	**asunto**
ear	**korva**	flower	**kukka**
earlier	**aikaisemmin**	follows	**seuraX-**
east	**itä**	food	**ruoka**
easy	**helppo**	foot, leg	**jalka**
eats	**syö-**	for example	**esimerkiksi**
elsewhere	**muualla**	for the last	**viimeksi**
empty	**tyhjä**	time	
end	**pää, loppu**	for a long time	**kauan**
ends (intr)	**päätty-**	foreigner	**ulkomaalainen**
English	**englanti**	forest	**metsä**
(language,		free	**vapaa**
country)		friend	**ystävä**
enough, is	**riittä-**	fruit	**hedelmä**
entry	**pääsy**	game	**peli**
evening	**ilta**	garden	**puutarha**
excuse me	**anteeksi**	gathers	**keräX-**
expensive	**kalliX**	gets, receives	**saa-**
fairly	**aika**	gets by	**pärjäX-**
fairly, quite	**melkein**	gets to know	**tutustu-**
family	**perheQ**	gift, present	**lahja**
far away	**kaukana**	girl	**tyttö**
farewell!	**hyvästi**	gives	**anta-**
father	**isä**	glass	**lasi**
fears	**pelkäX-**	god, God	**jumala**
feeling, mood	**tunnelma**	goes	**mene-**
feels, senses (tr)	**tunte-**	goes (and	**käy-**
feels (intr),	**tuntu-**	returns)	
seems		good	**hyvä**
feels like it	**viitsi-**	Goodbye!	**näkemiin**
fetches, applies	**hake-**	gradually	**vähitellen**
for		great, large	**suuri** *e*
finds	**löytä-**	ground	**maa**
fine, great,	**kiva**	happens	**tapahtu-**
lovely		hard	**kova**
Finland	**Suomi**	head	**pää**
Finnish	**suomi**	health	**terveys** *te*
(language)		healthy	**terveQ**
Finnish (adj)	**suomalainen**	hears	**kuule-**
first (adv)	**ensin**	helps, assists	**autta-**
first (adj)	**ensimmäinen**	Hi!; Bye!	**moi**

high	**korkea**	knows how	**osaX-**
hill	**mäki** *e*	(to X)	
hires, rents	**vuokraX-**	lake	**järvi** *e*
hobby, interest	**harrastus** *kse*	land	**maa**
holds; likes	**pitä-** (**-stA**)	landscape	**maisema**
home(ward)	**kotiin**	language	**kieli** *e*
hospital	**sairaala**	last (= final)	**viimeinen**
hot, warm	**kuuma**	last (= most	**viimeQ**
hour; lesson	**tunti**	recent)	
house; building	**talo**	lasts	**kestä-**
how	**kuinka, miten**	laughs	**naura-**
how much?	**paljonko**	leaf	**lehti** *e*
How are you?	**mitä kuuluu?**	learns, studies	**oppi-**
human being	**ihminen**	learns	**opettele-**
husband	**mies** (**miehe-**)	leaves (intr)	**lähte-**
ice	**jää**	leaves behind	**jättä-**
if	**jos**	left, on the	**vasemmalla**
ill	**sairaX**	left over	**jäljellä**
important	**tärkeä**	leg	**sääri** *e*
in general	**yleensä**	letter (of	**kirjain** *ime*
ink	**musteQ**	alphabet)	
inside	**sisällä**	letter (postal)	**kirjeQ**
inside, to	**sisälän**	life	**elämä**
instead of	**sijalan**	like, as	**niinkuin**
intends	**aiko-**	like that	**noin**
interesting	**mielenkiin-**	like this, in	**näin**
	toinen	this way	
interests	**kiinnosta-**	likes	**tykkäX-**
international	**kansainvälinen**	line	**viiva**
introduces	**esittele-**	listens	**kuuntele-**
invitation	**kutsu**	little	**pikku**
is	**ole-**	long	**pitkä**
is necessary	**täyty-**	looks at	**katso-**
is capable	**taita-**	loses	**kadotta-**
is able	**voi-, pysty-**	lots, many	**paljoln**
is likely	**taita-**	machine	**koneQ**
is worth while	**kannatta-**	mail; post	**posti**
journey, trip	**matka**	man	**mies** (**miehe-**)
just	**just, juuri**	many	**moni** *e*
knee	**polvi** *e*	map	**kartta**
knows (person)	**tunte-**	mark	**merkki**
knows (facts)	**tietä-**	Mark	**markka**

market	**tori, markkinalt**	next	**ensi**
married	**naimisissa**	next to	**vierelssä**
married woman,	**rouva**	nice, pleasant	**hauska**
Mrs		night	**yö**
matter, affair	**asia**	no	**ei**
maybe, perhaps	**kai, ehkä**	north(ern)	**pohjoinen**
means, signifies	**merkiTSE-**	notices	**huomaX-**
means (to an	**keino**	now	**nyt**
end)		nowadays	**nykyään**
means (to),	**meinaX-**	number	**numero**
intends		object	**esineQ**
means, intends	**tarkoitta-**	o'clock	**kello**
meat	**liha**	of course	**tietysti**
meets	**tapaX-**	old	**vanha**
mentions	**mainiTSE-**	on account of	**takia**
middle	**keski** *e*	once	**kerraln**
milk	**maito**	one	**yksi (yhte-)**
mind	**mieli** *e*	only	**vain**
mine, my	**minuln**	only, sole	**ainoa**
mixed up,	**sekaisin**	opens	**avaX-**
jumbled		opposite	**vastapäätä**
model, pattern	**malli**	or	**tai**
moment	**hetki** *e*,	or (in questions)	**vai**
	hetkinen	originally from	**kotoisin (X-**
money	**raha**		**stA)**
month	**kuukausi**	other	**muu**
moon	**kuu**	other (of two);	**toinen**
more, additional	**lisälä**	the other	
more	**enemmän**	over	**yli**
morning	**aamu**	own	**oma**
mother	**äiti**	package	**paketti**
mouth	**suu**	pair, a few	**pari**
myself	**itseni**	paper	**paperi**
name	**nimi** *e*	parents	**vanhemmalt**
nation, people	**kansa**	part	**osa**
near	**lähellä**	passport	**passi**
nearly	**lähes**	past	**ohli PP**
needs; is	**tarviTSE-**	pasty	**piirakka**
necessary		pays; costs	**maksa-**
never	**ei koskaan**	peace	**rauha**
new	**uusi** *te*	person	**henkilö,**
newspaper	**lehti** *e*		**ihminen**

picture	**kuva**	rests (intr)	**lepäX-**
piece	**pala**	rings, sounds	**soi-**
place	**paikka**	rises	**nouse-**
plant	**kasvi**	road	**tie**
plate, dish	**lautanen**	room	**huoneQ**
plays	**soitta-**	room, space	**tila**
pleasant	**mukava**	runs	**juokse-** (inf.
poem	**runo**		**juos|ta)**
political party	**puolueQ**	salary, wage,	**palkka**
pollutes	**säästä-**	pay	
popular	**suosittu**	same	**sama**
potato	**peruna**	says	**sano-**
pours	**kaata-**	school	**koulu**
power	**valta**	sea, ocean	**meri** (sP
prepares, makes	**laitta-**		**mer|ta)**
probably	**luultavasti**	sees	**näke-** (inf.
profession, trade	**ammatti**		**näh|dä)**
promises	**lupaX-**	sells	**myy-**
purpose	**tarkoitus** *kse*	sends	**lähettä-**
question	**kysymys** *kse*	seriously	**vakavasti**
quiet	**rauha**	settles in, fits in	**sopeutu-**
quite	**ihan**	ship	**laiva**
quite; precisely	**aivan**	shop	**kauppa**
railroad	**rautatie**	shore, coast	**ranta**
rain	**sateQ**	shows; looks,	**näyttä-**
rains	**sata-**	appears	
rare	**harva**	side	**puoli** *e*
rarely	**harvoin**	similar	**samanlainen**
reads	**luke-**	sings	**laula-**
ready; finished	**valmis**	sister	**sisko**
really, very	**oikein**	sits	**istu-**
reason	**syy**	sleeps	**nukku-**
recommends	**suosittele-**	small, little	**pieni** *e*
red	**punainen**	snow	**lumi** *e* (sP
region, area	**alueQ**		**lun|ta)**
relatives, kin	**suku**	so, therefore	**siis**
remains, stays	**jää-**	sometime(s)	**joskus**
behind		sore; ill	**kipeä**
remembers	**muista-**	sounds	**kuulosta-**
resides, inhabits,	**asu-**	south	**etelä**
lives		speaks	**puhu-**
restaurant	**ravintola**	spirits	**viina**

sport	urheilu	(subsequently)	
Spring	kevät (kevää-)	then (at that	silloin
stamp	postimerkki	time)	
starts, gets	rupeX-	thinks	ajattele-
stuck in		thinks (that ...)	luule-
state	valtio	thinks over	mietti-
station	asema	throws	heittä-
stays, tarries	viipy-	ticket	lippu
stays, doesn't	pysy-	time	aika (sG ajaln)
change		time, has enough	ehti-
still, yet	vielä	time, occasion	kerta
stone	kivi e	today	tänään
storey	kerros kse	together	yhdessä
story	tarina	tomorrow	huomenna
story; matter,	juttu	tongue	kieli e
affair		too (much)	liian
stranger; guest	vieraX	travels	matkusta-
street	katu	tree, wood	puu
student	opiskelija	tries	yrittä-
stuff	tavara	true, truly	tosi
subject	aineQ	two	kaksi
(matter)		type, sort, kind	laji
succeeds	onnistu-	understands	ymmärtä-
sufficiently,	tarpeeksi	unfortunately	valitettavasti
enough		university	yliopisto
Summer	kesä	until	kunnes
sun	aurinko	uses	käyttä-
supposedly	kuulemma	usual, customary	tavallinen
sure, certain	varma	various,	eri
surely, really	kyllä	different	
sweet	makea	vegetable	vihannes kse
table	pöytä	very	kovin
takes (away)	vie-	village	kylä
takes	otta-	voice; sound	ääni e
takes care of	hoita-	waits (for),	odotta-
tastes (good)	maistu-	expects	
telephone	puhelin ime	wants	haluX-
tells, recounts	kerto-	war	sota
thank you!	kiitos	wares	tavaralt
thanks!	kiitti	warm	lämmin
that (cj)	että		(lämpimä-)
then	sitten	watches	katso-

water	**vesi** *te*	whole, entire	**koko**
way, custom	**tapa**	wife	**vaimo**
weak	**heikko**	wind	**tuuli** *e*
weather	**sää**	window	**ikkuna**
week	**viikko**	wine	**viini**
weekend	**viikonloppu**	wins	**voitta-**
well	**hyvin**	Winter	**talvi** *e*
west	**länsi** *te*	without	**ilman**
what kind of?	**millainen**	wonder, miracle	**ihmeQ**
what about ...?	**entä(s)**	word	**sana**
what?	**mikä**	work	**työ**
when	**kun**	works, functions	**toimi-**
when?	**milloin**	world	**maailma**
where?	**missä**	writes	**kirjoitta-**
which? (of two)	**kumpi**	yeah	**joo**
white	**valkoinen**	year	**vuosi** *te*
who?	**kuka**	young	**nuori** *e*

Glossary of grammatical terms

abessive (case)
A case-suffix (-**ttA**) meaning 'without', e.g. **mitään sanomatta** 'without saying anything'; see Unit 15.

ablative (case)
A case suffix (-**ltA**) meaning '(away) from', e.g. **kirje isältä** 'a letter from father'; see Unit 4.

accusative
One of the cases which indicate the complete direct object of a sentence. Most words use the genitive suffix -**n** to mark the accusative, like the se**n** of **Se jätti sen kotiin** '(S)he left it home', unless the verb has no explicit subject person, in which case the nominative is used instead: **Jätä se kotiin!** 'Leave it at home!', **Se jätetään kotiin** 'One leaves it at home, We/people leave it at home'. The personal pronouns ('me', 'you', etc.) have their own special accusative suffix -**t Se jätti minut kotiin** '(S)he left me at home', **Minut jätettiin kotiin** 'They left me at home, I got left at home'. See Units 3 and 5.

adessive (case)
A case suffix (-**llA**) meaning 'located at/on', e.g. **asemalla** 'at the station'; see Unit 4.

citation form
This is the form of a nominal as it is listed in dictionaries. Its grammatical name is nominative singular, abbreviated as sN.

comitative (case)
A case suffix (-**ine**-) meaning 'in the company of', e.g. **lapsineen** 'with his/her children'; see Unit 15.

connegative
A verb form built with the suffix -Q, used with a negative verb to form negative statements or commands, e.g. **Älä sulje ovea** 'Don't close the door!'; see Unit 2.

consonant compression	The way in which Finnish consonants get 'squeezed' in certain contexts. For example, the long **kk** of **takki** 'jacket' gets squeezed to a short **k** when the genitive -**n** is added, as in **takin hinta** 'the price of the jacket'. The short **k** of **rikas** 'rich' is already compressed (by the **s** at the end of the word); it gets 'decompressed' when this **s** is absent, as in the plural, **rikkaat** 'the rich'; see Unit 1.
derivation	Making one word out of another. Finnish does this by adding derivational suffixes, so adding =**llinen** to **ystävä** 'friend', giving **ystävä=llinen**, is like adding English '=ly' to 'friend', giving 'friend=ly'.
diphthong	A Finnish diphthong is a sequence of two different vowels which is pronounced as one syllable. In Finnish, any vowel ending in i, u, or y is a diphthong (so ei, äi, ai, oi, ui, yi, öi, iu, eu, au, iy, ey, äy, öy are diphthongs), as are ie, uo, yö. Under certain circumstances, these last three are shortened to e, o, ö; see Unit 5 (plurals) and Unit 6 (past tense) for more details.
direct object	The direct object of a sentence is the part which has something done to it or at which the action is aimed. Examples of English direct objects are 'soup' in 'Edward heated up the soup', 'me' in 'She loves me' and 'bridge' in 'The engineer designed a bridge.' See Unit 5 for the various kinds of direct object which Finnish distinguishes.
elative (case)	A case suffix (-**stA**) meaning 'out of', e.g. **Mä otin lasin kaapista** 'I took a glass out of the cupboard', and 'about', e.g. **Se puhui hinnoista** '(S)he talked about prices'; see Units 1 and 4.
enclitics	These are little suffix-like elements (written in this book with prefixed double hyphen or dash) which can attach to just about any word in a sentence, depending on what is being added (--**kin**), subtracted (--**kAAn**), queried (--**kO**), or stressed (--**pA**, --**kin**). In colloquial Finnish, clitics often add emotional shadings to a sentence, such as --**hAn** in **Ethän polta** 'You're

not going to smoke, are you?' The clitic --**kin** adds **Jussi** in the sentence **Jussikin on säveltäjä** '*Jussi* is a composer, too (not just Pirjo)', but adds **säveltäjä** 'composer' in the sentence **Jussi on säveltäjäkin** 'Jussi is a *composer*, too (and not just a chartered accountant).' In the sentence **Jussi onkin säveltäjä,** 'Jussi really *is* a composer' the amazing fact that Jussi actually is a composer is stressed (We thought Jussi might be, and do you know what? . . .).

essive (case)	A case suffix (-**nA**) meaning 'being X; (functioning) as; in the form of', e.g. **Ulkomaalaisina meidän on hankittava viisumi** 'As foreigners, we must secure a visa'; see Unit 8.
genitive	A case which indicates the 'possessor', something like the apostrophe-plus-*s* of English in 'Peter's friends' or the preposition 'of' in 'the end of the road'. Finnish uses the suffix -**n** for singular nouns, so we have **Pekan ystävät** and **tien loppu** for these two phrases; for the genitive plural, see Unit 9. You'll find more on the genitive in Units 1 and 14.
illative (case)	A case suffix which means 'into'. This book uses a shorthand symbol -#**n** to refer to the illative suffix, because it has so many different forms. For example, it is -**än** in **metsään** 'into the forest', -**hun** in **puuhun** 'into a tree', and -**seen** in **huoneeseen** 'into a room'. See Units 4 and 5 for the details.
inessive (case)	A case suffix (-**ssA**) meaning '(located) inside', e.g. **sun huoneessa** 'in your room'; see Unit 4.
infinitives	These are verb forms which act like nouns. Finnish distinguishes several; they correspond, roughly, to English forms such as 'I like *to swim*', 'I can *swim*', and 'I like *swimming*'; you'll find a list of the various kinds of Finnish infinitive in the index.
instructive (case)	A case suffix meaning 'by means of, with', as in **omin käsin** 'with one's own hands'; see Unit 15.
modals	Special verbs which modify the meaning of the main verb in a sentence, introducing elements of possibility, ability, necessity, doubt and many

other shades. English examples are 'can', 'may', and 'must', as in 'I can swim' and 'You may be right.' For Finnish modals see Units 3 and 10.

nominative
: This is the case form of Finnish dictionary entries. Its suffix is zero. Its most common roles are (1) subject of the sentence (**Jussi asuu Turussa** 'Jussi lives in Turku') and (2) complete direct object of an imperative or indefinite verb form (**Hae Jussi asemalta** 'Fetch Jussi from the station!'); see Unit 1.

noun phrase
: Any group of words centred on a noun; the main noun is called the head noun. Thus 'bottle(s)' is the head noun in the noun phrases 'the bottle', 'a bottle', 'a glass bottle', 'in those green bottles'. In a Finnish noun phrase, adjectives have the same number (singular or plural) and case suffixes as the head noun; so the Finnish equivalent of the last example is **noissa vihreissä pulloissa**.

participles
: These are verb forms that act like adjectives. Finnish distinguishes several; they correspond, very roughly, to English forms such as 'rising' and 'broken' in 'rising prices' and 'broken promises'. You'll find a list of the various kinds of Finnish participle in the index.

partitive case
: An extremely frequent case, used to indicate negation, partialness or incompleteness, or indefinite quantity. Both subjects and objects can stand in the partitive. The partitive of 'water', **vettä**, is used in all the following sentences: **Se ei juonut vettä** '(S)he didn't drink the/any water' (negation), **Se joi vettä** '(S)he drank some water' (incomplete amount) or '(S)he was drinking (the) water' (incomplete action), **Eteisen lattialla oli vettä** 'There was (some) water on the floor of the entranceway' (indefinite quantity). See Units 2 and 5.

postpositions
: These are the mirror image of prepositions, i.e. they come *after* the words they go with, not before. Thus where English has '*in front of* the church', Finnish has **kirkon edessä**, literally 'church's front in', i.e. 'of-the-church in-front'.

See Unit 9 for more examples and discussion.

predicate — A term used in this book to refer to everything in a sentence other than the subject and the verb. For example, in the sentence **Te olette italialainen diplomaatti** 'You are an Italian diplomat', the predicate is **italialainen diplomaatti**, in **Mä olen kotoisin Espanjasta** 'I'm from Spain' the predicate is **kotoisin Espanjasta**, and in **Mä syön kaikki nämä voileivät** 'I'm going to eat up all of these sandwiches', it's **kaikki nämä voileivät**.

prolative (case) — A case suffix (**-tse**) meaning 'by way of; via', as in **puhelimitse** 'by telephone'; see Unit 15.

translative (case) — A case suffix (**-ksi**, **-kse-**) which indicates a change of state, as in **Vesi muuttui viiniksi** 'The water turned into wine', or the way in which someone or something is viewed or used, as in **Se luuli minua hulluksi** '(S)he thought I was a fool.' See Unit 8.

vowel harmony — This phrase refers to the way Finnish vowels have of adjusting to one another in a word. In English we do it with consonant sounds: the **s**-sound at the end of 'dogs' is really more of a **z** than an **s**, in 'harmony' with the **g**-sound to its immediate left; contrast the **s**-sound at the end of 'cats'. Finnish vowels adjust in a similar way, but they don't have to be in immediate contact to feel the need to harmonize: so for example the suffix meaning 'in' is **-ssa** in **Puolassa** 'in Poland' but **-ssä** in **Sveitsissä** 'in Switzerland'. For details see Units 1 and 10.

vowel lengthening (#) — Finnish short vowels become long in many contexts, e.g. **ä** becomes **ää** in **se elää** '(s)he lives', **e** becomes **ee** in **se menee** '(s)he/it goes', and **o** becomes **oo** in **se sanoo** '(s)he says'. In order to capture what is systematic about this process, this book uses the symbol # as a shorthand cover symbol: **se elä-#**, **se mene-#**, and **se sano-#** are simply a different way of writing **se elää**, **se menee**, and **se sanoo**, in which the suffix meaning '(s)he (does whatever)' is uniformly #. See Unit 2.

Index

The numbers refer to the lessons in which the topics are covered.

abessive (case) 15
ablative (case) 4
accusative 3, 5
adessive (case) 4
adverbs 6, 11
allative (case) 4
alternating stems 1
animals 14

citation form 1
colloquial pronunciation pp. 4–8;
    6, 7, 13
comitative (case) 15
commands 3, 16
comparative 8, 11
comparison 8
compass 13
computers 16
conditional mood 10
connegative 2
consonant compression 1, 2, 3, 5,
    6, 7, 8, 10, 11
customs 4

dental stems 2, 3, 5, 6, 8
dentals 2
derivation 2, 10
direct objects 5
directions 4

doctor 8

e-stems 1
economics 15
education 16
elative (case) 1, 4
emphasizing 6
essive (case) 8

family 4
foods 7, 11
foreign words 4

genitive 1, 9, 14
genitive plural 9
geography 14
goodbye 4, 5
greetings 1

'have' 2
hello 1
history 16
houses, flats 12, 13
how things seem 14
how you feel 15

illative (case) 4, 5
iME-stems 5
imperative 3

indefinite (verb) 5, 6
indefinite object 2
indefinite pronoun 15
indifferent 15
inessive (case) 4
infinitive, first 3
infinitive, second 13
infinitive, third 6, 15
instructive (case) 15
intentions 10
interrogative 15
introductions 1
invitations 9

kiosks 6

l-cases 4
languages 1, 10
'let's' 5
'let us' 16
likes and dislikes 2
linking clauses 11, 12
local cases 4

modals 3, 10
money 7
music 13

names Appendix
nationalities 1
necessity 13
negative verb 2
NeN-stems 1
nominative 1
non-alternating stems 1
nouns from verbs 10
numerals 2, 7, 11

occupations 1
off-licence 5
ordering at a bar 4
ordering in a restaurant 12

'other' 15

participial constructions 12
participle, past active 6, 7, 10, 12
participle, past passive 7, 10, 12
participle, present active 13, 16
participle, present passive 13, 16
participles, overview 13
participles as adjectives 16
partitive 2, 5
passport 4
past tense 6
perfect tense 7
permission 10
personal suffixes 10
pitä- 14
plans 10
plural (nouns) 5
politeness 1
politics 11, 15
possession 1, 2, 10
possessive suffixes 10
possibility 16
postpositions 9
potential mood 16
preferences 2
prepositions 9
present tense 2
privative 7
prohibition 3
prolative (case) 15
pronouns, demonstrative 6
pronouns, personal 1
pronouns, relative 11
proverbs 13
purpose 12

Q-stems 2
questions, yes/no 1
questions, other 3

religion 10

requests 3

sauna 9
s-cases 4
seasons 10
'self' 15
sequence 12
shopping 5, 6
sightseeing 13
simultaneity 13
sisu 16
social security 15
sport 8, 14
subject, submerged 14, 15
suggestions 5
superlative 8, 11

taxi 7
TE-stems 1
telephone 5
thanks 3
tight lid 1
time expressions 9
trains 4

translative (case) 8
travel agent's 11
Turku 15

uncertainty 16
UKsE-stems 5
UUTE-stems 8

vagueness 14
verb classes 3
verbal noun 3
verbs from nouns 10
verbs of motion 14
visiting 6, 8
vowel harmony 1, 10
vowel lengthening (#) 2

'without' 7
word order 2, 6
writers 15

X-stems 2

yes 1